Taste of Home

SIMPLE, EASY, FAST KITCHEN

TASTE OF HOME BOOKS • RDA ENTHUSIAST BRANDS, LLC • MILWAUKEE, WI

Taste of Home · Reader's digest

A TASTE OF HOME/READER'S DIGEST BOOK
©2015 RDA Enthusiast Brands, LLC, 1610 N. 2nd St., Suite 102, Milwaukee WI 53212-3906. All rights reserved.
Taste of Home and Reader's Digest are registered trademarks of The Reader's Digest Association, Inc.

EDITORIAL

Editor-in-Chief: Catherine Cassidy
Creative Director: Howard Greenberg
Editorial Operations Director: Kerri Balliet

Managing Editor, Print & Digital Books: Mark Hagen
Associate Creative Director: Edwin Robles Jr.

Editor: Janet Briggs
Art Director: Raeann Sundholm
Layout Designer: Catherine Fletcher
Editorial Production Manager: Dena Ahlers
Copy Chief: Deb Warlaumont Mulvey
Copy Editors: Dulcie Shoener, Mary-Liz Shaw
Contributing Copy Editor: Valerie Phillips
Content Operations Manager: Colleen King
Content Operations Assistant: Shannon Stroud
Executive Assistant: Marie Brannon

Chief Food Editor: Karen Berner
Food Editors: James Schend; Peggy Woodward, RD
Recipe Editors: Mary King; Annie Rundle; Jenni Sharp, RD; Irene Yeh

Test Kitchen & Food Styling Manager: Sarah Thompson
Test Cooks: Nicholas Iverson (lead), Matthew Hass, Lauren Knoelke
Food Stylists: Kathryn Conrad (senior), Leah Rekau, Shannon Roum
Prep Cooks: Megumi Garcia, Melissa Hansen, Bethany Van Jacobson, Sara Wirtz

Photography Director: Stephanie Marchese
Photographers: Dan Roberts, Jim Wieland
Photographer/Set Stylist: Grace Natoli Sheldon
Set Stylists: Stacey Genaw, Melissa Haberman, Dee Dee Jacq

Editorial Business Manager: Kristy Martin

BUSINESS

Vice President, Chief Sales Officer: Mark S. Josephson
General Manager, Taste of Home Cooking School: Erin Puariea
Vice President, Digital Experience & E-Commerce: Jennifer Smith

THE READER'S DIGEST ASSOCIATION, INC.

President and Chief Executive Officer: Bonnie Kintzer
Chief Financial Officer: Colette Chestnut
Vice President, Chief Operating Officer, North America: Howard Halligan
Vice President, Enthusiast Brands, Books & Retail: Harold Clarke
Vice President, North American Operations: Philippe Cloutier
Chief Marketing Officer: Leslie Dukker Doty
Vice President, North American Human Resources: Phyllis E. Gebhardt, SPHR
Vice President, Brand Marketing: Beth Gorry
Vice President, Global Communications: Susan Russ
Vice President, North American Technology: Aneel Tejwaney
Vice President, Consumer Marketing Planning: Jim Woods

For other Taste of Home books and products,
visit us at tasteofhome.com.

For more Reader's Digest products and information,
visit rd.com (in the United States) or see rd.ca (in Canada).

International Standard Book Number: 978-1-61765-362-9
Library of Congress Control Number: 2014948116

Cover Photographer: Grace Natoli Sheldon
Set Stylist: Melissa Haberman
Food Stylist: Kathryn Conrad

Pictured on front cover (clockwise from center right):
Romaine & Orange Salad with Lime Dressing, page 190; Chicken Artichoke Pasta, page 88; Easy Lemon Curd Bars, page 228; and Garlic-Cheese Crescent Rolls, page 152.

Pictured on back cover (top to bottom): Buffalo Turkey Burgers, page 83; Sweet BBQ Meatballs, page 63; Slow-Roasted Lemon Dill Chicken, page 108; and Berry Breakfast Parfaits, page 16.

Printed in China.
1 3 5 7 9 10 8 6 4 2

LIKE US
facebook.com/tasteofhome

TWEET US
@tasteofhome

FOLLOW US
pinterest.com/taste_of_home

SHOP WITH US
shoptasteofhome.com

SHARE A RECIPE
tasteofhome.com/submit

DATE-WALNUT
PINWHEELS, 242

BASIL
TORTELLINI SOUP, 184

OVEN-FRIED CHICKEN
DRUMSTICKS, 105

RIGATONI WITH
SAUSAGE & PEAS, 74

CONTENTS

PAIR IT!
Cheese Fries,
page 170,
with this sandwich
will be a hit with
your family!

Look for **PAIR IT!** for
helpful suggestions to
round out your meal.

**LOADED GRILLED
CHICKEN SANDWICH, 80**

Fabulous Dinners that are Easy on the Cook

Taste of Home Simple, Easy, Fast Kitchen has 400+ scrumptious dishes your family will love...and you'll enjoy making! This collection was created for families on the go because it features recipes with short ingredient lists, simple prep techniques, no-fuss cooking methods and easy-to-follow directions. Best of all, these dishes come from other family cooks who know how to make the most of their time in the kitchen.

Two at-a-glance icons highlight recipes every family cook needs:

(5)INGREDIENTS
With a maximum of 5 ingredients (plus pantry staples such as oil, water, salt or pepper), these recipes are quick to prepare.

SLOW COOKER
Slow cooker recipes are great for weekends when you're running about or for parties when the stovetop and oven are in use.

Simple, Easy, Fast Kitchen shows you that good food does not require hours of your time prepping and cooking. A few ingredients and no-fuss cooking methods are all you need for a family-pleasing meal!

**COCONUT ACORN
SQUASH, 175**

KEEP A WELL-STOCKED KITCHEN

Last-minute dinner decisions are easier to make when there is a variety of food in the kitchen. With a reasonably stocked pantry, refrigerator and freezer, you'll still be able to serve a delectable meal in short order. Here are some tips to help you stock up.

Quick-cooking meats such as boneless chicken breasts, chicken thighs, pork tenderloin, pork chops, ground meats, Italian sausage, sirloin and flank steaks, fish fillets, and shrimp should be stocked in the freezer. Wrap them individually (except shrimp), so you can remove only the amount you need.

Frozen vegetables prepackaged in plastic bags are a real time-saver. Simply pour out the amount needed. No preparation is required!

Pasta, rice, rice mixes and couscous are great staples to have in the pantry, and they generally have a long shelf life. Thinner pastas such as angel hair cook faster than thicker pastas. Fresh (refrigerated pastas) cook faster than dried or frozen pasta.

Dairy products like milk, sour cream, cheeses (shredded, cubed or crumbled), eggs, yogurt and butter are more perishable, so check the use-by date on packages and replace as needed.

Condiments such as ketchup, mustard, mayonnaise, salad dressings, salsa, taco sauce, soy sauce, stir-fry sauce, lemon juice, barbecue sauce and more add flavor to many dishes.

Fresh fruit and vegetables can make a satisfying predinner snack. Slices of oranges, bananas and apples are smart finger foods for kids. Ready-to-use salad greens are ideal for an instant salad.

Dried herbs, spices, vinegars and seasoning mixes add flavor and keep for months.

Pasta sauces, olives, beans, broths, canned tomatoes, canned vegetables and canned or dried soups are good to have on hand for a quick meal. Many of these items are also commonly used in recipes.

TIME-SAVING KITCHEN TIPS
Streamline your time by following these tips.

GET IT HOT.
When using an oven or grill, preheat it before beginning to prep the recipe.

GATHER ITEMS.
Pull out all the necessary ingredients and kitchen tools, then start the prep.

MAKE IT EASY.
Whenever possible, use convenience items such as prechopped garlic, onion and peppers, shredded or cubed cheese, seasoning mixes, jarred sauce, etc.

MULTITASK!
While the meat is simmering for a main dish, toss a salad, cook a side dish or start on the dessert.

DON'T RUN OUT.
Get your family into the habit of posting a grocery list. When an item is used up or is almost gone, just add it to the list for the next shopping trip.

ENCOURAGE HELPERS.
Have younger children set the table. Older kids can help with ingredient preparation or even assemble simple recipes themselves.

PAIR IT!
Berry Smoothies,
page 8,
are the perfect
companion for the
hearty waffles.

16 24 15

A.M. Express

Send your family off into the world with a **satisfying, quick breakfast.** Just add some **juice or milk** and they'll be raring to tackle the day.

OVERNIGHT MAPLE OATMEAL, 27

BERRY SMOOTHIES

(5) INGREDIENTS

Berry Smoothies

Smooth out the morning rush with a delightful boost of berries. Tart, tangy and sweet, this balanced beverage needs no additional sugar.

—**ELISABETH LARSEN**
PLEASANT GROVE, UT

START TO FINISH: 5 MIN.
MAKES: 5 SERVINGS

- 2 **cups cranberry juice**
- 2 **containers (6 ounces each) raspberry yogurt**
- 1 **cup frozen unsweetened raspberries**
- 1 **cup frozen unsweetened blueberries**
- 8 **ice cubes**

In a blender, add all ingredients; cover and process 30-45 seconds or until blended. Pour into chilled glasses; serve immediately.

Yogurt & Honey Fruit Cups

Fresh winter fruit gets dressed up in a sweet and creamy sauce. It will disappear as fast as it came together.

—*TASTE OF HOME* **TEST KITCHEN**

START TO FINISH: 10 MIN.
MAKES: 6 SERVINGS

- 4½ **cups cut-up fresh fruit (pears, apples, bananas, grapes, etc.)**
- ¾ **cup (6 ounces) mandarin orange, vanilla or lemon yogurt**
- 1 **tablespoon honey**
- ½ **teaspoon grated orange peel**
- ¼ **teaspoon almond extract**

Divide fruit among six individual serving bowls. Combine yogurt, honey, orange peel and extract; spoon over the fruit.

Chorizo Salsa Omelet

Just a few ingredients jazz up a basic omelet and make it delish!

—*TASTE OF HOME* TEST KITCHEN

START TO FINISH: 20 MIN.
MAKES: 1 SERVING

- 1 tablespoon butter
- 3 eggs
- 3 tablespoons water
- ⅛ teaspoon salt
- ⅛ teaspoon pepper
- ¼ cup cooked chorizo or sausage
- 2 tablespoons chunky salsa

1. In a small nonstick skillet, melt butter over medium-high heat. Whisk eggs, water, salt and pepper; add to skillet (mixture should set immediately at edges).

2. As eggs set, push cooked edges toward center, letting uncooked portion flow underneath. When eggs are set, spoon chorizo and salsa on one side; fold the other side over filling. Slide omelet onto a plate.

Overnight Cherry-Almond Oatmeal

Would you like breakfast ready for you when the sun comes up? If so, try my hot cereal. It's so simple...just place the ingredients in the slow cooker and turn it on before you go to bed. In the morning, enjoy a healthy, warm and filling dish.

—**GERALDINE SAUCIER**
ALBUQUERQUE, NM

PREP: 10 MIN. • **COOK:** 7 HOURS
MAKES: 6 SERVINGS

- 4 cups vanilla almond milk
- 1 cup steel-cut oats
- 1 cup dried cherries
- ⅓ cup packed brown sugar
- ½ teaspoon salt
- ½ teaspoon ground cinnamon

In a 3-qt. slow cooker coated with cooking spray, combine all the ingredients. Cover and cook on low 7-8 hours or until milk is absorbed.

Apple Pecan Crepes

This is a very easy, quick and delicious brunch item. When people taste the nutty apple pie filling tucked inside and the vanilla sauce draped over the tender crepes, everyone oohs and aahs between bites.

—**CAROLYN HAYES** MARION, IL

START TO FINISH: 15 MIN.
MAKES: 6 SERVINGS

- 1 can (21 ounces) apple pie filling
- ½ cup coarsely chopped pecans
- ½ teaspoon ground cinnamon
- 12 prepared crepes (7 inches each)
- 1 egg, lightly beaten
- ¾ cup half-and-half cream
- 2 tablespoons sugar
- ½ teaspoon vanilla extract
- ¼ teaspoon almond extract

1. Preheat oven to 375°. In a small bowl, combine pie filling, pecans and cinnamon. Spread 2 rounded tablespoonfuls down center of each crepe; roll up tightly.

2. Place in a greased 13x9-in. baking dish. Bake, uncovered, 10-14 minutes or until heated through.

3. Meanwhile, in a microwave-safe bowl, combine egg, cream, sugar and extracts. Cover and microwave at 50% power for 3½ to 4½ minutes or until thickened, stirring after each minute. Cool. Serve with crepes.

NOTE *This recipe was tested in a 1,100-watt microwave.*

CHORIZO SALSA OMELET

Cinnamon Breakfast Bites

These early-morning treats with a sweet, crispy coating are baked in the oven instead of being deep-fried.

—RUTH HASTINGS LOUISVILLE, IL

START TO FINISH: 30 MIN.
MAKES: 6 SERVINGS (1½ DOZEN)

- 1⅓ cups all-purpose flour
- 1 cup crisp rice cereal, coarsely crushed
- 2 tablespoons plus ½ cup sugar, divided
- 3 teaspoons baking powder
- ½ teaspoon salt
- ¼ cup butter-flavored shortening
- ½ cup milk
- 1 teaspoon ground cinnamon
- ¼ cup butter, melted

1. Preheat oven to 425°. In a large bowl, combine the flour, cereal, 2 tablespoons sugar, baking powder and salt; cut in shortening until mixture resembles coarse crumbs. Stir in milk just until moistened. Shape into 1-in. balls.
2. In a shallow bowl, combine cinnamon and remaining sugar. Dip balls in butter, then roll in cinnamon-sugar.
3. Arrange in a single layer in an 8-in. round baking pan. Bake 15-18 minutes or until a toothpick comes out clean.

Apple Walnut Crescents

A local apple orchard had a cook-off, so I created these golden cinnamon treats. They're a snap to assemble with convenient crescent roll dough.

—KAREN PETZOLD VASSAR, MI

PREP: 15 MIN. • **BAKE:** 20 MIN.
MAKES: 16 SERVINGS

- 2 packages (8 ounces each) refrigerated crescent rolls
- ¼ cup sugar
- 1 tablespoon ground cinnamon
- 4 medium tart apples, peeled and quartered
- ¼ cup chopped walnuts
- ¼ cup raisins, optional
- ¼ cup butter, melted

1. Preheat oven to 375°. Unroll crescent roll dough and separate into 16 triangles. Combine sugar and cinnamon; sprinkle about ½ teaspoon on each triangle. Place an apple quarter near the short side and roll up. Place in a lightly greased 15x10x1-in. baking pan.
2. Press walnuts and, if desired, raisins into top of dough. Drizzle with butter. Sprinkle with the remaining cinnamon-sugar. Bake 20-24 minutes or until golden brown. Serve warm.

Oh-So-Good Oatmeal

Lend extra nutrition to fiber-rich oatmeal by adding chopped apple with the peel and chopped almonds. My two boys demand seconds! At 1½ cups per serving, it's hearty and filling; and at zero cholesterol, what's not to love?

—DANIELLE PEPA ELGIN, IL

START TO FINISH: 20 MIN.
MAKES: 4 SERVINGS

- 3 cups water
- 2 medium tart apples, chopped
- 1½ cups old-fashioned oats
  Dash salt
- ¼ cup packed brown sugar
- ½ teaspoon ground cinnamon
- ½ teaspoon vanilla extract
- ¼ cup chopped almonds
  Maple syrup and/or fat-free milk, optional

1. In a large saucepan over medium heat, bring water to a boil. Add apples, oats and salt; cook and stir 5 minutes.
2. Remove from heat; stir in the brown sugar, cinnamon and vanilla. Cover and let stand for 2 minutes. Sprinkle each serving with almonds. Serve with maple syrup and/or milk if desired.

(5) INGREDIENTS
Waffle Sandwich

Keep going right through to lunchtime with this quick breakfast idea. I like to serve it with a crisp, juicy apple on the side.

—MICHELE MCHENRY BELLINGHAM, WA

START TO FINISH: 20 MIN.
MAKES: 1 SERVING

- 1 slice Canadian bacon
- 1 egg
- 1 green onion, chopped
- 2 frozen low-fat multigrain waffles
- 1 tablespoon shredded reduced-fat cheddar cheese
  Sliced tomato, optional

1. In a nonstick skillet coated with cooking spray, cook Canadian bacon over medium-high heat 1-2 minutes on each side or until lightly browned. Remove and keep warm.
2. In a small bowl, whisk egg and green onion; add to same pan. Cook and stir until egg is thickened and no liquid egg remains.
3. Meanwhile, prepare waffles according to package directions. Place one waffle on a plate. Top with Canadian bacon, scrambled egg, cheese and, if desired, tomato. Top with remaining waffle.

DID YOU KNOW?

Waffles have their own special days. National Waffle Day is August 24, the anniversary of the first U.S. patent for a waffle iron. International Waffle Day is March 25. It was first celebrated in Sweden, on the day marking both the beginning of spring and the Feast of the Annunciation. Either day offers a good excuse to eat waffles.

OH-SO-GOOD
OATMEAL

WAFFLE
SANDWICH

Strawberries 'n' Cream French Toast Sticks

I like to open my family's eyes with this luscious French toast breakfast that tastes like dessert. Ready in a flash, it disappears even faster.

—TARYN KUEBELBECK PLYMOUTH, MN

START TO FINISH: 15 MIN.
MAKES: 4 SERVINGS

- 1 **container (16 ounces) frozen sweetened sliced strawberries, thawed**
- ¼ **to ½ teaspoon ground cinnamon**
- 1 **teaspoon cornstarch**
- 2 **teaspoons water**
- 1 **package (12.7 ounces) frozen French toaster sticks**
- 2 **ounces cream cheese, softened**
- 1½ **teaspoons brown sugar**
- 1 **ounce white baking chocolate, melted and cooled**

1. In a small saucepan, combine strawberries and cinnamon. Combine cornstarch and water until smooth; stir into berries. Bring to a boil; cook and stir 2 minutes or until thickened.

2. Prepare French toast sticks according to package directions. Meanwhile, in a small bowl, beat cream cheese and brown sugar until light and fluffy. Stir in chocolate. Serve berry mixture over French toast; dollop with cream cheese topping.

NOTE *This recipe was tested with Eggo French Toaster Sticks.*

Easy Breakfast Quesadillas

We love Mexican food, and this was my attempt to have it for breakfast. If my kids will eat it, then I know it's a winner, and they all love this dish!

—JUDY PARKER MOORE, OK

START TO FINISH: 20 MIN.
MAKES: 6 SERVINGS

- 4 **eggs**
- 1 **cup egg substitute**
- 6 **whole wheat tortillas (8 inches)**
- 1 **cup (4 ounces) shredded reduced-fat cheddar cheese**
- 3 **turkey bacon strips, diced and cooked**
- 6 **tablespoons salsa**
- 6 **tablespoons fat-free sour cream**

1. In a small bowl, whisk eggs and egg substitute. Coat a large skillet with cooking spray. Add egg mixture; cook and stir over medium heat until completely set.

2. Heat another large nonstick skillet coated with cooking spray; add one tortilla. Top with ⅓ cup cheese, scant 2 tablespoons bacon, 1 cup egg mixture and one tortilla. Cook over medium heat for 2-3 minutes on each side or until lightly browned.

3. Repeat with the remaining tortillas, cheese, bacon and eggs, spraying pan as needed. Cut each quesadilla into six wedges. Serve with salsa and sour cream.

EASY BREAKFAST QUESADILLAS

HERB BREAKFAST FRITTATA

Herb Breakfast Frittata

One morning, I was staring into my fridge and wondering what I should make to eat. Gathering the items I had available, I came up with this recipe. Yukon Gold potatoes give the frittata a comforting bottom crust.
—**KATHERINE HANSEN** BRUNSWICK, ME

START TO FINISH: 30 MIN.
MAKES: 4 SERVINGS

- ¼ cup thinly sliced red onion
- 1 tablespoon olive oil
- 1 large Yukon Gold potato, peeled and thinly sliced
- 6 eggs
- 1 teaspoon minced fresh rosemary or ¼ teaspoon dried rosemary, crushed
- 1 teaspoon minced fresh thyme or ¼ teaspoon dried thyme
- ¼ teaspoon salt
- ⅛ teaspoon crushed red pepper flakes
- ⅛ teaspoon pepper
- 2 tablespoons shredded cheddar cheese

1. In an 8-in. ovenproof skillet, saute onion in oil until tender. Using a slotted spoon, remove onion and keep warm. Arrange potato in a single layer over bottom of pan.

2. In a small bowl, whisk eggs, seasonings and onion; pour over potatoes. Cover and cook 4-6 minutes or until nearly set.

3. Uncover skillet. Broil 3-4 in. from the heat 2-3 minutes or until eggs are completely set. Sprinkle with cheese. Let stand 5 minutes. Cut into wedges.

SWAP IT
Use basil and marjoram for the rosemary and thyme.

CINNAMON
APPLESAUCE
PANCAKES

BREAKFAST
BISCUITS 'N' EGGS

PBJ-STUFFED
FRENCH TOAST

Cinnamon Applesauce Pancakes

These fluffy, tender pancakes are so good, you just might skip the syrup. They were created for Christmas morning but have since wowed not only family and friends but also folks at church breakfasts. The cinnamon adds a pleasing touch.

—**RICHARD DEVORE** GIBSONBURG, OH

START TO FINISH: 20 MIN.
MAKES: 3 SERVINGS

- 1 **cup complete buttermilk pancake mix**
- 1 **teaspoon ground cinnamon**
- 1 **cup chunky cinnamon applesauce**
- ¼ **cup water**
  Maple syrup and butter

1. Combine pancake mix and cinnamon. Add applesauce and water; stir just until moistened.
2. Pour batter by ¼ cupfuls onto a greased hot griddle; turn when bubbles form on top. Cook until the second side is golden brown. Serve with syrup and butter.

(5)INGREDIENTS

Breakfast Biscuits 'n' Eggs

Using leftover biscuits from dinner the night before will make this sandwich even faster to make. Breakfast sandwiches are such a satisfying way to start the day.

—**TERESA HUFF** NEVADA, MO

START TO FINISH: 15 MIN.
MAKES: 4 BISCUITS

- 4 **individually frozen biscuits**
- 2 **teaspoons butter**
- 4 **eggs**
- 4 **slices process American cheese**
- 4 **thin slices deli ham**

1. Prepare biscuits according to package directions. Meanwhile, in a skillet, heat butter until hot. Add eggs; reduce heat to low. Fry until whites are completely set and yolks begin to thicken but are not hard.
2. Split biscuits. Layer the bottom of each biscuit with cheese, ham and an egg; replace top. Microwave, uncovered, 30-45 seconds or until cheese is melted.
NOTE *This recipe was tested in a 1,100-watt microwave.*

PBJ-Stuffed French Toast

I combined some of my favorite foods to create this delightfully different French toast. Now it's one of my go-to recipes when I have morning guests.

—**RUTH ANN BOTT** LAKE WALES, FL

START TO FINISH: 10 MIN.
MAKES: 2 SERVINGS

- 3 **tablespoons cream cheese, softened**
- 2 **tablespoons creamy peanut butter**
- 4 **slices Italian bread (¾ inch thick)**
- 2 **tablespoons red raspberry preserves**
- 2 **eggs**
- 1 **tablespoon evaporated milk**
  Maple syrup, optional

1. In a small bowl, combine cream cheese and peanut butter. Spread on two slices of bread; top with preserves and remaining bread. In a shallow bowl, whisk the eggs and milk. Dip the sandwiches into egg mixture.
2. In a greased large nonstick skillet, toast the sandwiches 2-3 minutes on each side or until golden brown. Serve with syrup if desired.

Fluffy Sausage Omelet

At Christmastime, we get family members together for a breakfast. I serve this omelet with fruit salad, hash brown casserole and biscuits.

—**JEAN TYNER** DARLINGTON, SC

START TO FINISH: 30 MIN.
MAKES: 2 SERVINGS

- ¼ **pound bulk pork sausage**
- 2 **tablespoons chopped onion**
- 2 **tablespoons chopped sweet red pepper**
- ¼ **cup sour cream**
- 3 **eggs, separated**
- 3 **tablespoons milk**
- ¼ **teaspoon salt**
- ¼ **teaspoon baking powder**
- ⅛ **teaspoon pepper**
- 1 **tablespoon butter**

1. Crumble sausage into a small microwave-safe dish; add onion and red pepper. Cover; microwave on high 2 minutes; drain. Stir in sour cream; set aside.
2. In a small bowl, whisk egg yolks, milk, salt, baking powder and pepper. In a large bowl, beat egg whites until stiff peaks form. Gently fold into egg yolk mixture.
3. Place the butter in a greased 9-in. microwave-safe pie plate. Microwave on high 30 seconds.
4. Pour egg mixture into plate. Microwave, uncovered, at 50% power for 3-5 minutes or until partially set. Lift the edges, letting uncooked portion flow underneath. Cook at 50% power 2-3 minutes longer or until eggs are set. Spoon sausage mixture over one side; fold omelet over filling.
NOTE *This recipe was tested in a 1,100-watt microwave.*

Lemon Blueberry Muffins

When my sister and I spent the night at our grandmother's house, we often requested these muffins for breakfast. Today, I bake them for my kids. The very aroma is a trip down memory lane.

—**KRIS MICHELS** WALLED LAKE, MI

START TO FINISH: 30 MIN.
MAKES: 1 DOZEN

- 2 cups biscuit/baking mix
- ½ cup plus 2 tablespoons sugar, divided
- 1 egg
- 1 cup (8 ounces) sour cream
- 1 cup fresh or frozen blueberries
- 2 teaspoons grated lemon peel

1. Preheat oven to 400°. In a large bowl, combine biscuit mix and ½ cup sugar. Whisk egg and sour cream; stir into dry ingredients just until moistened. Fold in the blueberries.
2. Fill greased or paper-lined muffin cups half full. Combine lemon peel and remaining sugar; sprinkle over batter.
3. Bake 20-25 minutes or until a toothpick inserted near the center comes out clean. Cool 5 minutes before removing from pan to a wire rack. Serve warm.
NOTE *If using frozen blueberries, use without thawing to avoid discoloring the batter.*

Microwave Egg Sandwich

If you're looking for a grab-and-go breakfast, this sandwich is high in protein. It keeps me full all morning, and it's only about 200 calories!

—**BRENDA OTTO** REEDSBURG, WI

START TO FINISH: 15 MIN.
MAKES: 1 SERVING

- 1 piece Canadian bacon
- ¼ cup egg substitute
- 1 tablespoon salsa
- 1 tablespoon shredded reduced-fat cheddar cheese
- 1 whole wheat English muffin, split, toasted
- 3 spinach leaves

1. Place Canadian bacon on the bottom of a 6-oz. ramekin or custard cup coated with cooking spray. Pour egg substitute over top. Microwave, uncovered, on high 30 seconds; stir. Microwave 15-30 seconds or until egg is almost set. Top with salsa; sprinkle with cheese. Microwave just until cheese is melted, about 10 seconds.
2. Line bottom of English muffin with spinach. Place egg and Canadian bacon over spinach; replace English muffin top.
NOTE *This recipe was tested in a 1,100-watt microwave.*

Peanut Butter Chip Pancakes

One day, I added peanut butter chips and pecans to my pancake recipe and everyone liked it!

—**MARGARET PACHE** MESA, AZ

START TO FINISH: 10 MIN.
MAKES: 4 SERVINGS

- 1½ cups pancake mix
- 2 tablespoons sugar
- 2 eggs, lightly beaten
- 1 cup milk
- ⅔ cup peanut butter chips
- ½ cup chopped pecans
  Pancake syrup and fresh strawberries

1. In a large bowl, combine the pancake mix and sugar. Whisk egg and milk; add to dry ingredients just until moistened. Stir in the chips and nuts.
2. Pour batter by ¼ cupfuls onto a greased hot griddle. Turn each pancake when bubbles form on top; cook until second side is golden brown. Serve with syrup and strawberries.

Berry Breakfast Parfaits

Are you short on time in the a.m.? My quick, delicious and beautiful parfaits are the perfect solution. Feel free to mix and match your favorite berries.

—**LISA SPEER** PALM BEACH, FL

START TO FINISH: 20 MIN.
MAKES: 8 SERVINGS

- 6½ cups frozen unsweetened raspberries
- ¼ cup packed brown sugar
- ¼ cup orange juice
- 2 tablespoons cornstarch
- ½ teaspoon grated orange peel
- 2 cups fresh blueberries
- 2 cups fresh blackberries
- 2 cups granola
- 4 cups vanilla Greek yogurt
  Additional brown sugar, optional

1. Place raspberries and brown sugar in a blender; cover and process until pureed. Press through a sieve; discard seeds.
2. In a small saucepan, combine the raspberry puree, orange juice, cornstarch and orange peel. Cook and stir over medium heat until thickened and bubbly. Reduce heat to low; cook and stir 2 minutes longer. Remove from heat; cool.
3. In eight parfait glasses, layer half of the raspberry sauce, berries, granola and yogurt. Repeat the layers. Sprinkle with additional brown sugar if desired. Serve immediately.

Chocolate-Peanut Granola Bars

Nutella and peanut butter meet to make some amazing granola bars. People always think they're eating something naughty when I serve these, but the bars are full of oats and healthy fats.

—**BRENDA L CAUGHELL** DURHAM, NC

START TO FINISH: 30 MIN.
MAKES: 2 DOZEN

- 2½ cups old-fashioned oats
- ¾ cup lightly salted dry roasted peanuts, coarsely chopped
- ¾ cup wheat germ
- ¾ cup sunflower kernels
- ½ cup honey
- ¼ cup packed brown sugar
- 3 tablespoons butter
- ⅓ cup creamy peanut butter
- ⅓ cup Nutella

1. Preheat oven to 400°. In an ungreased 15x10x1-in. baking pan, combine oats, peanuts, wheat germ and sunflower kernels. Bake 8-12 minutes or until toasted, stirring occasionally. Cool on a wire rack.
2. In a small saucepan, combine honey, brown sugar and butter. Cook and stir over medium heat until mixture comes to a boil; cook 2 minutes longer. Remove from heat; stir in peanut butter and Nutella until blended.
3. Transfer oat mixture to a large bowl; add honey mixture and toss to coat. Press into a greased 13x9-in. pan. Cool. Cut into bars.

SWAP IT
For a richer flavor, try chopped macadamia nuts for the peanuts.

BERRY BREAKFAST PARFAITS

CHOCOLATE-PEANUT GRANOLA BARS

SAUSAGE BREAKFAST HASH

CUBAN BREAKFAST SANDWICHES

Sausage Breakfast Hash

Served with dough well-done (toast) and dirty water (coffee), this makes a fun breakfast combo.

—JACOB KITZMAN SEATTLE, WA

START TO FINISH: 30 MIN.
MAKES: 4 SERVINGS

- 3 **tablespoons butter, divided**
- 1 **package (20 ounces) refrigerated diced potatoes with onion**
- 1 **package (7 ounces) frozen fully cooked breakfast sausage links, thawed and sliced**
- 1 **small green pepper, chopped**
- 1 **small sweet red pepper, chopped**
- ¼ **teaspoon salt**
  Dash cayenne pepper
- 1 **cup (4 ounces) shredded Swiss cheese**
- 8 **eggs**
- ¼ **teaspoon pepper**
  Hot pepper sauce, optional

1. In a skillet, melt 1 tablespoon butter over medium heat; stir in potatoes, sausage, green and red peppers, salt and cayenne. Cover and cook 12-14 minutes or until potatoes and vegetables are tender, stirring occasionally. Stir in cheese.
2. In a large skillet, fry eggs in remaining butter as desired. Sprinkle with pepper. Serve with hash and, if desired, pepper sauce.

⑤INGREDIENTS

Cuban Breakfast Sandwiches

Grab hold of breakfast time by serving these warm, energy-boosting sandwiches. They travel well for hectic mornings, and the hearty helping of protein will help keep hunger at bay.

—LACIE GRIFFIN AUSTIN, TX

START TO FINISH: 20 MIN.
MAKES: 4 SERVINGS

- 1 **loaf (1 pound) Cuban or French bread**
- 4 **eggs**
- 16 **pieces thinly sliced hard salami**
- 8 **slices deli ham**
- 8 **slices Swiss cheese**

1. Split bread in half lengthwise; cut into four pieces. Fry eggs in a large nonstick skillet coated with cooking spray until yolks are set. Layer bread bottoms with salami, ham, egg and cheese; replace tops.
2. Cook on a panini maker or indoor grill 2 minutes or until bread is browned and the cheese is melted.

DID YOU KNOW?

Egg grades are based on the exterior and interior quality of an egg. If you like fried eggs with thick whites and tall yolks purchase Grade AA eggs.

Mango-Peach Smoothies

This is my toddler son's favorite breakfast—he'll take one of these over pancakes any day! Get creative when mixing fruits and fruit-flavored yogurts; we love peach yogurt with mango, strawberry yogurt with blueberries or pina colada yogurt with mango and banana.

—**DANA HERRA** DEKALB, IL

START TO FINISH: 5 MIN.
MAKES: 4 SERVINGS

- 1 cup fat-free milk
- 12 ounces peach yogurt (about 1¼ cups)
- 2½ cups frozen mango chunks

Place all ingredients in a blender; cover and process until smooth. Serve immediately.

Strawberry Breakfast Shortcakes

I don't let a busy schedule stop me from eating healthfully! Protein, fruit, dairy and whole grains come together in a flash for a delectable start to the day.

—**PAULA WHARTON** EL PASO, TX

START TO FINISH: 10 MIN.
MAKES: 4 SERVINGS

- 8 frozen low-fat multigrain waffles
- 2 cups fresh strawberries, sliced
- 1 cup plain Greek yogurt
  Maple syrup

Prepare waffles according to package directions. Divide among two serving plates. Top with strawberries and yogurt. Serve with syrup.

Brown Sugar & Banana Oatmeal

Oatmeal is a popular breakfast food, quick, easy and filling. I came up with this version by using some of the same ingredients from my go-to breakfast smoothie. Add bran cereal for a heartier taste and more fiber. This is also good with a brown sugar substitute and soy milk.

—**JESSI RIZZI** ODENTON, MD

START TO FINISH: 15 MIN.
MAKES: 3 SERVINGS

- 2 cups fat-free milk
- 1 cup quick-cooking oats
- 1 large ripe banana, sliced
- 2 teaspoons brown sugar
- 1 teaspoon honey
- ½ teaspoon ground cinnamon
  Additional fat-free milk or ground cinnamon, optional

1. In a small saucepan, bring milk to a boil; stir in oats. Cook over medium heat 1-2 minutes or until thickened, stirring occasionally.
2. Stir in banana, brown sugar, honey and cinnamon. Divide among three serving bowls. Serve with additional milk and cinnamon if desired.

MANGO-PEACH SMOOTHIES

Scrambled Eggs with the Works

Loaded with fantastic flavors, my colorful, savory egg dish is perfect for hungry appetites.

—SUSAN ZIENTARA DECATUR, IL

START TO FINISH: 25 MIN.
MAKES: 5 SERVINGS

- ¼ pound bulk sage pork sausage
- 1¼ cups sliced fresh mushrooms
- 1 medium green pepper, chopped
- 1 small onion, chopped
- 10 eggs
- ⅔ cup shredded cheddar cheese
- ¼ cup water
- ¼ teaspoon salt
- ¼ teaspoon pepper
- 1 plum tomato, chopped

1. In a large skillet, cook sausage, mushrooms, green pepper and onion over medium heat until meat is no longer pink; drain.
2. In a large bowl, whisk the eggs, cheese, water, salt and pepper; add to skillet. Cook and stir over medium heat until eggs are set. Stir in tomato.

Peanut Butter & Banana Waffles

I love bananas and I love to make breakfast, too. These are a refreshing change from your everyday waffles. I frequently make big batches so I can freeze the leftovers and reheat them later for an even quicker breakfast.

—CHRISTINA ADDISON
BLANCHESTER, OH

PREP: 10 MIN. • **COOK:** 5 MIN./BATCH
MAKES: 16 WAFFLES

- 1¾ cups all-purpose flour
- 2 tablespoons sugar
- 3 teaspoons baking powder
- ¼ teaspoon salt
- ¾ cup creamy peanut butter
- ½ cup canola oil
- 2 eggs
- 1¾ cups 2% milk
- 1 cup mashed ripe bananas (about 2 medium)

1. In a large bowl, whisk the flour, sugar, baking powder and salt. Place the peanut butter in another bowl; gradually whisk in oil. Whisk in the eggs and milk. Add to the dry ingredients; stir just until moistened. Stir in the bananas.
2. Bake in a preheated waffle iron according to manufacturer's directions until golden brown.

Ham & Egg Pita Pockets

One day when the kids were running late for school, I needed a quick and portable breakfast, so I whipped up this egg sandwich. Because the eggs cook quickly in the microwave, breakfast is ready in 10 minutes.

—SUE OLSEN FREMONT, CA

START TO FINISH: 10 MIN.
MAKES: 1 SERVING

- 2 egg whites
- 1 egg
- ⅛ teaspoon smoked or plain paprika
- ⅛ teaspoon freshly ground pepper
- 1 slice deli ham, chopped
- 1 green onion, sliced
- 2 tablespoons shredded reduced-fat cheddar cheese
- 2 whole wheat pita pocket halves

In a microwave-safe bowl, whisk egg whites, egg, paprika and pepper until blended; stir in ham, green onion and cheese. Microwave, covered, on high 1 minute. Stir; cook on high 30-60 seconds longer or until almost set. Serve in pitas.
NOTE *This recipe was tested in a 1,100-watt microwave.*

Good-Morning Granola

This is ridiculously simple to make and has lots of healthy ingredients. It's a great way to start your day or to keep you going. With pretty packaging, it makes a nice gift or bake sale item.

—MARY BILYEU ANN ARBOR, MI

PREP: 15 MIN. • **BAKE:** 20 MIN. + COOLING
MAKES: 7½ CUPS

- 4 cups old-fashioned oats
- ½ cup toasted wheat germ
- ½ cup sliced almonds
- 2 teaspoons ground cinnamon
- ⅛ teaspoon salt
- ½ cup orange juice
- ½ cup honey
- 2 teaspoons canola oil
- 1 teaspoon vanilla extract
- 1 cup dried cherries
- 1 cup dried cranberries
  Reduced-fat plain yogurt, optional

1. Preheat oven to 350°. In a large bowl, combine the first five ingredients; set aside. In a small saucepan, combine orange juice, honey and oil. Bring to a boil, stirring constantly. Remove from heat; stir in vanilla. Pour over oat mixture and mix well.
2. Transfer to a 15x10x1-in. baking pan coated with cooking spray. Bake 20-25 minutes or until golden brown, stirring every 10 minutes. Cool completely on a wire rack.
3. Stir in dried fruits. Store in an airtight container. Serve with yogurt if desired.

SWAP IT
For an adult pocket, use cooked crumbled chorizo instead of the ham.

**PEANUT BUTTER &
BANANA WAFFLES**

**HAM & EGG
PITA POCKETS**

**GOOD-MORNING
GRANOLA**

FETA FRITTATA

Feta Frittata

Chopped tomatoes and feta cheese come together to make this frittata extra special. It's ideal for a lazy Sunday or to serve with a tossed salad for a light lunch.

—**MARJORIE DODERO** SEAL BEACH, CA

START TO FINISH: 25 MIN.
MAKES: 2 SERVINGS

- 1 **green onion, thinly sliced**
- 1 **small garlic clove, minced**
- 2 **eggs**
- ½ **cup egg substitute**
- 4 **tablespoons crumbled feta cheese, divided**
- ⅓ **cup chopped plum tomato**
- 4 **thin slices peeled avocado**
- 2 **tablespoons reduced-fat sour cream**

1. Heat a 6-in. nonstick skillet coated with cooking spray over medium heat. Saute onion and garlic until tender. Whisk the eggs, egg substitute and 3 tablespoons feta cheese. Add egg mixture to the skillet (mixture should set immediately at edges). Cover and cook for 4-6 minutes or until nearly set.

2. Sprinkle with tomato and remaining feta cheese. Cover and cook 2-3 minutes longer or until eggs are completely set. Let stand for 5 minutes. Cut in half; serve with avocado and sour cream.

LANCE'S OWN
FRENCH TOAST

A.M. RUSH ESPRESSO
SMOOTHIE

(5) INGREDIENTS
Lance's Own French Toast

When my young son, Lance, helps make this French toast, he knows the order to add the ingredients and how much to measure out. An avid cook, Lance calls this one of his specialties!
—**JANNA STEELE** MAGEE, MS

PREP: 10 MIN. • **COOK:** 10 MIN./BATCH
MAKES: 6 SERVINGS

- 4 eggs
- 1 cup 2% milk
- 1 tablespoon honey
- ½ teaspoon ground cinnamon
- ⅛ teaspoon pepper
- 12 slices whole wheat bread
  Sugar and additional ground cinnamon, optional

1. In a large bowl, whisk the eggs, milk, honey, cinnamon and pepper. Dip bread in egg mixture; cook on a greased hot griddle 3-4 minutes on each side or until golden brown.
2. Cut into decorative shapes and sprinkle with sugar and additional cinnamon if desired.

A.M. Rush Espresso Smoothie

Want an early-morning pick-me-up that's good for you, too? Fruit and flaxseed give this sweet espresso a nutritious twist.
—**AIMEE WILSON** CLOVIS, CA

START TO FINISH: 10 MIN.
MAKES: 1 SERVING

- ½ cup cold fat-free milk
- 1 tablespoon vanilla flavoring syrup
- 1 cup ice cubes
- ½ medium banana, cut up
- 1 to 2 teaspoons instant espresso powder
- 1 teaspoon ground flaxseed
- 1 teaspoon baking cocoa

In a blender, combine all the ingredients; cover and process 1-2 minutes or until blended. Pour into a chilled glass; serve immediately.
NOTE *This recipe was tested with Torani brand flavoring syrup. Look for it in the coffee section.*

Muesli

I received this authentic recipe from a New Zealand pen pal. My family loves the naturally sweet flavor of honey.
—**ANN BELCZAK** NORTH TONAWANDA, NY

PREP: 15 MIN. • **BAKE:** 40 MIN. + COOLING
MAKES: 11 CUPS

- 6 cups old-fashioned oats
- 1½ cups toasted wheat germ
- 1½ cups all-bran cereal
- ½ cup flaked coconut
- 1½ cups honey
- ½ cups chopped walnuts
- ⅓ cups chopped dried apricots

1. Preheat oven to 275°. In a large bowl, combine oats, wheat germ, cereal and coconut. Pour into two greased 13x9-in. baking pans.
2. Bake 20 minutes, stirring once. Heat honey in a saucepan until thin, about 5 minutes. Pour half into each pan; stir to coat evenly.
3. Bake 20-30 minutes longer or until golden; stir every 10 minutes. Stir in walnuts and apricots. Cool, stirring occasionally. Store in an airtight container.

Blueberry Oatmeal Pancakes

Wonderful blueberry flavor abounds in these thick and moist pancakes. My kids love them, and they are very nutritious, easy and inexpensive!

—AMY SPAINHOWARD
BOWLING GREEN, KY

PREP: 20 MIN. • **COOK:** 5 MIN./BATCH
MAKES: 14 PANCAKES (1¼ CUPS SYRUP)

- 2 cups all-purpose flour
- 2 packets (1.51 ounces each) instant maple and brown sugar oatmeal mix
- 2 tablespoons sugar
- 2 teaspoons baking powder
- ⅛ teaspoon salt
- 2 egg whites
- 1 egg
- 1½ cups fat-free milk
- ½ cup reduced-fat sour cream
- 2 cups fresh or frozen blueberries

BLUEBERRY SYRUP
- 1½ cups fresh or frozen blueberries
- ½ cup sugar

1. In a large bowl, combine the first five ingredients. In another bowl, whisk the egg whites, egg, milk and sour cream. Stir into dry ingredients just until moistened. Fold in blueberries.
2. Spoon batter by ¼ cupfuls onto a hot griddle coated with cooking spray. Turn when bubbles form on top of pancake; cook until the second side is golden brown.
3. In a microwave-safe bowl, combine the syrup ingredients.

Microwave, uncovered, on high 1 minute; stir. Microwave 1-2 minutes longer or until hot and bubbly. Serve warm with pancakes.
NOTE *If using frozen blueberries, do not thaw before adding to batter. This recipe was tested in a 1,100-watt microwave.*

Berry Nutritious Smoothies

We have committed our family to living a healthy lifestyle, which includes exercising regularly and eating healthfully. Breakfast is such an important meal of the day and should never be skipped. This recipe is always a fun experiment! I generally use whatever fresh or frozen fruit I have on hand, but I always include a frozen banana.

—JUDY PARKER MOORE, OK

START TO FINISH: 5 MIN.
MAKES: 3 SERVINGS

- 1 cup orange juice
- ½ cup fat-free plain yogurt
- ½ cup silken firm tofu
- 1 medium ripe banana, sliced and frozen
- ½ cup frozen unsweetened strawberries
- ½ cup frozen unsweetened raspberries
- 2 tablespoons toasted wheat germ

In a blender, combine all the ingredients; cover and process for 30 seconds or until smooth. Pour into chilled glasses; serve immediately.

Green Chili Breakfast Burritos

When I lived in the Southwest, we wrapped everything up in a tortilla. Breakfast burritos in every possible combination are very popular there, especially with green chilies.

—ANGELA SPENGLER
MECHANICSBURG, PA

START TO FINISH: 25 MIN.
MAKES: 6 SERVINGS

- 6 eggs
- 3 egg whites
- 1 jalapeno pepper, seeded and minced
  Dash cayenne pepper
- 4 breakfast turkey sausage links, casings removed
- ¾ cup shredded reduced-fat Mexican cheese blend
- 1 can (4 ounces) chopped green chilies, drained
- 6 whole wheat tortillas (8 inches), warmed
- 6 tablespoons salsa

1. In a small bowl, whisk the eggs, egg whites, jalapeno and cayenne; set aside.
2. Crumble sausage into a large skillet; cook over medium heat until no longer pink. Drain. Push sausage to the sides of pan. Pour egg mixture into center of pan. Cook and stir until set. Sprinkle with cheese and chilies. Remove from the heat; cover and let stand until cheese is melted.
3. Place ⅓ cup egg mixture off center on each tortilla. Fold sides and end over filling and roll up. Top with salsa.
NOTE *Wear disposable gloves when cutting hot peppers; the oils can burn skin. Avoid touching your face.*

HOW TO

FLIP PANCAKES
Turn pancakes over when edges become dry and bubbles on top begin to pop. Continue cooking pancakes until the bottoms are golden brown.

BERRY NUTRITIOUS SMOOTHIES

GREEN CHILI BREAKFAST BURRITOS

Biscuits with Turkey Sausage Gravy

My husband was diagnosed with diabetes, so I began using turkey sausage in this recipe, and it turned out extremely well. There are never any leftovers!

—**MARCIA SNYDER** BOONTON, NJ

START TO FINISH: 30 MIN.
MAKES: 4 SERVINGS

- 1 tube (16.3 ounces) large refrigerated flaky biscuits
- 1 pound Italian turkey sausage links, casings removed
- 3 tablespoons butter
- 3 tablespoons all-purpose flour
- ½ teaspoon ground mustard
- ¼ teaspoon salt
- ⅛ teaspoon pepper
- 2½ cups whole milk
- 1 tablespoon Worcestershire sauce

1. Bake biscuits according to package directions. Meanwhile, crumble sausage into a large saucepan; cook over medium heat until no longer pink. Drain and keep warm.

2. In the same saucepan, melt butter. Stir in flour, mustard, salt and pepper until smooth. Gradually add milk and the Worcestershire sauce. Bring to a boil; cook and stir 2 minutes or until thickened.

3. Stir in sausage; heat through. Place two biscuits on each serving plate; top with gravy.

Chocolate Challah French Toast

I serve up a decadent breakfast—with pleasure—from the kitchen of my family-run bed-and-breakfast.

—**MARIE PARKER** MILWAUKEE, WI

PREP: 15 MIN. + SOAKING • **COOK:** 10 MIN.
MAKES: 2 SERVINGS

- 4 slices challah or egg bread (¾ inch thick)
- ⅔ cup sugar
- ⅓ cup baking cocoa
- ¼ teaspoon salt
- ⅛ teaspoon baking powder
- 4 eggs
- 1 cup 2% milk
- 1 teaspoon vanilla extract
- 2 tablespoons butter
  Optional toppings: confectioners' sugar, fresh raspberries, sliced fresh strawberries, sliced ripe banana and maple syrup

1. Arrange bread slices in a 13x9-in. dish. In a small bowl, combine sugar, cocoa, salt and baking powder. In another bowl, whisk eggs, milk and vanilla. Gradually whisk into the dry ingredients until smooth. Pour over bread. Let stand 10 minutes, turning once.

2. In a large skillet, melt butter over medium heat. Cook bread for 3-4 minutes on each side or until toasted. Serve with toppings of your choice.

Ham and Cheddar Scones

This recipe came from a friend after she shared the scones with me. I like that you can see flecks of cheese, ham and green onions.

—**FELICITY LA RUE** PALMDALE, CA

PREP: 25 MIN. • **BAKE:** 20 MIN.
MAKES: 1 DOZEN

- 3 cups all-purpose flour
- ½ cup sugar
- 2 tablespoons baking powder
- ½ teaspoon salt
- 2 cups heavy whipping cream
- 1 cup diced fully cooked ham
- ½ cup diced cheddar cheese
- 4 green onions, thinly sliced

1. Preheat oven to 400°. In a large bowl, combine flour, sugar, baking powder and salt. Stir in cream just until moistened. Stir in ham, cheese and onions. Turn onto a floured surface; knead 10 times.

2. Transfer dough to a greased baking sheet. Pat into a 9-in. circle. Cut into 12 wedges, but do not separate. Bake 20-25 minutes or until golden brown. Serve warm.

HOW TO

SHAPE SCONES

❶ Most scone recipes suggest patting the dough into a circle. For proper baking, be sure the circle meets the dimensions noted in the recipe.

❷ Cut the dough into wedges with a dough scraper or knife. It may be helpful to flour the utensil's edge between cuts to prevent the dough from sticking to it.

OVERNIGHT
MAPLE OATMEAL

Overnight Maple Oatmeal

I first tasted muesli on a trip to Switzerland, and when I came home, I made it my way. Keep things interesting (and avoid the mid-morning munchies) by adding different fruits and nuts every day.
—**MADDIE KIRK** SPRINGFIELD, PA

PREP: 10 MIN. + CHILLING
MAKES: 6 SERVINGS

- 2 **cups old-fashioned oats**
- 1 **cup fat-free milk**
- ¼ **cup maple syrup**
- 2 **teaspoons vanilla extract**
- 1 **cup vanilla yogurt**
- ½ **cup chopped walnuts, toasted**
  Assorted fresh fruit

1. In a large bowl, combine the oats, milk, syrup and vanilla. Refrigerate, covered, overnight.
2. Just before serving, stir in yogurt. Top with walnuts and fruit.
NOTE *To toast nuts, spread in a 15x10x1-in. baking pan. Bake at 350° for 5-10 minutes or until lightly browned, stirring occasionally. Or, spread in a dry nonstick skillet and heat over low heat until lightly browned, stirring occasionally.*

PAIR IT!
A glass of cold milk is the perfect companion to this stick-to-your-ribs cereal.

PAIR IT!
Beef and Blue Cheese Crostini, page 39, and these chicken strips make a hearty snack spread.

CHICKEN SKEWERS WITH SWEET & SPICY MARMALADE, 47

42   40   48

Munchies

It's a breeze to whip up **no-fuss treats** for after-school snacking as well as **make-ahead bites** for grown-up get-togethers. Turn here for easy appetizers—many of which require only five ingredients!

Blue-Ribbon Beef Nachos

Chili powder and sassy salsa season a zesty mixture of ground beef and refried beans that's sprinkled with green onions, tomatoes and olives.

—**DIANE HIXON** NICEVILLE, FL

START TO FINISH: 20 MIN.
MAKES: 6 SERVINGS

- 1 pound ground beef
- 1 small onion, chopped
- 1 can (16 ounces) refried beans
- 1 jar (16 ounces) salsa
- 1 can (6 ounces) pitted ripe olives, chopped
- ½ cup shredded cheddar cheese
- 1 green onion, chopped
- 2 tablespoons chili powder
- 1 teaspoon salt
  Tortilla chips
  Sliced ripe olives, chopped green onions and tomatoes, optional

1. In a large skillet, cook the beef and onion over medium heat until meat is no longer pink; drain. Stir in the next seven ingredients and heat through.
2. Serve over tortilla chips. Top with olives, onions and tomatoes if desired.

Easy Three-Cheese Pesto Pizza

With a ready-made crust, this pizza can be on a serving tray in half an hour. The triple cheese blend will make these slices go fast.

—**PAT STEVENS** GRANBURY, TX

START TO FINISH: 30 MIN.
MAKES: 16 SLICES

- ½ cup finely chopped red onion
- ½ cup finely chopped sweet red pepper
- 1 tablespoon olive oil
- 1 prebaked 12-inch pizza crust
- ½ cup prepared pesto
- 1 cup (4 ounces) crumbled feta cheese
- 1 cup (4 ounces) shredded part-skim mozzarella cheese
- 1 cup (4 ounces) shredded Parmesan cheese
- 1 can (4¼ ounces) chopped ripe olives
- 1 medium tomato, thinly sliced

1. Preheat oven to 400°. In a small skillet, saute onion and red pepper in oil until tender. Remove from heat; set aside.
2. Place crust on an ungreased 14-in. pizza pan. Spread pesto to within ½ in. of edges. Layer with cheeses, onion mixture, olives and tomato.
3. Bake 15-18 minutes or until cheese is melted.

Turtle Chips

Salty-sweet, crunchy-chewy, so many sensations in one delectable bite. Both kids and adults will be reaching for this goodie. Best of all, it's the absolute easiest recipe to prepare!

—**LEIGH ANN STEWART** HOPKINSVILLE, KY

START TO FINISH: 25 MIN.
MAKES: 16 SERVINGS (½ CUP EACH)

- 1 package (11 ounces) ridged potato chips
- 1 package (14 ounces) caramels
- ⅓ cup heavy whipping cream
- 1 package (11½ ounces) milk chocolate chips
- 2 tablespoons shortening
- 1 cup finely chopped pecans

1. Arrange whole potato chips in a single layer on a large platter. In a saucepan, combine caramels and cream. Cook and stir over medium-low heat until caramels are melted. Drizzle over chips.
2. In a microwave, melt chocolate and shortening; stir until smooth. Drizzle over the caramel mixture; sprinkle with the pecans. Serve immediately.

⑤ INGREDIENTS

Basil & Sun-Dried Tomato Crescents

If your family is anything like mine, you may want to make a double batch of these crescents since they vanish so quickly. This is a low-fuss recipe that's meant to be shared.

—**MARA FLETCHER** BATESVILLE, IN

START TO FINISH: 30 MIN.
MAKES: 16 ROLLS

- 2 tubes (8 ounces each) refrigerated crescent rolls
- ⅔ cup butter, softened
- ½ cup minced fresh basil
- ¼ cup oil-packed sun-dried tomatoes, patted dry and finely chopped
- 1 teaspoon garlic powder

1. Preheat oven to 375°. Unroll each tube of crescent dough; separate dough into eight triangles. In a small bowl, mix remaining ingredients; spread over triangles.
2. Roll up and place 2 in. apart on ungreased baking sheets, point side down; curve to form crescents. Bake 11-13 minutes or until rolls are golden brown.

TOP TIP

After making Easy Three-Cheese Pesto Pizza, you may have a partially used container of pesto left over. Here are some easy ideas to put those leftovers to good use:
- Mix a little pesto with butter or mayonnaise for a sandwich spread.
- Stir a little into mashed potatoes.
- Add a dab to tuna or egg salad.

EASY THREE-CHEESE PESTO PIZZA

TURTLE CHIPS

BASIL & SUN-DRIED TOMATO CRESCENTS

CHICKEN NACHOS
FOR ONE

BANANAS FOSTER
CRUNCH MIX

Chicken Nachos for One

You will look forward to "me" time when you have the makings for these nachos on hand. I've had them many ways, and they're always so good!
—**REGINA MORALES** ORLANDO, FL

START TO FINISH: 10 MIN.
MAKES: 1 SERVING

- ¾ cup coarsely chopped ready-to-use grilled chicken breast strips
- 2 tablespoons water
- ¼ teaspoon taco seasoning
- ¼ cup shredded Mexican cheese blend
- 2 cups tortilla chips
- ½ cup refried black beans, warmed
- 1 tablespoon salsa

1. In a small skillet, combine the chicken, water and taco seasoning. Bring to a boil. Reduce heat; simmer, uncovered, 2 minutes, stirring occasionally. Remove from heat. Sprinkle with cheese; cover and let stand 1 minute or until melted.

2. Arrange chips on a serving plate; top with beans, chicken mixture and salsa.

Bananas Foster Crunch Mix

Bananas Foster is one of my favorite desserts. So, I thought that a crunchy, snackable version would be a hit.
—**DAVID DAHLMAN** CHATSWORTH, CA

PREP: 10 MIN. • **COOK:** 5 MIN. + COOLING
MAKES: 2½ QUARTS

- 3 cups Honey Nut Chex
- 3 cups Cinnamon Chex
- 2¼ cups pecan halves
- 1½ cups dried banana chips
- ⅓ cup butter, cubed
- ⅓ cup packed brown sugar
- ½ teaspoon ground cinnamon
- ½ teaspoon banana extract
- ½ teaspoon rum extract

1. In a large microwave-safe bowl, mix cereals, pecans and banana chips. In a small microwave-safe bowl, combine butter, brown sugar and cinnamon. Microwave,

uncovered, on high 2 minutes, stirring once. Stir in extracts. Pour over cereal mixture; toss to coat.

2. Cook, uncovered, on high 3 minutes, stirring after each minute. Spread mixture onto waxed paper to cool. Store in an airtight container.

NOTE *This recipe was tested in a 1,100-watt microwave.*

PAIR IT!
Italian Subs, page 35, and the snack mix will make a hearty treat for game day.

Pimiento Cheese Spread

A classic Southern comfort food, this cheese spread is often served as an appetizer with crackers or as a sandwich spread or burger topping.

—EILEEN BALMER SOUTH BEND, IN

PREP: 10 MIN. + CHILLING
MAKES: 1¼ CUPS

- 1½ cups (6 ounces) shredded cheddar cheese
- 1 jar (4 ounces) diced pimientos, drained and finely chopped
- ⅓ cup mayonnaise
  Assorted crackers

In a small bowl, combine cheese, pimientos and mayonnaise. Chill at least 1 hour. Serve with crackers.

Honey-Lime Yogurt Dip

When it comes to this tangy fruit dip, I don't mind my kids playing with their food. We like to dip strawberries, but pears and bananas are good, too.

—SHELLY L. BEVINGTON HERMISTON, OR

START TO FINISH: 5 MIN.
MAKES: 2 CUPS

- 2 cups (16 ounces) plain yogurt
- ¼ cup honey
- 2 tablespoons lime juice
- ½ teaspoon grated lime peel
  Assorted fresh fruit

Whisk yogurt, honey, lime juice and lime peel in a small bowl. Refrigerate until serving. Serve with fruit.

Sausage Wonton Cups

Here's a tasty hot appetizer for all those parties that feature fun finger foods and quick bites.

—SHIRLEY VAN ALLEN HIGH POINT, NC

START TO FINISH: 30 MIN.
MAKES: 2 DOZEN

- 4 Italian turkey sausage links (4 ounces each), casings removed
- 1 can (15 ounces) tomato sauce
- ½ teaspoon garlic powder
- ½ teaspoon dried basil
- 24 wonton wrappers
- 1 cup (4 ounces) shredded Italian cheese blend

1. Preheat oven to 350°. In a large skillet, cook sausage over medium heat until no longer pink; drain. Stir in the tomato sauce, garlic powder and basil. Bring to a boil. Reduce heat; simmer, uncovered, 8-10 minutes or until thickened.
2. Meanwhile, press wonton wrappers into miniature muffin cups coated with cooking spray. Bake for 8-9 minutes or until lightly browned.
3. Spoon sausage mixture into cups. Sprinkle with cheese. Bake 5-7 minutes longer or until cheese is melted. Serve warm.

PIMIENTO CHEESE SPREAD

EASY BUFFALO CHICKEN DIP

¾ cup flaked coconut, toasted
½ cup chopped macadamia nuts, toasted
2 tablespoons minced chives

Spread cream cheese over crackers. Top with crab, preserves, coconut, nuts and chives.

Little Mexican Pizzas

These little pizzas are perfect for lunch, snacks or parties. Whole wheat English muffins offer more fiber than regular pizza crust.
—**LINDA EGGERS** ALBANY, CA

START TO FINISH: 25 MIN.
MAKES: 1 DOZEN

1 package (13 ounces) whole wheat English muffins, split
¾ cup fat-free refried beans
¾ cup salsa
⅓ cup sliced ripe olives
2 green onions, chopped
2 tablespoons canned chopped green chilies
1½ cups (6 ounces) shredded part-skim mozzarella cheese

1. Spread cut sides of muffins with refried beans; top with the salsa, olives, onions, chilies and cheese.
2. Place on baking sheets; broil 4-6 in. from heat 2-3 minutes or until cheese is melted.

DID YOU KNOW?

The Anchor Bar in Buffalo, New York, is credited with serving the first Buffalo Wings. With some wings, a little imagination and a few handy ingredients, Teressa Bellissimo made a treat that's now enjoyed coast to coast.

---

(5) INGREDIENTS
Easy Buffalo Chicken Dip

With three simple ingredients, you can turn leftover chicken into the ultimate guy food. Perfect for a quick game-day snack, I often serve the dip with crackers or celery sticks.
—**JANICE FOLTZ** HERSHEY, PA

START TO FINISH: 30 MIN.
MAKES: 4 CUPS

1 package (8 ounces) reduced-fat cream cheese
1 cup (8 ounces) reduced-fat sour cream
½ cup Louisiana-style hot sauce
3 cups shredded cooked chicken breast
   Assorted crackers

1. Preheat oven to 350°. In a large bowl, beat the cream cheese, sour cream and hot sauce until smooth; stir in chicken.

2. Transfer to an 8-in.-square baking dish coated with cooking spray. Cover and bake 18-22 minutes or until heated through. Serve warm with crackers.

Hawaiian Crab Canapes

Treat your guests to a taste of paradise with crab, macadamia nuts, pineapple preserves and coconut. The sweet, crunchy canapes are a breeze to make and eat.
—**JAMIE MILLER** MAPLE GROVE, MN

START TO FINISH: 20 MIN.
MAKES: ABOUT 4 DOZEN

1 carton (8 ounces) spreadable chive and onion cream cheese
1 package (3.2 ounces) teriyaki rice crackers
1 can (6 ounces) lump crabmeat, drained
1 jar (12 ounces) pineapple preserves

Italian Subs

Olive lovers are sure to rejoice over this stacked sandwich! Stuffed and ripe olives are marinated in white wine vinegar and garlic before they are used to flavor these speedy salami, ham and provolone subs.

—DELORES CHRISTNER SPOONER, WI

PREP: 15 MIN. + CHILLING
MAKES: 10 SERVINGS

- ⅓ cup olive oil
- 4½ teaspoons white wine vinegar
- 1 tablespoon dried parsley flakes
- 2 to 3 garlic cloves, minced
- 1 can (2¼ ounces) sliced ripe olives, drained
- ½ cup chopped pimiento-stuffed olives
- 1 loaf (1 pound, 20 inches) French bread, unsliced
- 24 thin slices hard salami
- 24 slices provolone or mozzarella cheese
- 24 slices fully cooked ham
  Lettuce leaves, optional

1. In a small bowl, combine oil, vinegar, parsley and garlic. Stir in the olives. Cover and refrigerate 8 hours or overnight.

2. Cut bread in half lengthwise. Spread olive mixture on bottom of the bread. Top with salami, cheese and ham; add lettuce if desired. Replace top. Cut into 2-in. slices. Insert a toothpick into each slice.

LITTLE MEXICAN PIZZAS

ITALIAN SUBS

PARTY
SHRIMP

MOZZARELLA
RYE SNACKS

STROMBOLI
SLICES

Party Shrimp

An herby marinade makes the shrimp so flavorful, you won't even need a dipping sauce. I guarantee they'll disappear quickly.

—KENDRA DOSS
COLORADO SPRINGS, CO

PREP: 15 MIN. + MARINATING
BROIL: 10 MIN.
MAKES: ABOUT 2½ DOZEN

- 1 tablespoon olive oil
- 1½ teaspoons brown sugar
- 1½ teaspoons lemon juice
- 1 garlic clove, thinly sliced
- ½ teaspoon paprika
- ½ teaspoon Italian seasoning
- ½ teaspoon dried basil
- ¼ teaspoon pepper
- 1 pound uncooked large shrimp, peeled and deveined

1. In a large resealable plastic bag, combine the first eight ingredients. Add shrimp; seal bag and turn to coat. Refrigerate 2 hours.

2. Drain shrimp, discarding marinade. Place shrimp on an ungreased baking sheet. Broil 4 in. from heat 3-4 minutes on each side or until shrimp turn pink.

---

⑤INGREDIENTS

Mozzarella Rye Snacks

This creamy topping has a subtle tang that pairs perfectly with crisp rye bread. We enjoy my simple recipe at our summer deck parties. It's ideal for unexpected guests or as a snack.

—MISSIE KLEI CINCINNATI, OH

START TO FINISH: 20 MIN.
MAKES: 2 DOZEN

- 1 cup (4 ounces) shredded part-skim mozzarella cheese
- ½ cup mayonnaise
- ½ cup sour cream
- 1 tablespoon Italian salad dressing mix
- 1 loaf (16 ounces) snack rye bread

1. Preheat oven to 350°. In a small bowl, mix cheese, mayonnaise, sour cream and salad dressing mix until blended. Spread 1 tablespoonful over each slice of bread.

2. Place bread slices on greased baking sheets. Bake 5-7 minutes or until cheese is melted and bubbly. Serve immediately.

Stromboli Slices

I've served this dish to teens, college students and a women's group. Everyone has loved it, and many people have asked for the recipe. Easy and delicious, it's sure to please your guests!

—RACHEL JACKSON PENNSVILLE, NJ

START TO FINISH: 25 MIN.
MAKES: 1½ DOZEN

- 1 tube (11 ounces) refrigerated crusty French loaf
- 2 tablespoons olive oil
- ½ teaspoon dried basil
- 1 package (3½ ounces) sliced pepperoni
- 2 cups (8 ounces) shredded part-skim mozzarella cheese
- 1 cup meatless spaghetti sauce, warmed

1. Preheat oven to 350°. Unroll loaf of dough at the seam into a square; cut in half. Combine oil and basil; brush lengthwise down half of each rectangle to within ½ in. of edges. Layer brushed side with pepperoni and cheese. Fold plain dough over filling and pinch the edges to seal. Place on greased baking sheets.

2. Bake 10-15 minutes or until golden brown. Cut into slices. Serve warm with spaghetti sauce.

Cheesecake Phyllo Cups

I've been making these colorful cheesecake bites for years. Topped with kiwifruit and mandarin oranges, they are just delicious.

—LORRAINE CHEVALIER
MERRIMAC, MA

START TO FINISH: 25 MIN.
MAKES: 2½ DOZEN

- 4 ounces reduced-fat cream cheese
- ½ cup reduced-fat sour cream
  Sugar substitute equivalent to 2 tablespoons sugar
- 1 teaspoon vanilla extract
- 2 packages (2.1 ounces each) frozen miniature phyllo tart shells, thawed
- 1 can (11 ounces) mandarin orange slices, drained
- 1 kiwifruit, peeled, sliced and cut into quarters

1. In a small bowl, beat cream cheese, sour cream, sugar substitute and vanilla until mixture is smooth.

2. Pipe or spoon into phyllo shells. Top each with an orange segment and kiwi piece. Refrigerate shells until serving.

NOTE *This recipe was tested with Splenda sugar blend.*

SWAP IT
Try the phyllo cups with berries such as raspberries or blueberries.

BLACK BEAN & CORN SALSA

butter and nutmeg. Microwave, uncovered, on high 30-45 seconds or until butter is melted; brush over the pretzels. Transfer to an ungreased baking sheet.

2. Bake 3-4 minutes or until heated through. Serve with the warm preserves.

(5)INGREDIENTS

Mini White Pizzas

I make these savory pizzas in advance and freeze them. Then I can bake them whenever I need a quick appetizer or snack. They are so delicious!

—**JOCELYN HOOK** SWOYERSVILLE, PA

START TO FINISH: 20 MIN.
MAKES: 8 MINI PIZZAS

- 1⅓ cups shredded part-skim mozzarella cheese
- ½ cup mayonnaise
- 1½ teaspoons dried oregano
- ½ teaspoon garlic powder
- ¼ teaspoon salt
- ¼ teaspoon pepper
- 4 English muffins, split

In a small bowl, combine the first six ingredients. Spread over muffin halves; place on a baking sheet. Broil 3-4 in. from the heat for 5-8 minutes or until bubbly and golden brown.

(5)INGREDIENTS

Black Bean & Corn Salsa

Who knew adding a few ingredients to store-bought salsa could give it so much extra flavor? This one's perfect as a chip dip or on top of tacos, burritos or eggs.

—**PATRICIA SWART** GALLOWAY, NJ

START TO FINISH: 5 MIN.
MAKES: 4 SERVINGS

- 1 cup chunky salsa
- ½ cup canned black beans, rinsed and drained
- ½ cup canned whole kernel corn, drained
  Tortilla chips

In a small bowl, combine the salsa, beans and corn. Refrigerate until serving. Serve with tortilla chips.

(5)INGREDIENTS

Cinnamon Baked Pretzels

This delicious recipe is a great brunch starter or perfect for the morning after the kids have a slumber party.

—**MARINA HEPPNER**
ORCHARD PARK, NY

START TO FINISH: 15 MIN.
MAKES: 6 SERVINGS

- 3 tablespoons cinnamon-sugar
- 2 tablespoons butter
- ¼ teaspoon ground nutmeg
- 1 package (13 ounces) frozen baked soft pretzels
- ½ cup red raspberry preserves, warmed

1. Preheat oven to 400°. In a small microwave-safe bowl, combine the cinnamon-sugar,

DID YOU KNOW?

Crostini is Italian for "little toast." Crostini can be as simple as toast brushed or drizzled with olive oil and a sprinkle of salt. Or they can be more elegant and substantial like the Beef and Blue Cheese Crostini at right.

Beef and Blue Cheese Crostini

These little gems are easy, impressive and delicious. They are ridiculously easy and inexpensive to make. Seriously, you will look like a total rock star when you serve these!
—**MANDY RIVERS** LEXINGTON, SC

START TO FINISH: 30 MIN.
MAKES: 3 DOZEN

- 1 **French bread baguette (10½ ounces)**
  Cooking spray
- ½ **teaspoon coarsely ground pepper**
- ½ **cup reduced-fat sour cream**
- 2 **tablespoons minced chives**
- 1 **tablespoon horseradish**
- ¼ **teaspoon salt**
- 1¼ **pounds shaved deli roast beef**
- ⅓ **cup crumbled blue cheese**
  Additional minced chives

1. Preheat oven to 400°. Cut baguette into 36 slices. Place on ungreased baking sheets. Spritz with cooking spray. Sprinkle with pepper. Bake 4-6 minutes or until lightly browned.
2. Meanwhile, in a small bowl, combine sour cream, chives, horseradish and salt. Top toasts with beef; dollop with sour cream mixture. Sprinkle with cheese and additional chives.

⑤ INGREDIENTS
Sweet Pretzel Nuggets

This crowd-pleasing snack has been a tremendous hit both at home and at work. The fun, crunchy bites have a sweet cinnamon-toast taste and just a hint of saltiness that make them very munchable.

—**BILLIE SUE EBINGER** HOLTON, IN

START TO FINISH: 20 MIN.
MAKES: 12-16 SERVINGS

- 1 **package (16 ounces) sourdough pretzel nuggets**
- ⅔ **cup canola oil**
- ⅓ **cup sugar**
- 1 **to 2 teaspoons ground cinnamon**

1. Place pretzels in a microwave-safe bowl. In a small bowl, combine oil, sugar and cinnamon. Pour over pretzels; toss to coat.

2. Microwave, uncovered, on high 1½ minutes; stir. Microwave 2-3 minutes longer, stirring after each minute or until oil is absorbed. Cool to room temperature. Store in an airtight container.

NOTE *This recipe was tested in a 1,100-watt microwave.*

⑤ INGREDIENTS
Pesto Dip with Parmesan Toast

We created this easy dip at my office when we had leftover mayonnaise and pesto and weren't sure what to do with them.

—**LAUREL CHURCHMAN** WACO, TX

START TO FINISH: 20 MIN.
MAKES: 20 SERVINGS (2½ CUPS DIP)

- 1 **French bread baguette (10½ ounces), cut into ¼-inch slices**

PESTO DIP WITH PARMESAN TOAST

- 1 **cup grated Parmesan cheese, divided**
- 2 **cups mayonnaise**
- 1 **jar (8.1 ounces) prepared pesto**
- 1 **teaspoon garlic powder**

1. Place baguette slices on greased baking sheets. Broil 4-6 in. from heat 1-2 minutes or until toasted. Turn the slices over; sprinkle with ½ cup cheese. Broil 1 to 1½ minutes longer or until bread is lightly browned.

2. In a small bowl, combine the mayonnaise, pesto, garlic powder and remaining cheese. Serve with toast slices.

Antipasto Platter

Whenever I serve antipasto, I receive many compliments. Everyone loves that there are so many ingredients to nibble on.

—**TERI LINDQUIST** GURNEE, IL

PREP: 10 MIN. + CHILLING
MAKES: 14-16 SERVINGS

- 1 **jar (24 ounces) pepperoncini, drained**
- 1 **can (15 ounces) garbanzo beans or chickpeas, rinsed and drained**
- 2 **cups halved fresh mushrooms**
- 2 **cups halved cherry tomatoes**
- ½ **pound provolone cheese, cubed**
- 1 **can (6 ounces) pitted ripe olives, drained**
- 1 **package (3½ ounces) sliced pepperoni**
- 1 **bottle (8 ounces) Italian vinaigrette dressing Lettuce leaves**

1. In a large bowl, combine the pepperoncini, beans, mushrooms, tomatoes, cheese, olives and pepperoni. Pour vinaigrette over mixture; toss to coat.

2. Refrigerate at least 30 minutes or overnight. Arrange on a lettuce-lined platter. Serve with toothpicks.

ANTIPASTO PLATTER

SMOKED SAUSAGE APPETIZERS

⑤INGREDIENTS

Smoked Sausage Appetizers

A savory, sweet sauce with a touch of currant jelly glazes these yummy little sausages. They make a great appetizer, and both adults and kids seem to love these baby hot dogs.

—KATHRYN BAINBRIDGE
PENNSYLVANIA FURNACE, PA

START TO FINISH: 25 MIN.
MAKES: 8 DOZEN

- ¾ **cup red currant jelly**
- ¾ **cup barbecue sauce**
- 3 **tablespoons prepared mustard**
- 2 **packages (1 pound each) miniature smoked sausages, drained**

1. In a large saucepan, combine the jelly, barbecue sauce and mustard. Cook, uncovered, over medium heat for 15-20 minutes or until jelly is melted and mixture is smooth, stirring occasionally.
2. Add the sausages; stir to coat. Cover and cook 5-6 minutes longer or until heated through, stirring occasionally. Serve the sausages with toothpicks.

PAIR IT!
Sweet Pretzel Nuggets, page 40, will be a crunchy sidekick to the mini hot dogs.

Cranberry-Chili Cheese Spread

Appetizers just can't get much easier than this ritzy-looking cheese spread with its refreshing hint of lime. I turn to this recipe whenever unexpected guests drop in.
—**LAURIE LACLAIR** NORTH RICHLAND HILLS, TX

START TO FINISH: 10 MIN.
MAKES: 14 SERVINGS

- 2 packages (8 ounces each) cream cheese, softened
- 1 can (14 ounces) whole-berry cranberry sauce
- 1 can (4 ounces) chopped green chilies, drained
- 1 green onion, sliced
- 1 tablespoon lime juice
- ½ teaspoon garlic salt
- ½ teaspoon cayenne pepper
- ½ teaspoon chili powder
  Assorted crackers

Place cream cheese on a serving plate. In a small bowl, combine the cranberry sauce, green chilies, onion, lime juice and spices. Spoon mixture over cream cheese. Serve with crackers.

Reuben Dip

My rich, cheese-packed dip comes together so quickly, you can make it just before guests arrive. I often serve it with rye bread wedges.
—**MARY JO HAGEY** GLADWIN, MI

START TO FINISH: 15 MIN.
MAKES: 2½ CUPS

- 1 tablespoon butter
- 2 green onions, chopped
- 1½ cups (6 ounces) shredded Muenster cheese
- 4 ounces cream cheese, cubed
- 2 tablespoons ketchup
- 2 teaspoons Dijon mustard
- ¼ teaspoon pepper

- ½ pound cooked corned beef, chopped
- 1 cup sauerkraut, rinsed and well drained
  Assorted crackers

1. Place the butter in a small microwave-safe bowl and microwave on high 20 seconds or until melted. Add onions; cover and cook 1 minute longer.
2. Stir in the cheeses, ketchup, mustard and pepper. Cover and cook on high 1 minute; stir. Cook 45 seconds longer. Stir in beef.
3. Place the sauerkraut in a microwave-safe 1-qt. dish; top with beef mixture. Cover and microwave on high 2-3 minutes or until heated through. Serve with crackers.
NOTE *This recipe was tested in a 1,100-watt microwave.*

⑤INGREDIENTS
Waldorf Celery Sticks

This is my take on the traditional Waldorf salad. I added a strong, tangy cheese to give it a slightly sharper taste. I think the blue cheese works well with the sweetness of the apples.
—**STACIE HULL** SENECA, SC

START TO FINISH: 15 MIN.
MAKES: 1 DOZEN

- ½ cup finely chopped apple
- ¼ cup finely chopped walnuts
- 3 tablespoons mayonnaise
- 2 tablespoons crumbled blue cheese
- 12 celery ribs

In a small bowl, combine the apple, walnuts, mayonnaise and blue cheese. Cut celery ribs into smaller serving sizes, if desired. Fill celery with apple mixture. Chill sticks until serving.

CRANBERRY-CHILI CHEESE SPREAD

Touchdown Brat Sliders

It's game time when these minis make an appearance. Two things my husband loves—beer and brats—get stepped up a notch with crunchy flavored chips.

—**KIRSTEN SHABAZ** LAKEVILLE, MN

START TO FINISH: 30 MIN.
MAKES: 16 SLIDERS

- 5 thick-sliced bacon strips, chopped
- 1 pound uncooked bratwurst links, casings removed
- 1 large onion, finely chopped
- 2 garlic cloves, minced
- 1 package (8 ounces) cream cheese, cubed
- 1 cup dark beer or nonalcoholic beer
- 1 tablespoon Dijon mustard
- ¼ teaspoon pepper
- 16 dinner rolls, split and toasted
- 2 cups cheddar and sour cream potato chips, crushed

1. In a large skillet, cook bacon over medium heat until crisp. Remove to paper towels with a slotted spoon; drain, reserving drippings. Cook bratwurst and onion in drippings over medium heat until meat is no longer pink. Add garlic; cook 1 minute longer. Drain drippings from skillet.
2. Stir in the cream cheese, beer, mustard and pepper. Bring to a boil. Reduce heat; simmer, uncovered, 8-10 minutes or until thickened, stirring occasionally. Stir in bacon. Spoon ¼ cup onto each roll; sprinkle with chips. Replace tops.

Smoked Salmon Cheese Spread

Pretzels, chips and veggies all taste awesome with this creamy blend of salmon, cheese and herbs. Thanks to a food processor, it's ready in a hurry.

—**JILL CAMPBELL** HUNTSVILLE, TX

START TO FINISH: 15 MIN.
MAKES: 2½ CUPS

- 2 packages (8 ounces each) cream cheese, softened
- 1 package (4 ounces) smoked salmon or lox
- 3 tablespoons horseradish sauce
- 1 tablespoon lemon juice
- 1 tablespoon Worcestershire sauce
- ¼ teaspoon Creole seasoning
- ¼ teaspoon coarsely ground pepper
  Chopped walnuts and snipped fresh dill
  Assorted crackers

Place the first seven ingredients in a food processor; process until blended. Transfer to a serving dish; sprinkle with walnuts and dill. Refrigerate, covered, until serving. Serve with crackers.
NOTE *The following spices may be substituted for 1 teaspoon Creole seasoning: ¼ teaspoon each salt, garlic powder and paprika; and a pinch each of dried thyme, ground cumin and cayenne pepper.*

⑤ INGREDIENTS
Almond Chicken Strips

Teaching in the mornings allows me to have the afternoons to experiment with many recipes. This chicken is just as good cold, as a late night snack, as it is served hot for dinner. Unfortunately, there are seldom any leftovers.

—**WENDY THURSTON**
BOW ISLAND, AB

START TO FINISH: 25 MIN.
MAKES: 4 SERVINGS

- ¼ cup cornstarch
- 1 teaspoon sugar
- ½ teaspoon salt
- 4½ teaspoons water
- 2 egg whites, lightly beaten
- 1½ cups ground almonds
- 1 pound boneless skinless chicken breasts, cut into ½-inch strips
- 2 tablespoons canola oil
  Honey mustard, optional

1. In a shallow bowl, combine the cornstarch, sugar, salt and water; gradually stir in egg whites. Place almonds in another shallow bowl. Dip chicken in egg white mixture, then coat with almonds.
2. In a large skillet or wok, stir-fry chicken strips in oil 5-7 minutes or until no longer pink; drain on paper towels. Serve with honey mustard for dipping if desired.

TOP TIP

Traditional hamburger buns are too large for sliders, but there are many options that will work. Dinner rolls, which are used in the recipe above, are great. Other options are Hawaiian rolls; biscuits; frozen bread dough, shaped into small rolls and baked; and bread cut with a large round cookie cutter.

TOUCHDOWN
BRAT SLIDERS

SMOKED SALMON
CHEESE SPREAD

ALMOND CHICKEN
STRIPS

CORNY CHOCOLATE
CRUNCH

LAYERED
RANCH DIP

---

(5) INGREDIENTS

Corny Chocolate Crunch

This sweet treat tastes almost like candy, and it's gone in a flash when I serve it!

—**DELORES WARD** DECATUR, IN

START TO FINISH: 20 MIN.
MAKES: ABOUT 5 QUARTS

- 3 quarts popped popcorn
- 3 cups Corn Chex
- 3 cups broken corn chips
- 1 package (10 to 11 ounces) butterscotch chips
- 12 ounces dark chocolate candy coating, coarsely chopped

1. In a large bowl, combine the popcorn, cereal and corn chips; set aside. In a microwave, melt the butterscotch chips and candy coating; stir until smooth.
2. Pour over the popcorn mixture and toss to coat. Spread into two greased 15x10x1-in. baking pans. When cool enough to handle, break into pieces.

Layered Ranch Dip

I found something similar to this in one of my cookbooks for kids. It looked delicious, so I decided to try my own version.

—**PEGGY ROOS** MINNEAPOLIS, MN

PREP: 10 MIN. • **MAKES:** 8 SERVINGS

- 2 cups (16 ounces) sour cream
- 1 envelope ranch salad dressing mix
- 1 medium tomato, chopped
- 1 can (4 ounces) chopped green chilies, drained
- 1 can (2¼ ounces) sliced ripe olives, drained
- ¼ cup finely chopped red onion
- 1 cup (4 ounces) shredded Monterey Jack cheese
  Corn chips or tortilla chips

In a small bowl, mix sour cream and dressing mix; spread into a large shallow dish. Layer with tomato, green chilies, olives, onion and cheese. Refrigerate until serving. Serve with chips.

---

(5) INGREDIENTS

Fire-Roasted Salsa

Friends and family won't stray too far from your Cinco de Mayo buffet when this fiery treat is on the menu. Canned tomatoes speed preparation, and it is table-ready in just 15 minutes.

—**MISSY KAMPLING**
MOUNTAIN VIEW, CA

START TO FINISH: 15 MIN.
MAKES: 1½ CUPS

- 1 can (14½ ounces) fire-roasted diced tomatoes, drained
- ½ cup sliced onion
- ⅓ cup fresh cilantro leaves
- 1 tablespoon lime juice
- 1 teaspoon sugar
- ¼ teaspoon salt

In a food processor, combine the tomatoes, onion, cilantro, lime juice, sugar and salt. Cover and process until desired consistency.

Roast Beef Spirals

This savory appetizer is simple, addictive and a nice change of pace from familiar tortilla pinwheels.

—MARCIA ORLANDO BOYERTOWN, PA

PREP: 20 MIN. + CHILLING
MAKES: 4 DOZEN

- 2 **packages (8 ounces each) cream cheese, softened**
- 2 **garlic cloves, minced**
- 1 **teaspoon ground ginger**
- 6 **thin slices deli roast beef**

1. In a bowl, beat the cream cheese, garlic and ginger until blended. Spread over beef slices; roll up.
2. Wrap each in plastic wrap; refrigerate for at least 2 hours or until firm. Cut into 1-in. slices.

Chicken Skewers with Sweet & Spicy Marmalade

My father-in-law loved this chicken dish and said it reminded him of growing up in Southern California. What a great way to bring a dose of summer sunshine to cold winter days!

—LAUREL DALZELL MANTECA, CA

PREP: 25 MIN. + MARINATING
BROIL: 5 MIN.
MAKES: 8 SERVINGS (1 CUP SAUCE)

- 1 **pound boneless skinless chicken breasts**
- ¼ **cup olive oil**
- ¼ **cup reduced-sodium soy sauce**
- 2 **garlic cloves, minced**
- ⅛ **teaspoon pepper**

SAUCE
- 2 **teaspoons butter**
- 2 **tablespoons chopped seeded jalapeno pepper**
- 1 **teaspoon minced fresh gingerroot**
- ¾ **cup orange marmalade**
- 1 **tablespoon lime juice**
- 1 **tablespoon thawed orange juice concentrate**
- ¼ **teaspoon salt**

1. Preheat broiler. Pound chicken breasts with a meat mallet to ¼-in. thickness; cut lengthwise into 1-in.-wide strips. In a large resealable plastic bag, combine oil, soy sauce, garlic and pepper. Add chicken; seal bag and turn to coat. Refrigerate 4 hours or overnight.
2. In a small saucepan, heat butter over medium-high heat. Add the jalapeno; cook and stir until tender. Add ginger; cook 1 minute longer. Reduce heat; stir in marmalade, lime juice, orange juice concentrate and salt.
3. Drain chicken, discarding marinade. Thread chicken strips, weaving back and forth, onto eight metal or soaked wooden skewers. Place in a greased 15x10x1-in. baking pan. Broil 6 in. from heat 2-4 minutes on each side or until chicken is no longer pink. Serve with sauce.
NOTE *Wear disposable gloves when cutting hot peppers; the oils can burn skin. Avoid touching your face.*

ROAST BEEF SPIRALS

Garlic-Onion Pizza Wedges

Using a prebaked crust, you can have this delicious appetizer hot and ready to serve in 20 minutes. The wedges can even make a light main dish.
—**CLYDA CONRAD** YUMA, AZ

START TO FINISH: 20 MIN.
MAKES: 8 SERVINGS

- ½ cup grated Parmesan cheese
- ½ cup chopped red onion
- ½ cup mayonnaise
- ¼ cup minced fresh basil
- 4 garlic cloves, minced
  Pepper to taste
- 1 prebaked 12-inch thin pizza crust

1. Preheat oven to 450°. In a small bowl, combine cheese, onion, mayonnaise, basil, garlic and pepper; spread over crust.
2. Place on an ungreased baking sheet or pizza pan. Bake 8-10 minutes or until lightly browned. Cut into wedges.

Maple-Pecan Snack Mix

This is ideal when I need something healthy and portable for my kids to eat on the go. We love blueberry pancakes, and this recipe uses some of that flavor in a handy treat.
—**JACKIE GREGSTON** HALLSVILLE, TX

START TO FINISH: 20 MIN.
MAKES: 9 CUPS

- 5 cups Honey Nut Chex
- 1 cup granola without raisins
- 1 cup chopped pecans, toasted
- ¼ cup butter, cubed
- ¼ cup brown sugar
- ¼ cup maple syrup
- 1 package (3½ ounces) dried blueberries
- ¾ cup semisweet chocolate chips, optional

1. In a large microwave-safe bowl, combine the cereal, granola and pecans; set aside. In a small microwave-safe bowl, combine the butter, brown sugar and syrup. Microwave on high 2 minutes, stirring once. Pour over cereal mixture; toss to coat.
2. Microwave on high 4 minutes, stirring every minute. Spread onto waxed paper; cool 5 minutes. Sprinkle with blueberries and chocolate chips. Store in an airtight container.
NOTE *This recipe was tested in a 1,100-watt microwave.*

Italian Snack Mix

A sausage pizza inspired me to create this savory mix. It has great Italian flavors in a fun-to-eat snack version.
—**PRISCILLA YEE** CONCORD, CA

START TO FINISH: 10 MIN.
MAKES: 14 SERVINGS (2½ QUARTS)

- 7 cups Rice Chex
- 2 cups miniature pretzels
- 2 cups Parmesan and garlic-flavored snack crackers
- ¼ cup olive oil
- 1 tablespoon balsamic vinegar
- 2 teaspoons seasoned salt
- 2 teaspoons Italian seasoning
- ½ teaspoon fennel seed, crushed
- ½ cup grated Parmesan cheese

1. In a 3-qt. microwave-safe bowl, combine the cereal, pretzels and crackers. In a small bowl, combine the oil, vinegar, seasoned salt, Italian seasoning and fennel. Pour over cereal mixture and toss to coat. Stir in cheese.
2. Microwave, uncovered, on high 3 minutes, stirring every minute. Spread on waxed paper to cool. Store in an airtight container.
NOTE *This recipe was tested in a 1,100-watt microwave.*

GARLIC-ONION PIZZA WEDGES

Sun-Dried Tomato Dip

I love to serve this appetizer for just about any occasion. Here's why: It's thick, yet creamy enough to spread. It has simple ingredients with bold flavors, and the sun-dried tomatoes make it stand out from other dips.

—ANDREA REYNOLDS
ROCKY RIVER, OH

START TO FINISH: 10 MIN.
MAKES: 2 CUPS

- 1 package (8 ounces) cream cheese, softened
- ½ cup sour cream
- ½ cup mayonnaise
- ¼ cup oil-packed sun-dried tomatoes, drained and patted dry
- ½ teaspoon salt
- ¼ teaspoon pepper
- ¼ teaspoon hot pepper sauce
- 2 green onions, sliced
  Assorted crackers and/or fresh vegetables

Place the first seven ingredients in a food processor; cover and process until blended. Add green onions; cover and pulse until finely chopped. Serve with crackers and/or vegetables.

💬 TOP TIP

When serving dip on a hot day, it's important to keep it cool. It's easy to create a chilling bowl for dips. Fill a large glass or plastic serving bowl with ice cubes, crushed ice or ice packs. Fill a smaller bowl with dip and set on top of the ice. Replace the ice as it melts.

ITALIAN
SNACK MIX

SUN-DRIED
TOMATO DIP

PAIR IT!
Strawberry Cheesecake Sundaes, page 215, are an ideal ending to this enchilada dinner.

HONEY-LEMON CHICKEN ENCHILADAS, 76

74

97

101

30 Minutes to Dinner

Yes, you can make a **delicious entree** in just half an hour! From **beef, pork** and **chicken to seafood** and even **meatless dishes,** there are dozen of dinners here that are **perfect to add** to your meal rotation.

GRILLED BEEF & BLUE CHEESE SANDWICHES, 59

**JUICY & DELICIOUS
MIXED SPICE BURGERS**

Juicy & Delicious Mixed Spice Burgers

We like trying to make street foods at home, perfecting recipes for dishes like gyros and these spiced burgers, known as *kofta*.

—ANNE HENRY TORONTO, ON

START TO FINISH: 30 MIN.
MAKES: 6 SERVINGS

- 1 medium onion, finely chopped
- 3 tablespoons minced fresh parsley
- 2 tablespoons minced fresh mint
- 1 garlic clove, minced
- ¾ teaspoon ground allspice
- ¾ teaspoon pepper
- ½ teaspoon ground cinnamon
- ½ teaspoon salt
- ¼ teaspoon ground nutmeg
- 1½ pounds lean ground beef (90% lean)
  Refrigerated tzatziki sauce, optional

1. In a large bowl, combine the first nine ingredients. Add beef; mix lightly but thoroughly. Shape into six 4x2-in. oblong patties.
2. Grill patties, covered, over medium heat or broil 4 in. from heat 4-6 minutes on each side or until a thermometer reads 160°. If desired, serve with sauce.

Stovetop Italian Macaroni

It's not every day that a cost-conscious menu pleases both the eye and the stomach, but this scrumptious stovetop entree does just that.

—LAILA ZVEJNIEKS
STONEY CREEK, ON

START TO FINISH: 25 MIN.
MAKES: 5 SERVINGS

- 1 **pound ground beef**
- 1 **can (28 ounces) diced tomatoes, undrained**
- 2 **cups water**
- 1 **envelope onion soup mix**
- 1 **teaspoon Italian seasoning**
- ¼ **teaspoon crushed red pepper flakes, optional**
- 2 **cups uncooked elbow macaroni**
- ½ **cup grated Parmesan cheese**
- 1 **cup (4 ounces) shredded part-skim mozzarella cheese**

1. In a Dutch oven, cook beef over medium heat until no longer pink; drain. Add the tomatoes, water, soup mix, Italian seasoning and, if desired, pepper flakes. Bring to a boil. Stir in macaroni. Reduce heat; cover and simmer 8-9 minutes or until macaroni is tender.

2. Remove from heat; stir in Parmesan cheese. Sprinkle with mozzarella cheese. Cover; let stand 2 minutes or until cheese is melted.

Easy Beef Stroganoff

I lightened my mother-in-law's wonderful stroganoff and came up with this one. My family calls it "special noodles" in my house.

—JENNIFER RIORDAN ST. LOUIS, MO

START TO FINISH: 30 MIN.
MAKES: 6 SERVINGS

- 4½ **cups uncooked yolk-free noodles**
- 1 **pound lean ground beef (90% lean)**
- ½ **pound sliced fresh mushrooms**
- 1 **large onion, halved and sliced**
- 3 **garlic cloves, minced**
- 1 **tablespoon reduced-fat butter**
- 2 **tablespoons all-purpose flour**
- 1 **can (14½ ounces) reduced-sodium beef broth**
- 2 **tablespoons tomato paste**
- 1 **cup (8 ounces) fat-free sour cream**
- ¼ **teaspoon salt**
- ¼ **teaspoon pepper**

1. Cook noodles according to package directions.

2. Meanwhile, in a large saucepan, cook beef, mushrooms and onion over medium heat until the meat is no longer pink. Add garlic; cook 1 minute longer. Drain. Remove and keep warm.

3. In same pan, melt butter. Stir in flour until smooth; gradually add broth and tomato paste. Bring to a boil; cook and stir 2 minutes or until thickened.

4. Carefully return beef mixture to the pan. Add the sour cream, salt and pepper; cook and stir until heated through (do not boil). Drain noodles; serve with beef mixture.
NOTE *This recipe was tested with Land O'Lakes light stick butter.*

STOVETOP ITALIAN MACARONI

PAIR IT!

Bacon Tomato Salad, page 166, can be whipped together while the beefy macaroni simmers.

(5) INGREDIENTS
Quick Shepherd's Pie

Shepherd's pie is great with leftover homemade mashed potatoes, but it's tasty with ready-made mashed potatoes from the grocery store, too!
—**JENNIFER EARLY** EAST LANSING, MI

START TO FINISH: 20 MIN.
MAKES: 4 SERVINGS

- 1 tub (24 ounces) refrigerated cheddar mashed potatoes
- 1 pound lean ground beef (90% lean)
- 1 envelope mushroom gravy mix
- 1½ cups frozen mixed vegetables
- 1 cup water
- ⅛ teaspoon pepper

1. Heat potatoes according to package directions.
2. Meanwhile, in a large skillet, cook beef over medium heat 6-8 minutes or until no longer pink, breaking into crumbles; drain. Stir in gravy mix. Add vegetables and water; bring to boil. Reduce heat; simmer until heated through, stirring occasionally. Transfer to a 9-in.-square baking pan.
3. Spread the potatoes over top; sprinkle with pepper. Broil 4-6 in. from heat 10-15 minutes or until golden brown.

(5) INGREDIENTS
Grilled Italian Burgers

While trying to think of a new way to fix hamburgers with the same old ground beef, I came up with this recipe. A good dose of Italian seasonings and mozzarella makes them unique. They're great with a side salad or fresh green beans.
—**REBEKAH BEYER** SABETHA, KS

START TO FINISH: 20 MIN.
MAKES: 4 SERVINGS

- 1 cup (4 ounces) shredded part-skim mozzarella cheese, divided
- 1 teaspoon Worcestershire sauce
- ¼ teaspoon Italian seasoning
- ⅛ teaspoon salt
- ⅛ teaspoon pepper
- 1 pound ground beef
  Marinara or spaghetti sauce, warmed

1. In a large bowl, combine ½ cup cheese, Worcestershire sauce and seasonings. Add beef; mix lightly but thoroughly. Shape into four ½-in.-thick patties.
2. Grill burgers, covered, over medium heat or broil 4 in. from heat 4-5 minutes on each side or until a thermometer reads 160°.
3. Sprinkle with remaining cheese; grill, covered, 1-2 minutes longer or until cheese is melted. Serve with marinara sauce.

Southwest Steak & Potatoes

Bold seasonings give meat and potatoes a Southwestern twist. Feel free to adjust the heat factor by using more or less chili powder.
—**KENNY FISHER** CIRCLEVILLE, OH

START TO FINISH: 30 MIN.
MAKES: 4 SERVINGS

- 4 medium Yukon Gold potatoes
- 2 teaspoons cider vinegar
- 1 teaspoon Worcestershire sauce
- 1 beef top round steak (1 inch thick and about 1½ pounds)
- 1 tablespoon brown sugar
- 1 tablespoon chili powder
- 1½ teaspoons ground cumin
- 1 teaspoon garlic powder
- 1 teaspoon salt, divided
- ⅛ teaspoon cayenne pepper
- ⅛ teaspoon pepper

1. Pierce potatoes; place on a microwave-safe plate. Microwave, uncovered, on high 4-5 minutes or until almost tender, turning once. Cool slightly.
2. Meanwhile, mix vinegar and Worcestershire sauce; brush over steak. Mix brown sugar, chili powder, cumin, garlic powder, ½ teaspoon salt and cayenne until blended; sprinkle over both sides of steak.
3. Cut potatoes into ½-in. slices. Sprinkle with pepper and the remaining salt. Grill potatoes and steak, covered, over medium heat 12-17 minutes or until potatoes are tender and a thermometer inserted into beef reads 145° for medium-rare, turning occasionally.
4. Cut steak into thin slices. Serve with potatoes.

HOW TO

TEST THE GRILL TEMPERATURE

❶ For a covered grill, keep the cover down and open the vent slightly. Insert a grill thermometer through the vent.
❷ For an uncovered grill, cautiously hold the palm of your hand 3 to 4 inches above the grate. Count the number of seconds you can hold your hand there before the heat forces you to pull it away. At 2 seconds, the coals are hot, 450°. At 3 seconds, the coals are medium-hot, 400°. At 4 seconds, the coals are medium, 350°. At 5 seconds, the coals are medium-low, 300°.

GRILLED ITALIAN BURGERS

SOUTHWEST STEAK & POTATOES

BEEF AND BLUE CHEESE PENNE WITH PESTO

Flavorful Southwestern Chili

Here's a chili that is full of flavor, freezes beautifully and makes a complete last-minute meal. I top it with grated cheddar cheese and chopped black olives and serve tortilla chips on the side.

—**JENNY GREEAR** HUNTINGTON, WV

START TO FINISH: 30 MIN.
MAKES: 10 SERVINGS (2½ QUARTS)

- 2 **pounds lean ground beef (90% lean)**
- 1½ **cups chopped onions**
- 2 **cans (14½ ounces each) diced tomatoes, undrained**
- 1 **can (15 ounces) pinto beans, rinsed and drained**
- 1 **can (15 ounces) tomato sauce**
- 1 **package (10 ounces) frozen corn, thawed**
- 1 **cup salsa**
- ¾ **cup water**
- 1 **can (4 ounces) chopped green chilies**
- 1 **teaspoon ground cumin**
- ½ **teaspoon garlic powder**

In a Dutch oven, cook beef and onions over medium heat until meat is no longer pink; drain. Stir in the remaining ingredients. Bring to a boil. Reduce heat; simmer, uncovered, for 15 minutes.

FREEZE OPTION *Transfer cooled chili to freezer containers. Freeze up to 3 months. To use, thaw in the refrigerator. Place in a saucepan; heat through.*

Beef and Blue Cheese Penne with Pesto

Unique and simple to prepare, this delicious dish is filled with fresh flavors, and it's as healthy as it is hearty. Best of all, it takes just 30 minutes to set this meal on the table.

—**FRANCES PIETSCH**
FLOWER MOUND, TX

START TO FINISH: 30 MIN.
MAKES: 4 SERVINGS

- 2 **cups uncooked whole wheat penne pasta**
- 2 **beef tenderloin steaks (6 ounces each)**
- ¼ **teaspoon salt**
- ¼ **teaspoon pepper**
- 6 **cups fresh baby spinach, chopped**
- 2 **cups grape tomatoes, halved**
- 5 **tablespoons prepared pesto**
- ¼ **cup chopped walnuts**
- ¼ **cup crumbled Gorgonzola cheese**

1. Cook pasta according to the package directions.
2. Meanwhile, sprinkle steaks with salt and pepper. Grill, covered, over medium heat or broil 4 in. from the heat 5-7 minutes on each side or until meat reaches desired doneness (for medium-rare, a thermometer should read 145°; medium, 160°; well-done, 170°).
3. Drain pasta and transfer to a bowl. Add the spinach, tomatoes, pesto and walnuts; toss to coat. Thinly slice steaks. Divide pasta mixture among four serving plates. Top with beef; sprinkle with cheese.

FRENCH BREAD PIZZA

(5)INGREDIENTS

French Bread Pizza

Slices of this hearty French bread are guaranteed to please. I sometimes substitute spaghetti sauce for the pizza sauce, or add our favorite veggies to the toppings.
—**SUE MCLAUGHLIN** ONAWA, IA

START TO FINISH: 25 MIN.
MAKES: 6-8 SERVINGS

- ½ **pound ground beef**
- 1 **can (15 ounces) pizza sauce**
- 1 **jar (8 ounces) sliced mushrooms, drained**
- 1 **loaf (1 pound) French bread**
- 2 **cups (8 ounces) shredded part-skim mozzarella cheese**

1. Preheat oven to 400°. In a large skillet, cook the beef over medium heat until no longer pink; drain. Stir in pizza sauce and mushrooms; set aside.

2. Cut bread in half lengthwise, then into eight pieces. Spread meat sauce on bread; place on a greased baking sheet. Sprinkle with mozzarella. Bake, uncovered, for 10 minutes or until cheese is melted and bubbly.

SWAP IT
To lighten the pizza up a bit, use ground turkey in place of ground beef.

**GRILLED BEEF & BLUE
CHEESE SANDWICHES**

**ASIAN BEEF
WITH NOODLES**

**HASH BROWN-
TOPPED STEAK**

(5) INGREDIENTS
Grilled Beef & Blue Cheese Sandwiches

Roast beef, red onion and blue cheese really amp up this deluxe grilled sandwich. If you like a little heat, mix some horseradish into the spread.

—**BONNIE HAWKINS** ELKHORN, WI

START TO FINISH: 25 MIN.
MAKES: 4 SERVINGS

- 2 ounces cream cheese, softened
- 2 ounces crumbled blue cheese
- 8 slices sourdough bread
- ¾ pound thinly sliced deli roast beef
- ½ small red onion, thinly sliced
- ¼ cup olive oil

1. In a small bowl, mix cream cheese and blue cheese until blended. Spread over bread slices. Layer four of the slices with roast beef and onion; top with remaining bread slices.

2. Brush outsides of sandwiches with oil. In a large skillet, toast sandwiches over medium heat 4-5 minutes on each side or until golden brown.

Asian Beef with Noodles

Peanut butter, soy sauce and a surprise ingredient, Catalina salad dressing, make the yummy base for this dish.

—**DENISE PATTERSON** BAINBRIDGE, OH

START TO FINISH: 25 MIN.
MAKES: 6 SERVINGS

- 8 ounces uncooked spaghetti, broken in half
- 3 cups fresh sugar snap peas
- 1 cup julienned sweet red pepper
- ½ cup Catalina salad dressing
- 1 pound beef top sirloin steak, cut into thin strips
- 2 tablespoons creamy peanut butter
- 2 tablespoons soy sauce
- ½ cup thinly sliced green onions
- ½ cup dry roasted peanuts

1. In a large saucepan, cook the spaghetti according to package directions, adding snap peas and pepper during the last 2 minutes of cooking; drain.

2. Meanwhile, in a large skillet, heat salad dressing over medium-high heat. Add beef; cook 8-10 minutes or until meat reaches desired doneness (for medium-rare, a thermometer should read 145°; medium, 160°; well-done, 170°). Add peanut butter and soy sauce; cook 2 minutes or until thickened. Stir in the spaghetti mixture and onions; sprinkle with the peanuts.

Hash Brown-Topped Steak

My husband and I enjoy cooking together. One night, we were craving grilled steak and cheese-stuffed baked potatoes, but didn't want to wait for the baking. Here's what we invented.

—**JUDY ARMSTRONG** PRAIRIEVILLE, LA

START TO FINISH: 30 MIN.
MAKES: 4 SERVINGS

- 2 tablespoons butter
- 1 small onion, chopped
- 3 garlic cloves, minced
- 2 cups frozen shredded hash brown potatoes, thawed
- ¾ teaspoon salt, divided
- 1 cup (4 ounces) shredded Jarlsberg cheese
- 1 beef top sirloin steak (1 inch thick and 1½ pounds), cut into 4 portions
- ½ teaspoon pepper
- 2 tablespoons minced fresh chives

1. In a large skillet, heat butter over medium-high heat. Add onion; cook and stir 2-3 minutes or until tender. Add garlic; cook 2 minutes.

2. Stir in hash browns and ¼ teaspoon salt; spread in an even layer. Reduce heat to medium; cook 5 minutes. Turn hash browns over; cook, covered, 5-6 minutes longer or until heated through and the bottom is lightly browned. Sprinkle with cheese; cover and remove from heat. Keep warm.

3. Sprinkle beef with pepper and remaining salt. Grill, covered, over medium heat 5-7 minutes on each side or until meat reaches desired doneness (for medium-rare, a thermometer should read 145°; medium, 160°; well-done, 170°).

4. Remove steaks from heat; top each with a fourth of the potato mixture. Sprinkle with chives.

(5) INGREDIENTS
Garlicky Beef & Tomatoes with Pasta

We love this fast pasta dish of beef, tomatoes, spinach and white beans that easily feeds a hungry family.

—**LISA DIFFELL** CORINTH, ME

START TO FINISH: 20 MIN.
MAKES: 6 SERVINGS

- 1 package (16 ounces) uncooked bow tie pasta
- 1 pound ground beef
- ¼ teaspoon salt
- 2 cans (14½ ounces each) diced tomatoes with roasted garlic, undrained
- 1 can (15 ounces) white kidney or cannellini beans, rinsed and drained
- 1 package (10 ounces) frozen chopped spinach, thawed and squeezed dry

Cook pasta according to package directions. Meanwhile, in a large skillet, cook beef over medium heat 6-8 minutes or until no longer pink, breaking into crumbles; drain. Sprinkle beef with salt. Stir in the remaining ingredients; heat through. Serve with pasta.

Sirloin Steak with Rich Mushroom Gravy

Toasting the flour to a light tan color gives this gravy a rich taste and thickness, without overloading on fat. The gravy is thick and can be thinned to taste with additional broth.

—*TASTE OF HOME* TEST KITCHEN

START TO FINISH: 30 MIN.
MAKES: 4 SERVINGS

- ¼ cup all-purpose flour
- 1 cup reduced-sodium beef broth
- 1 beef top sirloin steak (1¼ pounds)
- ½ teaspoon salt
- ¼ teaspoon pepper
- 1 tablespoon canola oil
- ½ pound sliced fresh mushrooms
- 1 garlic clove, minced
- ½ teaspoon dried rosemary, crushed
- ⅛ teaspoon salt
- ¼ cup sherry or additional reduced-sodium beef broth
- 1 tablespoon butter

1. In a large skillet over medium-high heat, cook and stir flour 4-5 minutes or until light tan in color. Immediately transfer to a small bowl; whisk in broth until smooth. Set aside.
2. Sprinkle beef with salt and pepper. In the same skillet, cook beef in oil over medium heat for 5-6 minutes on each side or until meat reaches desired doneness (for medium-rare, a meat thermometer

should read 145°; medium, 160°; well-done, 170°). Remove and keep warm.
3. In the same skillet, saute the mushrooms until tender. Add garlic, rosemary and salt; saute 1 minute longer. Stir in sherry. Stir flour mixture; add to pan. Bring to a boil; cook and stir 1 minute or until thickened. Stir in butter until melted. Serve with steak.

Meatball Pizza

I always keep meatballs and pizza crusts in the freezer to make this pizza at the spur of the moment. Add a tossed salad and you have a delicious dinner.

—**MARY HUMENIUK-SMITH**
PERRY HALL, MD

START TO FINISH: 25 MIN.
MAKES: 6-8 SLICES

- 1 prebaked 12-inch pizza crust
- 1 can (8 ounces) pizza sauce
- 1 teaspoon garlic powder
- 1 teaspoon Italian seasoning
- ¼ cup grated Parmesan cheese
- 1 small onion, halved and sliced
- 12 frozen fully cooked homestyle meatballs (½ ounce each), thawed and halved
- 1 cup (4 ounces) shredded part-skim mozzarella cheese
- 1 cup (4 ounces) shredded cheddar cheese

1. Preheat oven to 350°. Place the crust on an ungreased 12-in. pizza pan. Spread with pizza sauce; top with garlic powder, Italian

seasoning, Parmesan cheese and onion. Arrange meatball halves over top; sprinkle with cheeses.
2. Bake 12-17 minutes or until pizza is heated through and cheese is melted.

Tater Tot-chos

Playing with food is loads of fun when you have Tater Tots and taco toppings. Let kids build their own for smiles all around.

—**ELEANOR MIELKE** MITCHELL, SD

START TO FINISH: 30 MIN.
MAKES: 6 SERVINGS

- 4 cups frozen miniature Tater Tots
- 1 pound ground beef
- 1 envelope reduced-sodium taco seasoning
- ⅔ cup water
- ½ cup shredded cheddar cheese
- 2 cups shredded lettuce
- ¼ cup sliced ripe olives, optional
- ¼ cup taco sauce
- ½ cup sour cream

1. Bake Tater Tots according to package directions.
2. Meanwhile, in a large skillet, cook beef over medium heat 6-8 minutes or until no longer pink, breaking into crumbles; drain. Stir in taco seasoning and water. Bring to a boil; cook and stir 2 minutes or until thickened.
3. To serve, top Tater Tots with beef mixture, cheese, lettuce and, if desired, olives. Serve with taco sauce and sour cream.

TOP TIP

If you're watching your calories, you may wish to remove fat from canned broth before using. You will need to plan ahead since the broth should be chilled in the refrigerator. Once the can is cooled, remove the lid, lift off the cold fat from the top and discard.

Salisbury Steak Deluxe

This recipe is so good that I truly enjoy sharing it with others. I've always liked Salisbury steak, but I had to search a long time to find a recipe this tasty. It's handy, too, because it can be prepared ahead, kept in the refrigerator and warmed up later.

—**DENISE BARTEET** SHREVEPORT, LA

START TO FINISH: 30 MIN.
MAKES: 6 SERVINGS

- 1 can (10¾ ounces) condensed cream of mushroom soup, undiluted
- 1 tablespoon prepared mustard
- 2 teaspoons Worcestershire sauce
- 1 teaspoon prepared horseradish
- 1 egg
- ¼ cup dry bread crumbs
- ¼ cup finely chopped onion
- ½ teaspoon salt
  Dash pepper
- 1½ pound ground beef
- 1 to 2 tablespoons canola oil
- ½ cup water
- 2 tablespoons chopped fresh parsley

1. In a small bowl, combine the soup, mustard, Worcestershire sauce and horseradish. Set aside. In another bowl, lightly beat the egg. Add the bread crumbs, onion, salt, pepper and ¼ cup of the soup mixture. Crumble beef over mixture and mix well. Shape into six patties.

2. In a large skillet, brown patties in oil; drain. Mix remaining soup mixture with water; pour over patties. Cover and cook over low heat 10-15 minutes or until meat is no longer pink and a thermometer reads 160°. Remove patties to a serving platter; serve sauce with meat. Sprinkle with parsley.

TATER TOT-CHOS

SALISBURY STEAK DELUXE

FLANK STEAK WITH CILANTRO SALSA VERDE

BEEF GYROS

Flank Steak with Cilantro Salsa Verde

Even though steak is always a winner in our house, to make it even more special I add jarred salsa verde and top with freshly chopped tomato and avocado.

—LILY JULOW LAWRENCEVILLE, GA

START TO FINISH: 25 MIN.
MAKES: 4 SERVINGS

- 1 **beef flank steak or top sirloin steak, 1 inch thick (about 1¼ pounds)**
- ¼ **teaspoon salt**
- ¼ **teaspoon pepper**
- 1 **cup salsa verde**
- ½ **cup fresh cilantro leaves**
- 1 **medium ripe avocado, peeled and cubed**
- 1 **medium tomato, seeded and chopped**

1. Sprinkle steak with salt and pepper. Grill steak, covered, over medium heat or broil 4 in. from heat 6-9 minutes on each side or until meat reaches desired doneness (for medium-rare, a thermometer should read 145°; medium, 160°; well-done, 170°). Let stand 5 minutes.
2. Meanwhile, place salsa and cilantro in a food processor; process until blended. Slice steak thinly across the grain; serve with salsa mixture, avocado and tomato.

Beef Gyros

Going out to restaurants for gyros can be expensive, so I came up with this homemade version. Usually I set out the fixings so everyone can assemble his or her own.

—SHERI SCHEERHORN HILLS, MN

START TO FINISH: 30 MIN.
MAKES: 5 SERVINGS

- 1 **cup ranch salad dressing**
- ½ **cup chopped seeded peeled cucumber**
- 1 **pound beef top sirloin steak, cut into thin strips**
- 2 **tablespoons olive oil**
- 5 **whole pita breads, warmed**
- 1 **medium tomato, chopped**
- 1 **can (2¼ ounces) sliced ripe olives, drained**
- ½ **small onion, thinly sliced**
- 1 **cup (4 ounces) crumbled feta cheese**
- 2½ **cups shredded lettuce**

1. In a small bowl, combine salad dressing and cucumber; set aside. In a large skillet, cook the beef in oil over medium heat until no longer pink.
2. Layer half of each pita with steak, tomato, olives, onion, cheese, lettuce and dressing mixture. Fold each pita over filling; secure with toothpicks.

PAIR IT!
Cheery Cherry Parfaits, page 224, will add a fun sweet to your meal.

Sweet BBQ Meatballs

These sauced-up meatballs have big Asian flair. If your family likes sweet-and-sour chicken, this beefy version is bound to hit the spot.
—*TASTE OF HOME* TEST KITCHEN

START TO FINISH: 25 MIN.
MAKES: 6 SERVINGS

- 2 teaspoons olive oil
- ½ pound sliced fresh mushrooms
- 1 medium green pepper, cut into 1-inch pieces
- 1 medium onion, cut into 1-inch pieces
- 1 package (12 ounces) frozen fully cooked Italian meatballs, thawed
- 1 bottle (18 ounces) barbecue sauce
- 1 jar (10 ounces) apricot preserves
- 1 cup unsweetened pineapple chunks
- ½ cup water
- ¾ teaspoon ground mustard
- ⅛ teaspoon ground allspice
  Hot cooked rice

1. In a Dutch oven, heat the oil over medium-high heat. Add mushrooms, pepper and onion; cook and stir 7-9 minutes or until vegetables are tender.

2. Stir in meatballs, barbecue sauce, preserves, pineapple, water, mustard and allspice. Reduce heat to medium; cook and stir 6-8 minutes or until meatballs are heated through. Serve with rice.

SWEET BBQ MEATBALLS

⑤ INGREDIENTS

Beef Teriyaki Noodles

At our house, we love to combine fresh ingredients with a pantry product. This version starts with beef, onions, peppers and mushrooms, since we always have them on hand, but make the dish your own—bring out your inner chef!
—**RICHARD ROBINSON**
PARK FOREST, IL

START TO FINISH: 20 MIN.
MAKES: 4 SERVINGS

- 1 envelope (4.6 ounces) lo mein noodles and teriyaki sauce mix
- 1 beef flat iron steak or top sirloin steak (1 pound), cut into bite-size pieces
- ¼ teaspoon salt
- ¼ teaspoon pepper
- 2 tablespoons canola oil, divided
- 2 cups frozen pepper and onion stir-fry blend
- 1 cup sliced fresh mushrooms

1. Prepare noodle mix according to package directions.

2. Meanwhile, sprinkle beef with salt and pepper. In a skillet, heat 1 tablespoon oil over medium-high heat. Add beef; stir-fry 6-8 minutes or until no longer pink. Remove from pan; discard drippings.

3. Stir-fry vegetable blend and mushrooms in remaining oil 3-4 minutes or until vegetables are tender.

4. Return beef to pan. Stir in noodle mixture; heat through.

Cheese-Topped Sloppy Joes

I got this recipe for quick-to-fix sandwiches from my Aunt Nellie. A busy farm wife, she used to serve them to their hungry harvest crew. Microwaved leftovers taste delicious the next day.

—MARY DEMPSEY
OVERLAND PARK, KS

START TO FINISH: 25 MIN.
MAKES: 6 SERVINGS

- 1 **pound ground beef**
- 2 **celery ribs, chopped**
- 1 **tablespoon chopped onion**
- 1 **tablespoon all-purpose flour**
- 1 **tablespoon brown sugar**
- ½ **teaspoon ground mustard**
- ¾ **cup ketchup**
- 6 **hamburger buns, split**
- 6 **slices Swiss cheese**

1. In a large skillet, cook the beef, celery and onion over medium heat until meat is no longer pink; drain. Stir in flour, brown sugar, mustard and ketchup.

2. Bring to a boil. Reduce heat; simmer, uncovered, 10 minutes, stirring occasionally. Serve on buns with cheese.

Chili Hash

A little micro time, a dash in the pan and you'll have a satisfying meal for those where-did-the-time-go nights, so you can put up your feet and relax!

—TASTE OF HOME TEST KITCHEN

START TO FINISH: 30 MIN.
MAKES: 4 SERVINGS

- 1 **pound medium potatoes, cubed**
- ½ **cup water**
- 1 **pound ground beef**
- 1 **medium onion, chopped**
- 1 **can (15½ ounces) chili starter**
- 1 **cup frozen peas**
- 2 **tablespoons minced fresh parsley**
- ¼ **teaspoon salt**
- **Sour cream, optional**

1. Place potatoes and water in a microwave-safe dish. Cover and microwave on high 7 minutes or until tender.

2. Meanwhile, in a large skillet, cook beef and onion over medium heat until the meat is no longer pink; drain.

3. Drain potatoes and add to the skillet. Stir in the chili starter, peas, parsley and salt. Bring to a boil. Reduced the heat; simmer, uncovered, 5 minutes. Serve with sour cream if desired.

NOTE: *This recipe was tested in a 1,100-watt microwave.*

Cheeseburger Macaroni Skillet

Here's the ultimate simple and filling dinner that uses items I typically have right in my own pantry. It's so easy to prepare and cooks in one skillet, which makes cleanup a snap.

—JULI MEYERS HINESVILLE, GA

START TO FINISH: 30 MIN.
MAKES: 6 SERVINGS

- 1 **pound lean ground beef (90% lean)**
- 8 **ounces uncooked whole wheat elbow macaroni**
- 3 **cups reduced-sodium beef broth**
- ¾ **cup fat-free milk**
- 3 **tablespoons ketchup**
- 2 **teaspoons Montreal steak seasoning**
- 1 **teaspoon prepared mustard**
- ¼ **teaspoon onion powder**
- 1 **cup (4 ounces) shredded reduced-fat cheddar cheese**
  Minced chives

1. In a large skillet, cook the beef over medium heat 6-8 minutes or until no longer pink, breaking into crumbles; drain.

2. Stir in macaroni, broth, milk, ketchup, steak seasoning, mustard and onion powder; bring to a boil. Reduce heat; simmer, uncovered, 10-15 minutes or until macaroni is tender. Stir in cheese until melted. Sprinkle with chives.

(5)INGREDIENTS

Super Spaghetti Sauce

We never know how many we'll have for dinner. That's why this sauce is one of my favorites—flavorful, filling and fast. Smoked kielbasa gives it depth, and salsa adds the kick.

—BELLA ANDERSON CHESTER, SC

START TO FINISH: 30 MIN.
MAKES: 2½ QUARTS

- 1 **pound ground beef**
- 1 **pound smoked kielbasa, cut into ¼-inch slices**
- 2 **jars (24 ounces each) spaghetti sauce with mushrooms**
- 1 **jar (16 ounces) chunky salsa**
  Hot cooked pasta

1. In a Dutch oven, cook beef over medium heat until no longer pink; drain and set aside. In the same pan, cook sausage over medium heat 5-6 minutes or until browned.

2. Stir in the spaghetti sauce, salsa and reserved beef; heat through. Serve with pasta.

CHILI HASH

CHEESEBURGER
MACARONI SKILLET

SUPER
SPAGHETTI SAUCE

Provolone-Stuffed Pork Chops with Tarragon Vinaigrette

Provolone cheese and a fresh tarragon vinaigrette give these stuffed pork chops the savory feel of dining in Provence.

—BARBARA PLETZKE HERNDON, VA

START TO FINISH: 25 MIN.
MAKES: 4 SERVINGS

- ½ **cup olive oil**
- ¼ **cup white balsamic vinegar**
- 2 **tablespoons minced fresh tarragon or 2 teaspoons dried tarragon**
- 2 **garlic cloves, minced**
- ¼ **teaspoon salt**
- ¼ **teaspoon pepper**

PORK CHOPS

- 4 **bone-in pork loin chops (8 ounces each and ¾ inch thick)**
- 4 **slices provolone cheese, cut into eighths**
- 2 **tablespoons olive oil**
- 2 **teaspoons minced fresh tarragon or ½ teaspoon dried tarragon**
- ¼ **teaspoon salt**
- ¼ **teaspoon pepper**
- 2 **large tomatoes, each cut into 6 wedges**

1. In a small bowl, whisk the first six ingredients. Set aside ¼ cup vinaigrette for serving.

2. For pork chops, cut a pocket in each chop by slicing almost to the bone; fill pockets with cheese. Combine the oil, tarragon, salt and pepper; brush onto both sides of chops.

3. Moisten a paper towel with cooking oil; using long-handled tongs, rub on grill rack to coat lightly. Brush tomato wedges with some of the remaining vinaigrette. Grill, uncovered, over medium

heat or broil 4 in. from heat 1-3 minutes on each side or until lightly browned. Set aside.

4. Grill chops, covered, over medium heat or broil 4-5 in. from heat 4-5 minutes on each side or until meat reaches desired doneness (for medium-rare, a thermometer should read 145°; medium, 160°). Baste frequently with remaining vinaigrette during last 3 minutes of cooking. Let stand 5 minutes. Serve with tomatoes and reserved vinaigrette.

⑤ INGREDIENTS

Pineapple Cranberry Ham

Tired of the same-old, same-old meals for dinner? Try something new tonight with this dish! A sweet and tangy relish of cranberries and pineapple tops these ham steaks, adding lots of flavor and color.

—RITA BROWER EXETER, CA

START TO FINISH: 25 MIN.
MAKES: 4 SERVINGS

- 4 **boneless fully cooked ham steaks (6 ounces each)**
- 1½ **teaspoons canola oil**
- ½ **cup jellied cranberry sauce**
- ½ **cup undrained crushed pineapple**
- 3 **tablespoons brown sugar**
- ⅛ **teaspoon ground cloves**

1. Cut each ham steak in half. In a skillet over medium heat, cook ham in oil in batches 3-5 minutes on each side or until browned and heated through. Set aside; keep warm.

2. Meanwhile, in a small saucepan, mash cranberry sauce; stir in the remaining ingredients. Bring to a boil; cook and stir 3-5 minutes or until slightly thickened. Serve with the ham.

Hearty Sausage 'n' Beans

Our son, Will, is a brand new dad. He cooked this blend of sausage, beans, tomatoes and rice when we came to visit our newborn granddaughter, Jenna. The beauty of the dish is the simplicity: Toss the ingredients in one pan, simmer, and you've got dinner. Add corn bread and a tossed salad on the side.

—WILL OWEN WACO, TX

START TO FINISH: 25 MIN.
MAKES: 6 SERVINGS

- 1 **pound smoked sausage, sliced**
- 1 **medium onion, chopped**
- 2 **tablespoons canola oil**
- 2 **cans (15 ounces each) pinto beans, rinsed and drained**
- ½ **cups water**
- 1 **can (14½ ounces) diced tomatoes with mild green chilies, undrained**
- 1 **tablespoon ranch salad dressing mix**
- 2 **cups uncooked instant rice**

In a Dutch oven, cook sausage and onion in oil over medium heat until onion is tender. Add the beans, water, tomatoes and salad dressing mix. Bring to a boil; stir in rice. Reduce heat; cover and simmer for 5 minutes or until rice is tender.

TOP TIP

A pork loin chop has a T-bone-shaped bone, with meat on both sides of the bone. The rib chop has meat nestled between the rib and backbone. The bones make an L shape. Center cut chops are boneless and a blade chop has bones from the shoulder blade.

**PROVOLONE-STUFFED PORK CHOPS
WITH TARRAGON VINAIGRETTE**

**PINEAPPLE
CRANBERRY HAM**

**HEARTY
SAUSAGE 'N' BEANS**

CREAMY HAM PENNE

APPLE-BALSAMIC PORK CHOPS & RICE

(5) INGREDIENTS

Creamy Ham Penne

Mixing spreadable cheese with whole wheat pasta, broccoli and fat-free milk for a main dish is a healthier use of this convenience product than simply spreading it on crackers.

—**BARBARA PLETZKE** HERNDON, VA

START TO FINISH: 30 MIN.
MAKES: 4 SERVINGS

- 2 cups uncooked whole wheat penne pasta
- 2 cups fresh broccoli florets
- 1 cup fat-free milk
- 1 package (6½ ounces) reduced-fat garlic-herb spreadable cheese
- 1 cup cubed fully cooked ham
- ¼ teaspoon pepper

In a large saucepan, cook penne according to package directions, adding broccoli during the last 5 minutes of cooking; drain. Remove and set aside. In same pan, mix milk and spreadable cheese. Cook and stir over medium heat 3-5 minutes or until cheese is melted. Add the ham, pepper and penne mixture; heat through.

Apple-Balsamic Pork Chops & Rice

Thanks to tangy balsamic vinegar and sweet apples, this one-pot dish lets you have a little something special anytime.

—**GREG HAGELI** ELMHURST, IL

START TO FINISH: 30 MIN.
MAKES: 4 SERVINGS

- 4 boneless pork loin chops (6 ounces each)
- ½ teaspoon salt, divided
- ½ teaspoon pepper, divided
- 1 tablespoon canola oil
- 2 medium Gala apples, cut into ½-inch pieces
- 2 cups sliced fresh mushrooms
- 1 medium onion, chopped
- 1½ cups instant brown rice
- 1 cup reduced-sodium chicken broth
- 2 tablespoons balsamic vinegar
- ¼ teaspoon dried thyme

1. Sprinkle pork chops with ¼ teaspoon salt and ¼ teaspoon pepper. In a large skillet, heat oil over medium heat. Brown pork chops on both sides; remove from pan.

2. In same skillet, add apples, mushrooms and onion; cook and stir 4-5 minutes or until tender. Stir in rice, broth, vinegar, thyme and remaining salt and pepper. Bring to a boil. Reduce heat; cook, covered, 5 minutes.

3. Place pork chops over top; cook, covered, 4-6 minutes or until a thermometer inserted into pork reads 145°. Let stand 5 minutes before serving.

> **PAIR IT!**
> *Chocolate-Raspberry Angel Food Torte, page 224, will be great with the pork chops and rice.*

Breaded Pork Chops

For our birthday, we got to choose dinner and Mom would prepare it. I always chose these breaded pork chops as part of my dinner.

—**DEBORAH AMRINE** FORT MYERS, FL

START TO FINISH: 20 MIN.
MAKES: 6 SERVINGS

- 1 egg, lightly beaten
- ½ cup 2% milk
- 1½ cups crushed saltine crackers
- 6 boneless pork loin chops
  (1 inch thick and 4 ounces each)
- ¼ cup canola oil

1. In a shallow bowl, mix egg and milk. Place crumbs in another bowl. Dip each pork chop in egg mixture, then coat with crumbs, patting to make a thick coating.

2. In a skillet, cook chops in oil 4-5 minutes on each side or until a thermometer reads 145°. Let meat stand 5 minutes before serving.

Potato Kielbasa Skillet

Smoky kielbasa steals the show in this hearty, home-style all-in-one meal. This is perfect for those cold late fall and early winter nights.

—*TASTE OF HOME* TEST KITCHEN

START TO FINISH: 30 MIN.
MAKES: 4 SERVINGS

- 1 pound red potatoes, cubed
- 3 tablespoons water
- ¾ pound smoked kielbasa or Polish sausage, cut into ¼-inch slices
- ½ cup chopped onion
- 1 tablespoon olive oil
- 2 tablespoons brown sugar
- 2 tablespoons cider vinegar
- 1 tablespoon Dijon mustard
- ½ teaspoon dried thyme
- ¼ teaspoon pepper
- 4 cups fresh baby spinach
- 5 bacon strips, cooked and crumbled

1. Place potatoes and water in a microwave-safe dish. Cover and microwave on high for 4 minutes or until tender; drain.

2. In a large skillet, saute kielbasa and onion in oil until onion is tender. Add potatoes; saute 3-5 minutes longer or until kielbasa and potatoes are lightly browned.

3. Combine the brown sugar, vinegar, mustard, thyme and pepper; stir into skillet. Bring to a boil. Reduce heat; simmer, uncovered, for 2-3 minutes or until heated through. Add spinach and bacon; cook and stir until spinach is wilted.

DID YOU KNOW?

Red potatoes are a great all-purpose potato. Their waxy texture allows them to hold their shape during cooking. They are ideal for roasting, soups, stews, salads and mashing.

BREADED PORK CHOPS

⑤ INGREDIENTS
Pork Medallions with Cranberry Sauce

A little bit tangy, a little bit smoky, this special weeknight recipe takes pork medallions from ordinary to extraordinary.

—CATHERINE HIGGINS
BOUNTIFUL, UT

START TO FINISH: 25 MIN.
MAKES: 4 SERVINGS

- 1 pork tenderloin (1 pound), cut into 1-inch slices
- ⅛ teaspoon salt
- ⅛ teaspoon pepper
- ½ cup whole-berry cranberry sauce
- 2 tablespoons barbecue sauce
- 1 tablespoon water
- 2 garlic cloves, minced
- ½ teaspoon Chinese five-spice powder

1. Sprinkle pork with salt and pepper. In a large nonstick skillet coated with cooking spray, cook pork in batches over medium heat for 3-5 minutes on each side or until juices run clear. Remove and keep warm.
2. Add cranberry sauce, barbecue sauce, water, garlic and five-spice powder to skillet. Bring to a boil. Reduce heat; simmer, uncovered, for 1-2 minutes or until thickened. Serve with pork.

Quick Golden Stew

This complete meal can be prepared in a hurry. Yet it has a rich goodness that tastes elegant.

—MERRY MCNALLY IONIA, MI

START TO FINISH: 30 MIN.
MAKES: 4 SERVINGS

- 4 medium carrots, cut into 1-inch pieces
- 1½ cups diced peeled potatoes
- 2 medium onions, cut into chunks
  Water

- 1 package (10 ounces) frozen peas, thawed
- 2 cups cubed fully cooked ham
- 1 can (10¾ ounces) condensed cream of celery soup, undiluted
- 1 jar (8 ounces) process cheese spread

1. In a large saucepan or Dutch oven, combine carrots, potatoes, onions and just enough water to cover. Bring to a boil. Reduce heat; cover and cook 10 minutes or until vegetables are tender.
2. Add the peas and ham; cover and cook 5 minutes longer. Drain water. Stir in the soup and cheese; heat through.

Skewerless Stovetop Kabobs

My family loves this quick and easy recipe so much, we never have any leftovers. It's also great on the grill.

—JENNIFER MITCHELL ALTOONA, PA

START TO FINISH: 30 MIN.
MAKES: 4 SERVINGS

- 1 pound pork tenderloin, cut into ¾-inch cubes
- ¾ cup fat-free Italian salad dressing, divided
- 2 large green peppers, cut into ¾-inch pieces
- 2 small zucchini, cut into ½-inch slices
- ½ pound medium fresh mushrooms, halved
- 1 large sweet onion, cut into wedges
- 1 cup cherry tomatoes
- ¼ teaspoon pepper
- ⅛ teaspoon seasoned salt

1. In a large nonstick skillet, saute pork in ¼ cup salad dressing until no longer pink. Remove from skillet and keep warm.
2. In the same pan, cook the peppers, zucchini, mushrooms, onion, tomatoes, pepper and seasoned salt in remaining salad dressing until vegetables are tender. Return pork to skillet; heat through.

⑤ INGREDIENTS
Salsa Skillet Pork Chops

There's nothing better than turning out a super-quick skillet supper. This recipe delivers a meal that'll please the whole family on a busy weeknight. It's a keeper.

—DEANNA ELLETT
BOYNTON BEACH, FL

START TO FINISH: 30 MIN.
MAKES: 6 SERVINGS

- 6 boneless pork loin chops (6 ounces each)
- ½ teaspoon salt
- ¼ teaspoon pepper
- 2 cups fresh whole kernel corn
- 1 can (15 ounces) pinto beans, rinsed and drained
- 1¼ cups chunky salsa
- 2 tablespoons water
- 1 teaspoon ground cumin

1. Sprinkle pork chops with salt and pepper. Heat a large nonstick skillet coated with cooking spray over medium heat. Brown chops on both sides in batches.
2. Return all chops to pan. Add remaining ingredients; bring to a boil. Reduce heat; simmer, covered, 6-8 minutes or until thermometer inserted into pork reads 145°. Let stand 5 minutes before serving.

TOP TIP

Pork tenderloin is a versatile cut of meat and it cooks quickly. For cutlets, cut the tenderloin into 3-ounce portions and pound to 1/4-inch thick. For stir-fries, cut into 1/2-inch slices, then into strips. And for kabobs, cubes of tenderloin will grill in minutes.

SALSA SKILLET PORK CHOPS

SKEWERLESS STOVETOP KABOBS

**PORK &
POTATO SUPPER**

**FETTUCCINE
CARBONARA**

**RAVIOLI WITH SAUSAGE &
TOMATO CREAM SAUCE**

Pork & Potato Supper

If you're looking for a down-home dinner that can be easily made on a weeknight, then this recipe is for you. My husband made sure that I added it to the list of Allen family favorites.

—**MACEY ALLEN** GREEN FOREST, AR

START TO FINISH: 30 MIN.
MAKES: 4 SERVINGS

- 2 tablespoons butter, divided
- 1 pork tenderloin (1 pound), cut into ¼-inch slices
- 1 cup sliced fresh mushrooms
- 2 garlic cloves, minced
- 8 small red potatoes, quartered
- 1 can (14½ ounces) reduced-sodium chicken broth, divided
- 2 teaspoons Worcestershire sauce
- ¼ teaspoon salt
- ¼ teaspoon pepper
- 2 tablespoons all-purpose flour
- 4 green onions, sliced

1. In a 12-in. skillet, heat 1 tablespoon butter over medium heat. Cook pork 2-4 minutes on each side or until tender. Remove from pan.

2. In same pan, heat remaining butter over medium-high heat. Add mushrooms; cook and stir until almost tender. Add garlic; cook 1 minute longer. Stir in potatoes, 1½ cups broth, Worcestershire sauce, salt and pepper. Bring to a boil. Reduce heat; simmer, covered, 10-15 minutes or until potatoes are tender.

3. In a bowl, mix the flour and remaining broth until smooth. Stir into mushroom mixture. Bring to a boil; cook and stir until sauce is thickened. Stir in green onions. Return pork to pan and heat through.

Fettuccine Carbonara

When a man at church found out how much my family likes fettuccine carbonara, he shared his Italian grandmother's recipe with us. I've made it my own over the last 25 years. Grated Parmesan cheese works just as well as Romano.

—**KRISTINE CHAYES** SMITHTOWN, NY

START TO FINISH: 30 MIN.
MAKES: 6 SERVINGS

- ½ pound bacon strips, chopped
- 1 package (16 ounces) fettuccine
- 1 small onion, finely chopped
- 2 garlic cloves, minced
- 1 cup half-and-half cream
- 4 eggs, lightly beaten
- ½ cup grated Romano cheese
- ½ teaspoon salt
- ¼ teaspoon pepper
- 1 tablespoon minced fresh parsley
  Additional grated Romano cheese, optional

1. In a large skillet, cook bacon over medium heat until crisp, stirring occasionally. Remove with a slotted spoon; drain on paper towels. Discard drippings, reserving 1 tablespoon in pan.

2. Meanwhile, in a Dutch oven, cook fettuccine according to package directions. Drain; return to pan.

3. Add onion to drippings in skillet; cook and stir over medium heat 2-3 minutes or until tender. Add garlic; cook 1 minute longer. Reduce heat to medium-low. Stir in cream. In a small bowl, whisk a small amount of warm cream into eggs; return all to pan, whisking constantly. Cook 8-10 minutes or until a thermometer reads 160°, stirring constantly.

4. Stir cheese, salt, pepper and bacon into sauce. Add to fettuccine and toss to combine. Sprinkle with parsley and, if desired, additional cheese. Serve immediately.

Ravioli with Sausage & Tomato Cream Sauce

It tastes like you spent all day preparing this quick pasta recipe, but it's ready in just 30 minutes! Family and friends request my ravioli often.

—**CHERYL WEGENER** FESTUS, MO

START TO FINISH: 25 MIN.
MAKES: 4 SERVINGS

- 1 package (9 ounces) refrigerated cheese ravioli
- ¾ pound bulk Italian sausage
- 1 jar (24 ounces) tomato basil pasta sauce
- ½ cup heavy whipping cream
- 2 bacon strips, cooked and crumbled
- 2 tablespoons grated Parmesan cheese
  Minced fresh parsley

1. Cook ravioli according to the package directions.

2. Meanwhile, cook sausage in a large skillet over medium heat until no longer pink; drain. Stir in pasta sauce, cream and bacon. Bring mixture to a boil; reduce heat. Simmer, uncovered, for 2 minutes or until slightly thickened.

3. Drain ravioli; stir into sauce. Top with the Parmesan cheese and parsley.

> **HOW TO**

CHOP BACON

Bacon fat tends to smear onto the cutting board and knife when you are chopping it. An easier way to chop it is to use kitchen shears that have been sprayed with cooking spray. Cut the bacon into long strips, then stack the strips and cut crosswise into pieces directly over the skillet.

(5) INGREDIENTS
Ham & Zucchini Italiano

I believe dinner should be healthy, delicious and simple. With fresh zucchini, ham and marinara sauce baked with mozzarella, you can accomplish all three.
—**MADISON MAYBERRY** AMES, IA

START TO FINISH: 30 MIN.
MAKES: 4 SERVINGS

- 3 medium zucchini, cut diagonally into ¼-inch slices
- 1 tablespoon olive oil
- 1 teaspoon dried basil
- ½ teaspoon salt
- ¼ teaspoon pepper
- ½ pound smoked deli ham, cut into strips
- 1 cup marinara or spaghetti sauce
- ¾ cup shredded part-skim mozzarella cheese

1. Preheat oven to 450°. In a skillet, saute zucchini in oil until crisp-tender. Sprinkle with basil, salt and pepper.
2. Place half of the zucchini in a greased 8-in.-square baking dish. Layer with half of the ham, marinara sauce and cheese. Repeat layers.
3. Bake, uncovered, 10-12 minutes or until heated through and the cheese is melted. Serve with a slotted spoon.

(5) INGREDIENTS
Southwest Pork Tenderloin

When living in Europe, I missed classic Southwestern flavors. Using what I had, I made spicy pork tenderloin.
—**JOHN COX** SEGUIN, TX

START TO FINISH: 30 MIN.
MAKES: 8 SERVINGS

- 2 pork tenderloins (1 pound each)
- 2 tablespoons canola oil
- 1 envelope taco seasoning
- 3 medium limes, cut into wedges

1. Preheat oven to 400°. Rub tenderloins with oil; sprinkle with taco seasoning. Place on a rack in a shallow roasting pan.
2. Roast 20-25 minutes or until a thermometer reads 145°. Remove tenderloins from oven; tent with foil. Let stand 10 minutes before slicing. Squeeze lime wedges over pork.

Rigatoni with Sausage & Peas

With a tomato-y meat sauce and tangy goat cheese, this weeknight wonder is my version of comfort food.
—**LIZZIE MUNRO** BROOKLYN, NY

START TO FINISH: 30 MIN.
MAKES: 6 SERVINGS

- 12 ounces uncooked rigatoni or large tube pasta
- 1 pound bulk Italian sausage
- 4 garlic cloves, minced
- ¼ cup tomato paste
- 1 can (28 ounces) crushed tomatoes
- ½ teaspoon dried basil
- ¼ to ½ teaspoon crushed red pepper flakes
- 1½ cups frozen peas
- ½ cup heavy whipping cream
- ½ cup crumbled goat or feta cheese
- Thinly sliced fresh basil, optional

1. Cook rigatoni according to the package directions.
2. Meanwhile, in a Dutch oven, cook sausage over medium heat 6-8 minutes or until no longer pink, breaking into crumbles. Add garlic; cook 1 minute longer. Drain.
3. Add tomato paste; cook and stir 2-3 minutes or until meat is coated. Stir in tomatoes, dried basil and pepper flakes; bring to a boil. Reduce heat; simmer, uncovered, 10-15 minutes or until thickened, stirring occasionally.
4. Drain rigatoni; stir into sausage mixture. Add peas and cream; heat through. Top with cheese and basil.

HAM & ZUCCHINI ITALIANO

SOUTHWEST
PORK TENDERLOIN

RIGATONI WITH
SAUSAGE & PEAS

**HONEY-LEMON
CHICKEN ENCHILADAS**

Honey-Lemon Chicken Enchiladas

Honey, lemon and chili flavors blend wonderfully in enchiladas. My family devours this dish, so I also use the delicious chicken filling for soft tacos with toppings.

—**KRISTI MOAK** GILBERT, AZ

START TO FINISH: 30 MIN.
MAKES: 6 SERVINGS

- ¼ **cup honey**
- 2 **tablespoons lemon or lime juice**
- 1 **tablespoon canola oil**
- 2 **teaspoons chili powder**
- ¼ **teaspoon garlic powder**
- 3 **cups shredded cooked chicken breast**
- 2 **cans (10 ounces each) green enchilada sauce, divided**
- 12 **corn tortillas (6 inches), warmed**
- ¾ **cup shredded reduced-fat cheddar cheese**
  Sliced green onions and chopped tomatoes, optional

1. In a large bowl, whisk the first five ingredients. Add the chicken and toss to coat. Pour 1 can of enchilada sauce into a greased microwave-safe 11x7-in. dish. Place ¼ cup chicken mixture off center on each tortilla. Roll up and place enchiladas, seam side down, in the prepared dish. Top with remaining enchilada sauce.

2. Microwave, covered, on high 11-13 minutes or until heated through. Sprinkle with cheese. If desired, top with green onions and tomatoes.

Thai Red Chicken Curry

After experimenting in the kitchen, I re-created a favorite dish from a Thai restaurant, and now I cook it almost weekly for my family. On a busy night, frozen stir-fry veggies speed things up.
—**MARY SHENK** DEKALB, IL

START TO FINISH: 25 MIN.
MAKES: 4 SERVINGS

- 1 **can (13.66 ounces) coconut milk**
- ⅓ **cup chicken broth**
- 2 **tablespoons brown sugar**
- 2 **tablespoons fish sauce**
- 1 **tablespoon red curry paste**
- 2 **cups frozen stir-fry vegetable blend**
- 3 **cups cubed cooked chicken breast**
  Cooked jasmine rice
  Minced fresh cilantro, optional

1. Mix the first five ingredients in a large skillet. Bring to a boil; reduce heat and simmer 5 minutes.

2. Stir in vegetables; return to a boil. Reduce heat and simmer, uncovered, 9-11 minutes or until vegetables are tender and sauce thickens slightly.

3. Add chicken; heat through. Serve with rice. Sprinkle with cilantro if desired.

Pineapple-Mango Chicken

Combining pineapple, mango and spices makes a sauce for chicken that is so unique. This has become a favorite of so many friends and family members. We like to grill the chicken with vegetable kabobs.
—**KIM WAITES** RUTHERFORDTON, NC

START TO FINISH: 30 MIN.
MAKES: 4 SERVINGS

- 1½ **cups undrained crushed pineapple**
- ½ **cup golden raisins**
- ¼ **teaspoon ground cinnamon**
- ¼ **teaspoon ground cloves**
- ⅛ **teaspoon ground nutmeg**
- 2 **medium mangoes, peeled and chopped**
- 4 **boneless skinless chicken breast halves (5 ounces each)**
- ½ **teaspoon salt**
- ⅛ **teaspoon pepper**
  Hot cooked rice

1. In a small saucepan, combine the first five ingredients; bring to a boil over medium heat. Reduce heat; simmer, uncovered, 4-6 minutes or until sauce is thickened and raisins are plumped, stirring occasionally. Stir in mangoes; heat through. Set aside.

2. Moisten a paper towel with cooking oil; using long-handled tongs, rub on grill rack to coat lightly. Sprinkle chicken with salt and pepper. Grill chicken, covered, over medium heat or broil 4 in. from heat 5-8 minutes on each side or until a thermometer reads 165°. Serve with sauce and rice.

THAI RED CHICKEN CURRY

PAIR IT!
Blueberry Shortcake Sundaes, page 208, will cool the heat from the delicious curry.

White Chili with Chicken

Folks who enjoy a change from traditional tomato-based chilis will enjoy this version. The flavorful blend has tender chunks of chicken, white beans and just enough zip.

—**CHRISTY CAMPOS** RICHMOND, VA

START TO FINISH: 30 MIN.
MAKES: 6 SERVINGS

- 1 **medium onion, chopped**
- 1 **jalapeno pepper, seeded and chopped, optional**
- 1 **tablespoon canola oil**
- 2 **garlic cloves, minced**
- 4 **cups chicken broth**
- 2 **cans (15½ ounces each) great northern beans, rinsed and drained**
- 2 **tablespoons minced fresh parsley**
- 1 **tablespoon lime juice**
- 1 **to 1¼ teaspoons ground cumin**
- 2 **tablespoons cornstarch**
- ¼ **cup cold water**
- 2 **cups cubed cooked chicken**

1. In a large saucepan, cook the onion and jalapeno if desired in oil until tender. Add the garlic; cook 1 minute longer. Stir in the broth, beans, parsley, lime juice and cumin; bring to a boil. Reduce heat; cover and simmer 10 minutes, stirring occasionally.

2. Combine cornstarch and water until smooth; gradually stir into the chili. Add the chicken. Bring to a boil; cook and stir 2 minutes or until thickened.

NOTE *Wear disposable gloves when cutting hot peppers; the oils can burn skin. Avoid touching your face.*

Turkey Tortellini Toss

One night I had frozen tortellini on hand and didn't have a clue what I was going to make. I scanned my cupboards and refrigerator, and soon I was happily cooking away. So fresh-tasting and simple, this combination is now a go-to recipe!

—**LEO PARR** NEW ORLEANS, LA

START TO FINISH: 30 MIN.
MAKES: 4 SERVINGS

- 2 **cups frozen cheese tortellini (about 8 ounces)**
- 1 **pound ground turkey**
- 2 **medium zucchini, halved lengthwise and sliced**
- 2 **garlic cloves, minced**
- 1½ **cups cherry tomatoes, halved**
- 1 **teaspoon dried oregano**
- ½ **teaspoon salt**
- ¼ **teaspoon crushed red pepper flakes**
- 1 **cup shredded Asiago cheese, divided**
- 1 **tablespoon olive oil**

1. Cook tortellini according to the package directions.

2. Meanwhile, in a large skillet, cook turkey, zucchini and garlic over medium heat 7-9 minutes or until turkey is no longer pink, breaking up turkey into crumbles; drain. Add tomatoes, oregano, salt and pepper flakes; cook 2 minutes longer. Stir in ¾ cup cheese.

3. Drain tortellini; add to skillet and toss to combine. Drizzle with the oil; sprinkle with remaining Asiago cheese.

Balsamic Chicken with Broccoli Couscous

This quick-fix recipe's all about saving time thanks to a couple of packaged convenience items and an ingenious shortcut: The broccoli cooks right with the couscous. The result is pure satisfaction on a plate.

—*TASTE OF HOME* TEST KITCHEN

START TO FINISH: 30 MIN.
MAKES: 4 SERVINGS

- 4 **boneless skinless chicken breast halves (4 ounces each)**
- ½ **teaspoon salt**
- ¼ **teaspoon pepper**
- 1 **tablespoon olive oil**
- 2 **tablespoons balsamic vinegar**
- 1 **tablespoon honey**
- ¼ **teaspoon Italian seasoning**

COUSCOUS

- 1 **can (14½ ounces) chicken broth**
- ¼ **teaspoon garlic powder**
- ¼ **teaspoon pepper**
- 3 **cups frozen chopped broccoli, thawed and drained**
- 1 **cup uncooked couscous**
- ¼ **cup grated Parmesan cheese**

1. Sprinkle chicken with salt and pepper. In a large skillet, heat oil over medium heat. Add chicken; cook 4-6 minutes on each side or until a thermometer reads 165°. Stir in vinegar, honey and Italian seasoning; heat through.

2. Meanwhile, in a small saucepan, bring broth, garlic powder and pepper to a boil. Stir in broccoli and couscous. Remove from heat; let stand, covered, 5-10 minutes or until broth is absorbed. Stir in the cheese. Serve with chicken.

TOP TIP

To reduce the heat of jalapenos and other hot peppers, cut the peppers in half; remove and discard the seeds and membranes. If you like very spicy foods, add the seeds to the dish you're making instead of discarding them.

TURKEY TORTELLINI TOSS

BALSAMIC CHICKEN WITH BROCCOLI COUSCOUS

Mediterranean Turkey Skillet

I've always heard that it's important to eat a rainbow of colors to get all of the nutrients we need. Thanks to my garden-grown veggies, this dish certainly fits the bill.
—NICOLE EHLERT BURLINGTON, WI

START TO FINISH: 30 MIN.
MAKES: 6 SERVINGS

- 1 tablespoon olive oil
- 1 package (20 ounces) lean ground turkey
- 2 medium zucchini, quartered lengthwise and cut into ½-inch slices
- 1 medium onion, chopped
- 2 banana peppers, seeded and chopped
- 3 garlic cloves, minced
- ½ teaspoon dried oregano
- 1 can (15 ounces) black beans, rinsed and drained
- 1 can (14½ ounces) diced tomatoes, undrained
- 1 tablespoon balsamic vinegar
- ½ teaspoon salt

1. In a large skillet, heat oil over medium-high heat. Add the turkey, zucchini, onion, peppers, garlic and oregano; cook 10-12 minutes or until turkey is no longer pink and vegetables are tender, breaking up turkey into crumbles; drain.

2. Stir in remaining ingredients; heat through, stirring occasionally.

SWAP IT
If you don't have black beans on hand, use cannellini or red beans.

LOADED GRILLED CHICKEN SANDWICH

Loaded Grilled Chicken Sandwich

I threw these ingredients together on a whim and the sandwich turned out so well, I surprised myself! If you're in a rush, microwave the bacon. Just cover it with paper towel to keep it from splattering too much.
—DANA YORK KENNEWICK, WA

START TO FINISH: 30 MIN.
MAKES: 4 SERVINGS

- 4 boneless skinless chicken breast halves (4 ounces each)
- 2 teaspoons Italian salad dressing mix
- 4 slices pepper jack cheese
- 4 ciabatta or kaiser rolls, split
- 2 tablespoons mayonnaise
- ¾ teaspoon Dijon mustard
- 4 cooked bacon strips, halved
- 4 slices tomato
- ½ medium ripe avocado, peeled and thinly sliced
- ½ pound deli coleslaw (about 1 cup)

1. Pound the chicken breasts with a meat mallet to flatten slightly; sprinkle both sides with the dressing mix. Moisten a paper towel with cooking oil; using long-handled tongs, rub on the grill rack to coat lightly.

2. Grill chicken, covered, over medium heat or broil 4 in. from heat 4-6 minutes on each side or until a thermometer reads 165°. Place cheese on chicken; grill, covered, 1-2 minutes longer or until cheese is melted. Meanwhile, grill rolls, cut side down, 1-2 minutes or until toasted.

3. Mix mayonnaise and mustard; spread on roll tops. Layer roll bottoms with chicken, bacon, tomato, avocado and coleslaw. Replace tops.

Chicken Thighs with Shallots & Spinach

This moist and tender chicken comes complete with its own creamy and flavorful vegetable side. It makes a pretty presentation and comes together quickly for a nutritious weeknight meal.
—**GENNA JOHANNES**
WRIGHTSTOWN, WI

START TO FINISH: 30 MIN.
MAKES: 6 SERVINGS

- 6 boneless skinless chicken thighs (about 1½ pounds)
- ½ teaspoon seasoned salt
- ½ teaspoon pepper
- 1½ teaspoons olive oil
- 4 shallots, thinly sliced
- ⅓ cup white wine or reduced-sodium chicken broth
- 1 package (10 ounces) fresh spinach
- ¼ teaspoon salt
- ¼ cup fat-free sour cream

1. Sprinkle chicken with seasoned salt and pepper. In a large nonstick skillet coated with cooking spray, heat oil over medium heat. Add the chicken; cook 6 minutes on each side or until a thermometer reads 165°. Remove from the pan and keep warm.

2. In same pan, cook and stir shallots until tender. Add wine; bring to a boil. Cook until wine is reduced by half. Add the spinach and salt; cook and stir just until the spinach is wilted. Stir in the sour cream; serve with chicken.

CHICKEN THIGHS WITH SHALLOTS & SPINACH

**BUFFALO
TURKEY BURGERS**

**TURKEY CUTLETS IN
LEMON WINE SAUCE**

**COLA BBQ
CHICKEN**

Buffalo Turkey Burgers

Celery and blue cheese dressing help tame the hot sauce on these juicy burgers. For an even lighter version, pass on the buns and serve with lettuce leaves, sliced onion and chopped tomato.

—MARY PAX-SHIPLEY BEND, OR

START TO FINISH: 25 MIN.
MAKES: 4 SERVINGS

- 2 tablespoons Louisiana-style hot sauce, divided
- 2 teaspoons ground cumin
- 2 teaspoons chili powder
- 2 garlic cloves, minced
- ½ teaspoon salt
- ⅛ teaspoon pepper
- 1 pound lean ground turkey
- 4 whole wheat hamburger buns, split
- 1 cup shredded lettuce
- 2 celery ribs, chopped
- 2 tablespoons fat-free blue cheese salad dressing

1. In a large bowl, mix 1 tablespoon hot sauce, cumin, chili powder, garlic, salt and pepper. Add turkey; mix lightly but thoroughly. Shape into four ½-in.-thick patties.
2. In a large nonstick skillet coated with cooking spray, cook burgers over medium heat 4-6 minutes on each side or until a thermometer reads 165°.
3. Serve burgers on buns with lettuce, celery, salad dressing and remaining hot sauce.
FREEZE OPTION *Place patties on a plastic wrap-lined baking sheet; wrap and freeze until firm. Remove from pan and transfer to a large resealable plastic bag; return to freezer. To use, grill frozen patties as directed, increasing time as necessary for a thermometer to read 165°.*

(5)INGREDIENTS
Turkey Cutlets in Lemon Wine Sauce

After I ate something like this at a local Italian restaurant, I figured out how to make it at home for my family. Now I serve it a lot since it's so quick to make—and they're so happy I do.

—KATHIE WILSON WARRENTON, VA

START TO FINISH: 25 MIN.
MAKES: 4 SERVINGS

- ½ cup all-purpose flour
- ½ teaspoon salt
- ½ teaspoon paprika
- ¼ teaspoon pepper
- 4 turkey breast cutlets (2½ ounces each)
- 1 tablespoon olive oil
- 1 cup white wine or chicken broth
- ¼ cup lemon juice

1. In a shallow bowl, mix flour, salt, paprika and pepper. Dip turkey in flour mixture to coat both sides; shake off excess.
2. In a large skillet, heat oil over medium heat. Add turkey and cook in batches 1-2 minutes on each side or until turkey is no longer pink. Remove from pan.
3. Add wine and lemon juice to skillet, stirring to loosen browned bits from pan. Bring to a boil; cook until liquid is reduced by half. Return cutlets to pan; turn to coat and heat through.

Cola BBQ Chicken

My dad has been making a basic version of this family favorite for years. I've recently made it my own by spicing it up a bit with hoisin sauce and red pepper flakes. Sometimes I let the chicken and sauce simmer in my slow cooker.

—BRIGETTE SCHROEDER YORKVILLE, IL

START TO FINISH: 30 MIN.
MAKES: 6 SERVINGS

- 1 cup cola
- ⅓ cup finely chopped onion
- ⅓ cup barbecue sauce
- 2 teaspoons hoisin sauce
- 1 garlic clove, minced
- ⅛ teaspoon salt
- ⅛ teaspoon pepper
- ⅛ teaspoon crushed red pepper flakes
- 6 boneless skinless chicken thighs (about 1½ pounds) Hot cooked rice

1. In a saucepan, combine the first eight ingredients; bring to a boil. Reduce heat; simmer, uncovered, 10-15 minutes or until slightly thickened, stirring occasionally. Reserve ¾ cup for serving.
2. Grill the chicken, covered, over medium heat or broil 4 in. from the heat 5-7 minutes on each side or until a thermometer reads 170°, basting occasionally with the remaining sauce during the last 5 minutes of cooking. Serve chicken with rice and reserved sauce.

▸ TOP TIP

The United States Department of Agriculture recommends that you don't wash or rinse chicken before cooking. If you do, bacteria can spread to kitchen surfaces and utensils and contaminate other foods.

Chicken with Cherry Pineapple Sauce

Sweet and colorful, this tender, lower-fat chicken dish is simply fantastic! The quick prep time, fresh flavors, cherries and chunks of pineapple will make it a family favorite in no time.

—SALLY MALONEY DALLAS, GA

START TO FINISH: 25 MIN.
MAKES: 4 SERVINGS

- 4 boneless skinless chicken breast halves (4 ounces each)
- ½ teaspoon garlic salt
- ¼ teaspoon ground ginger
- 2 teaspoons canola oil
- 1 can (8 ounces) unsweetened pineapple chunks
- ½ cup sweet-and-sour sauce
- ¼ cup dried cherries
- 2 green onions, sliced

1. Sprinkle chicken with garlic salt and ginger. In a large nonstick skillet coated with cooking spray, brown chicken in oil.
2. Drain pineapple, reserving ¼ cup juice. In a small bowl, combine the sauce, cherries and reserved juice; pour over chicken. Bring to a boil. Reduce heat; cover and simmer 8-10 minutes or until a thermometer reads 165°, turning chicken once. Stir in pineapple and onions; heat through.

Broccoli Chicken Skillet

You're only 25 minutes from a comforting, cheesy veggie and chicken dish that the whole family will love! And since it's all in one skillet, cleanup is a breeze.

—*TASTE OF HOME* TEST KITCHEN

START TO FINISH: 25 MIN.
MAKES: 4 SERVINGS

- 1½ pounds boneless skinless chicken breasts, cubed
- 2 cups frozen broccoli florets, thawed
- 1 cup julienned carrots
- ½ cup chopped onion
- 1 tablespoon olive oil
- 1 can (10¾ ounces) condensed cream of broccoli soup, undiluted
- 1 cup stuffing mix
- 1 cup milk
- ¼ cup raisins
- ⅛ teaspoon pepper
- 1 cup (4 ounces) shredded Colby cheese

1. In a large skillet, saute the chicken, broccoli, carrots and onion in oil for 5-6 minutes or until chicken is no longer pink.
2. Stir in the soup, stuffing mix, milk, raisins and pepper. Cook, uncovered, over medium heat 8-10 minutes or until heated through. Sprinkle with cheese. Remove from heat; cover and let stand until cheese is melted.
FREEZE OPTION *Before adding cheese, cool casserole; cover and freeze. To use, partially thaw in refrigerator overnight. Remove from refrigerator 30 minutes before reheating. Preheat oven to 350°. Cover casserole with foil; bake 20-30 minutes or until heated through and a thermometer inserted into center reads 165°. Sprinkle with cheese.*

Turkey Picadillo

I serve this over short-cut pasta or egg noodles and garnish it with sour cream and a sprinkling of chopped green onions.

—ANITA PINNEY SANTA ROSA, CA

START TO FINISH: 30 MIN.
MAKES: 4 SERVINGS

- 5⅓ cups uncooked whole wheat egg noodles
- 1 pound lean ground turkey
- 1 medium green pepper, chopped
- 1 small onion, chopped
- 2 garlic cloves, minced
- 2 teaspoons chili powder
- ¼ teaspoon pepper
- 1 can (14½ ounces) Italian diced tomatoes, undrained
- ½ cup golden raisins
  Reduced-fat sour cream and chopped green onions, optional

1. Cook noodles according to the package directions.
2. Meanwhile, in a large nonstick skillet, cook turkey, green pepper and onion over medium heat until turkey is no longer pink, breaking up the turkey into crumbles; drain. Add the garlic, chili powder and pepper; cook 1 minute longer. Stir in the tomatoes and raisins; heat through.
3. Drain the noodles; serve with turkey mixture. Garnish with sour cream and green onions if desired.

Cashew Chicken with Noodles

I tried this recipe with some friends one night when we were doing freezer meals. I was smitten! It's quick, easy and so delicious.

—ANITA BEACHY BEALETON, VA

START TO FINISH: 20 MIN.
MAKES: 4 SERVINGS

- 8 **ounces uncooked thick rice noodles**
- ¼ **cup soy sauce**
- 2 **tablespoons cornstarch**
- 3 **garlic cloves, minced**
- 1 **pound boneless skinless chicken breasts, cubed**
- 1 **tablespoon peanut oil**
- 1 **tablespoon sesame oil**
- 6 **green onions, cut into 2-inch pieces**
- 1 **cup unsalted cashews**
- 2 **tablespoons sweet chili sauce**

1. Cook rice noodles according to package directions.

2. Meanwhile, in a small bowl, combine soy sauce, cornstarch and garlic. Add the chicken. In a large skillet, saute chicken mixture in peanut and sesame oils until no longer pink. Add onions and cook 1 minute longer.

3. Drain noodles; stir into skillet. Add cashews and chili sauce and heat through.

DID YOU KNOW?

Picadillo is considered to be Latin American in origin. Some of the areas where it is served regularly are Cuba, Mexico, Puerto Rico, the Dominican Republic and the Philippines. Each culture has its own variation, but one standard item is ground or minced meat.

TURKEY PICADILLO

CASHEW CHICKEN WITH NOODLES

CHIPOTLE CITRUS-GLAZED
TURKEY TENDERLOINS

SIMPLE SESAME
CHICKEN WITH COUSCOUS

Chipotle Citrus-Glazed Turkey Tenderloins

This simple skillet recipe makes it easy to cook turkey on a weeknight. The combination of sweet, spicy and smoky flavors from orange, peppers and molasses is amazing.

—DARLENE MORRIS
FRANKLINTON, LA

START TO FINISH: 30 MIN.
MAKES: 4 SERVINGS (½ CUP SAUCE)

- 4 **turkey breast tenderloins (5 ounces each)**
- ¼ **teaspoon salt**
- ¼ **teaspoon pepper**
- 1 **tablespoon canola oil**
- ¾ **cup orange juice**
- ¼ **cup lime juice**
- ¼ **cup packed brown sugar**
- 1 **tablespoon molasses**
- 2 **teaspoons minced chipotle peppers in adobo sauce**
- 2 **tablespoons minced fresh cilantro**

1. Sprinkle turkey with salt and pepper. In a large skillet, brown turkey in oil on all sides.
2. Meanwhile, in a small bowl whisk the juices, brown sugar, molasses and chipotle peppers; add to skillet. Reduce heat and simmer 12-16 minutes or until turkey reaches 165°. Transfer turkey to a cutting board; let rest 5 minutes.
3. Simmer glaze until thickened, about 4 minutes. Slice turkey and serve with glaze. Top with cilantro.

Simple Sesame Chicken with Couscous

I created this after my three kids tried Chinese takeout and wanted more. I use a rotisserie chicken from the deli.

—NAYLET LAROCHELLE MIAMI, FL

START TO FINISH: 25 MIN.
MAKES: 4 SERVINGS

- 1½ **cups water**
- 1 **cup uncooked whole wheat couscous**
- 1 **tablespoon olive oil**
- 2 **cups coleslaw mix**
- 4 **green onions, sliced**
- 2 **tablespoons plus ½ cup reduced-fat Asian toasted sesame salad dressing, divided**
- 2 **cups shredded cooked chicken breast**
- 2 **tablespoons minced fresh cilantro**
  Chopped peanuts, optional

1. In a small saucepan, bring water to a boil. Stir in couscous. Remove from heat; let stand, covered, 5-10 minutes or until water is absorbed. Fluff with a fork.
2. Meanwhile, in a large nonstick skillet, heat oil over medium heat. Add coleslaw mix; cook and stir 3-4 minutes or just until tender. Add green onions, 2 tablespoons dressing and couscous; heat through. Remove mixture from pan; keep warm.
3. In same skillet, add the chicken and remaining dressing; cook and stir over medium heat until heated through. Serve over couscous; top with the cilantro and, if desired, chopped peanuts.

Quick Chicken and Dumplings

Ready in 30 minutes, this easy chicken and dumplings recipe takes advantage of convenience items like canned soup and uses time-saving, drop-style dumplings.

—**WILLIE DEWAARD** CORALVILLE, IA

START TO FINISH: 30 MIN.
MAKES: 6 SERVINGS

- 1½ cups 2% milk
- 1½ cups frozen mixed vegetables, thawed
- 2½ cups cubed cooked chicken
- 1 can (10¾ ounces) condensed cream of chicken soup, undiluted
- ½ teaspoon garlic powder
- ¼ teaspoon poultry seasoning

DUMPLINGS

- 1 cup biscuit/baking mix
- ⅓ cup French-fried onions, coarsely chopped
- 7 tablespoons 2% milk
- ½ teaspoon dried parsley flakes

1. In a Dutch oven, combine the first six ingredients; bring to a boil, stirring occasionally.
2. Meanwhile, in a small bowl, combine biscuit mix, onions, milk and parsley just until moistened. Drop by heaping teaspoonfuls onto simmering stew. Cook, uncovered, 10 minutes.
3. Cover and simmer 10-12 minutes longer or until a toothpick inserted into a dumpling comes out clean (do not lift the cover while simmering).

Pecan-Crusted Chicken Nuggets

I loved chicken nuggets as a child. This baked version is healthier than the original, a great snack for kids.

—**HAILI CARROLL** VALENCIA, CA

START TO FINISH: 30 MIN.
MAKES: 6 SERVINGS

- 1½ cups cornflakes
- 1 tablespoon dried parsley flakes
- ½ teaspoon garlic powder
- ½ cup panko (Japanese) bread crumbs
- ½ cup finely chopped pecans
- 3 tablespoons 2% milk
- 1½ pounds boneless skinless chicken breasts, cut into 1-inch pieces
- ½ teaspoon salt
- ¼ teaspoon pepper
  Cooking spray

1. Preheat oven to 400°. Place cornflakes, parsley and garlic powder in a blender; cover and pulse until finely ground. Transfer to a bowl; stir in bread crumbs and pecans. Place milk in another bowl. Sprinkle chicken with salt and pepper; dip in milk, then roll in crumb mixture to coat.
2. Place on a greased baking sheet; spritz chicken with cooking spray. Bake 12-16 minutes or until chicken is no longer pink, turning once halfway through cooking.

QUICK CHICKEN AND DUMPLINGS

Sweet Onion 'n' Sausage Spaghetti

Sweet onion seasons the turkey, adding rich flavor to this pasta dish.
—MARY RELYEA CANASTOTA, NY

START TO FINISH: 30 MIN.
MAKES: 5 SERVINGS

- 6 ounces uncooked whole wheat spaghetti
- ¾ pound Italian turkey sausage links, casings removed
- 2 teaspoons olive oil
- 1 sweet onion, thinly sliced
- 1 pint cherry tomatoes, halved
- ½ cup loosely packed fresh basil leaves, thinly sliced
- ½ cup half-and-half cream
    Shaved Parmesan cheese, optional

1. Cook spaghetti according to package directions.
2. Meanwhile, in a large nonstick skillet over medium heat, cook sausage in oil for 5 minutes. Add onion; cook 8-10 minutes longer or until meat is no longer pink and onion is tender.
3. Stir in tomatoes and basil; heat through. Add cream; bring to a boil. Drain spaghetti; toss with sausage mixture. Top with cheese if desired.

Chicken Artichoke Pasta

Here's a colorful, delicious chicken dish easy enough for weeknights, but special enough for guests. A light wine sauce adds lovely flavor.
—CATHY DICK ROANOKE, VA

START TO FINISH: 30 MIN.
MAKES: 4 SERVINGS

- 6 ounces uncooked fettuccine
- 1 pound boneless skinless chicken breasts, cut into thin strips
- 3 teaspoons olive oil, divided
- ½ cup fresh broccoli florets
- ½ cup sliced fresh mushrooms
- ½ cup cherry tomatoes, halved
- 2 garlic cloves, minced

- 1 can (14 ounces) water-packed artichoke hearts, rinsed, drained and halved
- ½ teaspoon salt
- ½ teaspoon dried oregano
- 2 teaspoons all-purpose flour
- ¼ cup reduced-sodium chicken broth
- ⅓ cup white wine or additional reduced-sodium chicken broth
- 1 tablespoon minced fresh parsley
- 1 tablespoon shredded Parmesan cheese

1. Cook the pasta according to the package directions; drain.
2. Meanwhile, in a large nonstick skillet coated with cooking spray, cook chicken in 2 teaspoons oil over medium heat until no longer pink. Remove; keep warm.
3. In same skillet, saute broccoli in remaining oil 2 minutes. Stir in mushrooms, tomatoes and garlic; cook 2 minutes. Add artichokes, salt and oregano; heat through.
4. Combine flour with broth and wine until smooth; stir into pan. Bring to a boil; cook and stir 1-2 minutes or until thickened. Add parsley and reserved chicken. Add fettuccine to chicken mixture and toss to coat. Sprinkle with cheese.

Tuscan Chicken and Beans

Who doesn't like flavorful meals that are quick and easy to make? I particularly like the combination of rosemary and beans in this rustic Italian dish.
—MARIE RIZZIO INTERLOCHEN, MI

START TO FINISH: 30 MIN.
MAKES: 4 SERVINGS

- 1 pound boneless skinless chicken breasts, cut into ¾-inch pieces
- 2 teaspoons minced fresh rosemary or ½ teaspoon dried rosemary
- ¼ teaspoon salt

- ¼ teaspoon coarsely ground pepper
- 1 cup reduced-sodium chicken broth
- 2 tablespoons sun-dried tomatoes (not packed in oil), chopped
- 1 can (15½ ounces) white kidney or cannellini beans, rinsed and drained

1. In a small bowl, combine the chicken, rosemary, salt and pepper. In a large nonstick skillet coated with cooking spray, cook chicken over medium heat until browned.
2. Stir in broth and tomatoes. Bring to a boil. Reduce heat; simmer, uncovered, 3-5 minutes or until chicken juices run clear. Add the beans; heat through.

Creole Blackened Chicken

I love blackened chicken and was thrilled when I discovered I could cook it at home. I adjusted an old recipe, making it a little spicier.
—LAUREN HARDY JACKSONVILLE, FL

START TO FINISH: 30 MIN.
MAKES: 8 SERVINGS

- 2 tablespoons ground cumin
- 2 tablespoons Creole seasoning
- 2 tablespoons salt-free Southwest chipotle seasoning blend
- 4 teaspoons lemon-pepper seasoning
- 1 teaspoon cayenne pepper
- 8 boneless skinless chicken breast halves (6 ounces each)
- 2 tablespoons canola oil

1. Preheat oven to 350°. Mix the first five ingredients; sprinkle over chicken. In a large skillet, heat oil over medium-high heat. Brown chicken in batches on both sides; transfer to a greased 15x10x1-in. baking pan.
2. Bake, uncovered, 12-15 minutes or until a thermometer reads 165°.

CHICKEN
ARTICHOKE PASTA

TUSCAN CHICKEN
AND BEANS

CREOLE BLACKENED
CHICKEN

THAI CHICKEN PIZZA

Thai Chicken Pizza

This is a recipe I make for my friends on a girls' night filled with fun and laughter. It is simple to prepare but is full of flavor.

—KIMBERLY KNUPPENBURG
MENOMONEE FALLS, WI

START TO FINISH: 25 MIN.
MAKES: 6 SERVINGS

- 1 prebaked 12-inch pizza crust
- ⅔ cup Thai peanut sauce
- 2 tablespoons reduced-sodium soy sauce
- 2 tablespoons creamy peanut butter
- 1 cup shredded cooked chicken breast
- 1 cup (4 ounces) shredded part-skim mozzarella cheese
- 3 green onions, chopped
- ½ cup bean sprouts
- ½ cup shredded carrot

1. Preheat oven to 400°. Place crust on an ungreased 12-in. pizza pan or baking sheet. In a small bowl, combine the peanut sauce, soy sauce and peanut butter. Add the chicken; toss to coat. Spread over crust; sprinkle with cheese and onions.

2. Bake 10-12 minutes or until cheese is melted. Top with bean sprouts and carrot.

PAIR IT!

Winter Salad, page 169, **is a delicious way to add a little more nutrition to the meal.**

Chicken Sausages with Polenta

I get a kick out of serving this dish—everyone's always on time for dinner when they know it's on the menu.
—**ANGELA SPENGLER**
MECHANICSBURG, PA

START TO FINISH: 30 MIN.
MAKES: 6 SERVINGS

- 4 teaspoons olive oil, divided
- 1 tube (1 pound) polenta, cut into ½-inch slices
- 1 each medium sweet red, yellow and green peppers, thinly sliced
- 1 medium onion, thinly sliced
- 1 package (12 ounces) fully cooked Italian chicken sausage links, thinly sliced
- ¼ cup grated Parmesan cheese
- 1 tablespoon minced fresh basil

1. In a large nonstick skillet, heat 2 teaspoons oil over medium heat. Add polenta; cook 9-11 minutes on each side or until golden brown. Keep warm.

2. Meanwhile, in another large skillet, heat remaining oil over medium-high heat. Add peppers and onion; cook and stir until tender. Remove from pan.

3. Add sausages to same pan; cook and stir 4-5 minutes or until browned. Return pepper mixture to pan; heat through. Serve with polenta; sprinkle with the cheese and basil.

(5)INGREDIENTS
Apricot Chicken Drumsticks

During the summer months, you can find my family gathered around the grill enjoying delicious bites like this.
—**MARY ANN SKLANKA** BLAKELY, PA

START TO FINISH: 25 MIN.
MAKES: 6 SERVINGS

- 12 chicken drumsticks (3 pounds)
- 1 teaspoon salt
- ¼ teaspoon pepper
- ¼ cup canola oil
- ¼ cup apricot jam, warmed
- ¼ cup prepared mustard
- 1 tablespoon brown sugar

1. Sprinkle chicken with salt and pepper. For sauce, in a bowl, combine the remaining ingredients.

2. Moisten a paper towel with cooking oil; using long-handled tongs, rub on grill rack to coat lightly. Grill the chicken, covered, over medium heat 15-20 minutes or until a thermometer reads 170°-175°, turning occasionally and basting with sauce during the last 5 minutes of cooking. Serve immediately, or serve cold.

NOTE *To bake drumsticks, coat a foil-lined baking sheet with cooking spray. Arrange drumsticks in a single layer. Baste with sauce. Bake at 400° for 25 minutes or until a thermometer reads 170°-175°. Serve warm or chilled.*

CHICKEN SAUSAGES WITH POLENTA

Catfish with Brown Butter-Pecan Sauce

My husband is from the Midwest and grew up eating fried catfish. The rich, toasty pecans and tangy citrus are a perfect complement to any fish.
—TRISHA KRUSE EAGLE, ID

START TO FINISH: 25 MIN.
MAKES: 4 SERVINGS

- ⅓ cup all-purpose flour
- ½ teaspoon salt
- ½ teaspoon cayenne pepper
- ¼ teaspoon pepper
- 4 catfish fillets (6 ounces each)
- 6 tablespoons butter, divided
- ¾ cup chopped pecans
- 2 teaspoons grated lemon peel
- 2 teaspoons lemon juice
  Lemon wedges

1. In a large resealable plastic bag, combine the flour, salt, cayenne and pepper. Add catfish, one fillet at a time, and shake to coat. In a large skillet, cook fillets in 2 tablespoons butter over medium-high heat 2-4 minutes on each side or until fish flakes easily with a fork. Remove fish to a serving platter and keep warm.
2. In the same skillet, melt remaining butter. Add pecans and cook over medium heat until toasted, about 2-3 minutes. Stir in lemon peel and juice. Serve with fish and lemon wedges.

Eastern Shore Crab Cakes

In Delaware, we're surrounded by an abundance of fresh seafood, particularly terrific crab. The secret to great crab cakes is fresh crab meat, not too much filler and not breaking up the crab too much.
—CYNTHIA BENT NEWARK, DE

START TO FINISH: 25 MIN.
MAKES: 3 SERVINGS

- 1 egg, lightly beaten
- ½ cup dry bread crumbs
- ½ cup mayonnaise
- ¾ teaspoon seafood seasoning
- ½ teaspoon lemon juice
- ½ teaspoon Worcestershire sauce
- ⅛ teaspoon white pepper
- 1 pound fresh lump crabmeat
- 2 tablespoons canola oil

1. In a large bowl, combine the egg, bread crumbs, mayonnaise, seafood seasoning, lemon juice, Worcestershire sauce and pepper. Fold in crab. Shape into six patties.
2. In a large skillet, cook the crab cakes in oil 4-5 minutes on each side or until browned.

Caramel Glazed Salmon

Your kids don't like fish? Try a touch of sugar. My salmon dish has a brilliant combination of brown sugar and Dijon mustard.
—ATHENA RUSSELL FLORENCE, SC

START TO FINISH: 25 MIN.
MAKES: 4 SERVINGS

- 4 salmon fillets (6 ounces each)
- ½ teaspoon salt
- ⅛ teaspoon cayenne pepper
- ¼ cup packed brown sugar
- 2 tablespoons Dijon mustard
- 1 tablespoon butter, melted
- 2 teaspoons dill weed

1. Sprinkle salmon with salt and cayenne; set aside.
2. In a small bowl, combine the brown sugar, mustard, butter and dill. Place salmon skin side down on a greased broiler pan. Broil 4-6 in. from heat 5 minutes. Brush half of the glaze mixture over fillets. Broil 7-10 minutes longer or until fish flakes easily with a fork, brushing occasionally with remaining glaze.

Cajun Fish Tacos

Classic fish tacos often feature deep-fried fish, a corn tortilla, cabbage and a thin mayo-based sauce. But we found that fish + pita bread = total yumminess in this streamlined version using lemon-flavored fish with a Cajun twist.
—TASTE OF HOME TEST KITCHEN

START TO FINISH: 25 MIN.
MAKES: 4 SERVINGS

- 2 packages (7.6 ounces each) frozen lemon butter grilled fish fillets
- 3 cups broccoli coleslaw mix
- ½ cup thinly sliced sweet orange pepper
- ½ cup mayonnaise
- 1 tablespoon lemon juice
- 1 teaspoon sugar
- 1¾ teaspoons Cajun seasoning, divided
- 4 whole pita breads, warmed
  Lemon wedges, optional

1. Cook fish according to package directions.
2. Meanwhile, in a small bowl, combine the coleslaw mix, pepper, mayonnaise, lemon juice, sugar and 1½ teaspoons of the Cajun seasoning.
3. Slice fillets. Spoon coleslaw mixture onto pita breads, top with fish. Sprinkle with remaining Cajun seasoning. Serve with lemon wedges if desired.

EASTERN SHORE
CRAB CAKES

CARAMEL
GLAZED SALMON

CAJUN
FISH TACOS

**CRUMB-TOPPED
BAKED FISH**

**HERB-ROASTED
SALMON FILLETS**

Crumb-Topped Baked Fish

Flaky cod is treated to a coating of bread crumbs, cheese and seasonings in this savory entree that's sure to please!

—**JEAN BARCROFT** CLARKSVILLE, MI

START TO FINISH: 25 MIN.
MAKES: 4 SERVINGS

- 4 haddock or cod fillets (6 ounces each)
  Salt and pepper to taste
- 1¼ cups seasoned bread crumbs
- ¼ cup shredded cheddar cheese
- ¼ cup butter, melted
- 1 tablespoon minced fresh parsley
- ½ teaspoon dried marjoram
- ¼ teaspoon garlic powder
- ¼ teaspoon dried rosemary, crushed

Preheat oven to 400°. Place fillets on a greased baking sheet; season with salt and pepper. In a bowl, mix the remaining ingredients; pat onto fillets. Bake 15-20 minutes or until fish flakes easily with a fork.

⑤ INGREDIENTS
Herb-Roasted Salmon Fillets

This roasted salmon is simple but elegant enough to serve to company. I make it on days when I have less than an hour to cook.

—**LUANNE ASTA** NEW YORK, NY

START TO FINISH: 30 MIN.
MAKES: 4 SERVINGS

- 4 salmon fillets (6 ounces each)
- 4 garlic cloves, minced
- 1 tablespoon minced fresh rosemary or 1 teaspoon dried rosemary, crushed
- 1 tablespoon olive oil
- 2 teaspoons minced fresh thyme or ½ teaspoon dried thyme
- ¾ teaspoon salt
- ½ teaspoon pepper

Preheat oven to 425°. Place salmon in a greased 15x10x1-in. baking pan, skin side down. Combine remaining ingredients; spread over fillets. Roast 15-18 minutes or until desired doneness.

⑤ INGREDIENTS
Mediterranean Tilapia

I recently became a fan of tilapia because of its mild taste; it's also low in calories and fat. Plus, it's easy to top with my favorite ingredients.

—**ROBIN BRENNEMAN** HILLIARD, OH

START TO FINISH: 25 MIN.
MAKES: 6 SERVINGS

- 6 tilapia fillets (6 ounces each)
- 1 cup canned Italian diced tomatoes
- ½ cup water-packed artichoke hearts, chopped
- ½ cup sliced ripe olives
- ½ cup crumbled feta cheese

Preheat oven to 400°. Place fillets in a 15x10x1-in. baking pan coated with cooking spray. Top with tomatoes, artichoke, olives and cheese. Bake 15-20 minutes or until fish flakes easily with a fork.

Cajun Pecan Catfish

This is one of our favorite recipes. Just serve with a side salad and biscuits, with mixed fruit for dessert.

—JAN WILKINS BLYTHEVILLE, AR

START TO FINISH: 25 MIN.
MAKES: 4 SERVINGS

- 2 **tablespoons olive oil**
- 2 **teaspoons lemon juice**
- 1 **teaspoon Cajun seasoning**
- ½ **teaspoon dried thyme**
- ⅓ **cup finely chopped pecans**
- 2 **tablespoons grated Parmesan cheese**
- 1 **tablespoon dry bread crumbs**
- 1 **tablespoon dried parsley flakes**
- 4 **catfish fillets (6 ounces each)**

1. Preheat oven to 425°. In a small bowl, combine oil, lemon juice, Cajun seasoning and thyme. In another bowl, combine pecans, cheese, bread crumbs, parsley and 1 tablespoon oil mixture.

2. Place catfish on a greased 15x10x1-in. baking pan. Brush with remaining oil mixture. Spread pecan mixture over fillets. Bake 10-15 minutes or until fish flakes easily with a fork.

> **PAIR IT!**
> *Honey Mustard Coleslaw, page 169* is a classic go-with for fish.

⑤INGREDIENTS
Ginger-Chutney Shrimp Stir-Fry

When I was juggling college, work and a growing family, I made this recipe often. It takes only minutes to pull together.

—SALLY SIBTHORPE
SHELBY TOWNSHIP, MI

START TO FINISH: 25 MIN.
MAKES: 4 SERVINGS

- 2 **tablespoons peanut oil**
- 1 **pound uncooked medium shrimp, peeled and deveined, tails removed**
- 1 **tablespoon minced fresh gingerroot**
- 3 **cups frozen pepper and onion stir-fry blend, thawed**
- ¾ **cup mango chutney**
- 2 **tablespoons water**
- ¾ **teaspoon salt**

In a large skillet, heat oil over medium-high heat. Add shrimp and ginger; stir-fry 4-5 minutes or until shrimp turn pink. Stir in remaining ingredients; cook until vegetables are tender, stirring occasionally.

CAJUN
PECAN CATFISH

Super-Quick Shrimp & Green Chili Quesadillas

If I am really short on time, I head to the grocery store for prepared guacamole. Swap in shredded rotisserie chicken for shrimp for another fun option.

—ANGIE RESSA CHENEY, WA

START TO FINISH: 10 MIN.
MAKES: 4 SERVINGS (½ CUP GUACAMOLE)

- 1¾ cups shredded cheddar cheese
- 1 cup peeled and deveined cooked small shrimp
- 1 can (4 ounces) chopped green chilies, drained
- 2 green onions, thinly sliced
- 8 flour tortillas (8 inches)
- 1 medium ripe avocado, peeled and pitted
- 2 tablespoons salsa
- ¼ teaspoon garlic salt

1. In a bowl, combine the cheese, shrimp, green chilies and green onions. Place half of the tortillas on a greased griddle; sprinkle with cheese mixture. Top with the remaining tortillas. Cook over medium heat 1-2 minutes on each side or until golden brown and cheese is melted.
2. Meanwhile, in a small bowl, mash avocado with salsa and garlic salt. Serve with quesadillas.

Italian Tilapia

Fresh Italian flavors turn mild-tasting tilapia fillets into a family-pleasing meal. You could also use a sprinkling of Parmesan cheese in place of the fresh mozzarella.

—TASTE OF HOME TEST KITCHEN

START TO FINISH: 25 MIN.
MAKES: 6 SERVINGS

- 6 tilapia fillets (6 ounces each)
- 1 cup diced tomatoes with roasted garlic
- ½ cup julienned roasted sweet red peppers
- ½ cup sliced fresh mushrooms
- ½ cup diced fresh mozzarella cheese
- ½ teaspoon dried basil

Preheat oven to 400°. Place fillets in a 15x10x1-in. baking pan coated with cooking spray. Top with tomatoes, peppers, mushrooms, cheese and basil. Bake 15-20 minutes or until fish flakes easily with a fork.

Crispy Scallops with Tarragon Cream

You'll flip for these tender, crisp-coated scallops. The easy, creamy tarragon sauce truly makes this dish a star.

—KAREN KUEBLER DALLAS, TX

START TO FINISH: 25 MIN.
MAKES: 4 SERVINGS

- 1 egg
- 2 teaspoons water
- ⅔ cup Italian-style panko (Japanese) bread crumbs
- ⅓ cup mashed potato flakes
- 1 pound sea scallops
- ¼ cup olive oil
- 2 tablespoons butter
- 1 tablespoon all-purpose flour
- ¼ teaspoon salt
- ⅛ teaspoon pepper
- ¾ cup heavy whipping cream
- 2 tablespoons minced fresh tarragon or 2 teaspoons dried tarragon

1. In a shallow bowl, whisk egg and water. In another shallow bowl, combine bread crumbs and potato flakes. Dip scallops in egg mixture, then coat with crumb mixture.
2. Heat oil in a large skillet over medium-high heat. Cook scallops in batches 2 minutes on each side or until golden brown.
3. Meanwhile, in a small saucepan, melt butter. Stir in flour, salt and pepper until smooth; gradually add cream. Bring to a boil; cook and stir 1-2 minutes or until thickened. Stir in tarragon. Serve with scallops.

Lemony Parsley Baked Cod

If there's one thing I hate, it's overcooking a good piece of fish. The trick is to cook it at a high temperature for a short amount of time. It'll keep the fish moist and tender.

—SHERRY DAY PINCKNEY, MI

START TO FINISH: 25 MIN.
MAKES: 4 SERVINGS

- 3 tablespoons minced fresh parsley
- 2 tablespoons lemon juice
- 1 tablespoon grated lemon peel
- 1 tablespoon olive oil
- 2 garlic cloves, minced
- ¼ teaspoon salt
- ⅛ teaspoon pepper
- 4 cod fillets (6 ounces each)
- 2 green onions, chopped

Preheat oven to 400°. In a small bowl, mix the first seven ingredients. Place cod in an ungreased 11x7-in. baking dish; top with parsley mixture. Sprinkle with green onions. Bake, covered, 10-15 minutes or until fish flakes easily with a fork.

Seared Scallops with Citrus Herb Sauce

Be sure to pat the scallops with a paper towel to remove any excess moisture. This helps create that perfectly browned and flavorful scallop your guests will love.

—**APRIL LANE** GREENEVILLE, TN

START TO FINISH: 20 MIN.
MAKES: 4 SERVINGS

- 1½ **pounds sea scallops**
- ½ **teaspoon salt**
- ½ **teaspoon pepper**
- ¼ **teaspoon paprika**
- 6 **tablespoons butter, divided**
- 2 **garlic cloves, minced**
- ¼ **cup dry sherry or chicken broth**
- 2 **tablespoons lemon juice**
- ¼ **teaspoon minced fresh oregano**
- ¼ **teaspoon minced fresh tarragon**

1. Pat scallops dry with paper towels; sprinkle with salt, pepper and paprika. In a large skillet, heat 2 tablespoons butter over medium-high heat. Add half of scallops; sear 1-2 minutes on each side or until golden brown and firm. Remove from the skillet; keep warm. Repeat with 2 tablespoons butter and remaining scallops.
2. Wipe skillet clean if necessary. Saute garlic in remaining butter until tender; stir in sherry. Cook until liquid is almost evaporated; stir in the remaining ingredients. Serve with scallops.

DID YOU KNOW?

Scallops vary in color from creamy white to tan and should have a sweet, fresh odor. Scallops should be used within 24 hours of purchase.

LEMONY PARSLEY BAKED COD

SEARED SCALLOPS WITH CITRUS HERB SAUCE

FISH &
VEGETABLE PACKETS

Fish & Vegetable Packets

Try this traditional cooking technique to keep the contents moist. I like to serve fish still wrapped in parchment for each person to open.
—**JILL ANDERSON** SLEEPY EYE, MN

START TO FINISH: 25 MIN.
MAKES: 4 SERVINGS

- 1½ cups julienned carrots
- 1½ cups fresh snow peas
- 2 green onions, cut into 2-inch pieces
- 4 cod fillets (6 ounces each)
- 2 teaspoons lemon juice
- ¼ teaspoon salt
- ¼ teaspoon dried thyme
- ¼ teaspoon crushed red pepper flakes
- ¼ teaspoon pepper
- 4 teaspoons butter

1. Preheat oven to 450°. In a small bowl, combine carrots, snow peas and green onions. Cut parchment paper or heavy-duty foil into four 18x12-in. pieces; place a fish fillet off center on each. Drizzle with lemon juice and top with carrot mixture. Sprinkle with seasonings; dot with butter.

2. Fold parchment paper over fish. Bring edges of paper together on all sides and crimp to seal, forming a large packet. Repeat for remaining packets. Place on baking sheets.

3. Bake 10-15 minutes or until fish just begins to flake easily with a fork. Open packets carefully to allow steam to escape.

SWAP IT
Replace the snow peas with fresh green beans.

(5) INGREDIENTS
Haddock with Lime-Cilantro Butter

In Louisiana we broil fish and serve it with lime juice, cilantro and butter.
—DARLENE MORRIS
FRANKLINTON, LA

START TO FINISH: 15 MIN.
MAKES: 4 SERVINGS

- 4 **haddock fillets (6 ounces each)**
- ½ **teaspoon salt**
- ¼ **teaspoon pepper**
- 3 **tablespoons butter, melted**
- 2 **tablespoons minced fresh cilantro**
- 1 **tablespoon lime juice**
- 1 **teaspoon grated lime peel**

1. Preheat broiler. Sprinkle fillets with salt and pepper. Place on a greased broiler pan. Broil 4-5 in. from heat 5-6 minutes or until fish flakes easily with a fork.
2. In a small bowl, mix remaining ingredients. Serve over fish.

(5) INGREDIENTS
Shrimp Tortellini Pasta Toss

Cheese tortellini might seem indulgent, but when you bulk it up with shrimp and vegetables you have on hand, it's a fast and healthy meal.
—TASTE OF HOME TEST KITCHEN

START TO FINISH: 20 MIN.
MAKES: 4 SERVINGS

- 1 **package (9 ounces) refrigerated cheese tortellini**
- 1 **cup frozen peas**
- 3 **tablespoons olive oil, divided**
- 1 **pound uncooked medium shrimp, peeled and deveined**
- 2 **garlic cloves, minced**
- ¼ **teaspoon salt**
- ¼ **teaspoon dried thyme**
- ¼ **teaspoon pepper**

1. Cook tortellini according to package directions, adding peas during last 5 minutes of cooking.

2. Meanwhile, in a large nonstick skillet, heat 2 tablespoons oil over medium-high heat. Add shrimp; cook and stir 2 minutes. Add garlic; cook 1-2 minutes longer or until shrimp turn pink.
3. Drain tortellini mixture; add to skillet. Stir in salt, thyme, pepper and remaining oil; toss to coat.

(5) INGREDIENTS
Strawberry-Teriyaki Glazed Salmon

This is the best recipe I've ever made. Strawberry jam might seem like a surprise in an Asian-inspired dish, but the sweet-savory glaze is a hit.
—KRYSTINA CAHALAN
WINTER PARK, FL

START TO FINISH: 25 MIN.
MAKES: 4 SERVINGS

- ¼ **cup seedless strawberry jam**
- 2 **tablespoons reduced-sodium soy sauce**
- 1 **garlic clove, minced**
- ½ **teaspoon ground ginger**
- 4 **salmon fillets (4 ounces each)**
- ¼ **teaspoon salt**
- ¼ **teaspoon pepper**

1. Preheat broiler. In a small saucepan, combine jam, soy sauce, garlic and ginger; cook and stir until mixture comes to a boil. Reduce heat; simmer, uncovered, 6-8 minutes or until mixture is reduced by half.
2. Sprinkle salmon with salt and pepper. Place in an ungreased 15x10x1-in. baking pan. Broil 4-6 in. from heat 8-10 minutes or until fish just begins to flake easily with a fork, brushing with 2 tablespoons jam mixture during the last 2 minutes of cooking. Just before serving, brush with the remaining jam mixture.

SHRIMP TORTELLINI PASTA TOSS

**BLACK BEAN &
CORN QUINOA**

Black Bean &
Corn Quinoa

My daughter's college asked parents for a favorite healthy recipe to use in the dining halls. My quinoa recipe fit the bill.
—**LINDSAY MCSWEENEY**
WINCHESTER, MA

START TO FINISH: 30 MIN.
MAKES: 4 SERVINGS

2 **tablespoons canola oil**
1 **medium onion, finely chopped**
1 **medium sweet red pepper, finely chopped**
1 **celery rib, finely chopped**
2 **teaspoons chili powder**
¼ **teaspoon salt**
¼ **teaspoon pepper**
2 **cups vegetable stock**
1 **cup frozen corn**
1 **cup quinoa, rinsed**
1 **can (15 ounces) black beans, rinsed and drained**
⅓ **cup plus 2 tablespoons minced fresh cilantro, divided**

1. In a large skillet, heat oil over medium-high heat. Add onion, red pepper, celery and seasonings; cook and stir 5-7 minutes or until vegetables are tender.
2. Stir in stock and corn; bring to a boil. Stir in quinoa. Reduce heat; simmer, covered, 12-15 minutes or until liquid is absorbed.
3. Add beans and ⅓ cup cilantro; heat through, stirring occasionally. Sprinkle with remaining cilantro.
NOTE *Look for quinoa in the cereal, rice or organic food aisle.*

PAIR IT!
End the quinoa dinner on a sweet note with *Glazed Pear Shortcakes,* page 207.

Hearty Portobello Linguine

If you like Mediterranean cuisine, you'll love this entree! It turns any night into a special occasion when it's on the menu. I like to serve it with fresh bread and a crisp white wine.
—**TRE BALCHOWSKY** SAUSALITO, CA

START TO FINISH: 25 MIN.
MAKES: 4 SERVINGS

- 1 package (9 ounces) refrigerated linguine
- 4 large portobello mushroom caps (about ¾ pound), halved and thinly sliced
- ¼ cup olive oil
- 3 garlic cloves, minced
- 3 plum tomatoes, chopped
- ⅓ cup pitted Greek olives, halved
- 1 teaspoon Greek seasoning
- ¾ cup crumbled tomato and basil feta cheese

1. Cook linguine according to package directions.

2. Meanwhile, in a large skillet, cook and stir mushrooms in oil over medium-high heat until tender. Add garlic; cook 1 minute. Stir in tomatoes, olives and Greek seasoning; cook and stir 2 minutes.

3. Drain linguine; add to pan and toss to coat. Serve with cheese.

Saucy Vegetable Tofu

This is my daughter Tonya's favorite meal. Sometimes we make it with rigatoni and call it "Riga-Tonya." Either way, it's a great, quick way to prepare some tasty vegetables.
—**SANDRA ECKERT** POTTSTOWN, PA

START TO FINISH: 20 MIN.
MAKES: 6 SERVINGS

- 8 ounces uncooked whole wheat spiral pasta
- 1 large onion, coarsely chopped
- 1 large green or sweet red pepper, coarsely chopped
- 1 medium zucchini, halved lengthwise and sliced
- 1 tablespoon olive oil
- 1 package (16 ounces) firm tofu, drained and cut into ½-inch cubes
- 2 cups meatless spaghetti sauce

1. Cook pasta according to the package directions.

2. Meanwhile, in a large skillet, saute onion, pepper and zucchini in oil until crisp-tender.

3. Stir in tofu and spaghetti sauce; heat through. Drain pasta; serve with tofu mixture.

Ravioli with Creamy Squash Sauce

Store-bought ravioli speeds assembly of this cozy, restaurant-quality dish that tastes so good, your family won't notice it's meatless.
—*TASTE OF HOME* TEST KITCHEN

START TO FINISH: 20 MIN.
MAKES: 4 SERVINGS

- 1 package (9 ounces) refrigerated cheese ravioli
- 3 garlic cloves, minced
- 2 tablespoons butter
- 1 package (12 ounces) frozen cooked winter squash, thawed
- 1 package (6 ounces) fresh baby spinach
- 1 cup heavy whipping cream
- ⅓ cup vegetable broth
- ¼ teaspoon salt
- 1 cup chopped walnuts, toasted

1. Cook ravioli according to the package directions.

2. Meanwhile, in a Dutch oven, saute garlic in butter 1 minute. Add the squash and spinach; cook 2-3 minutes longer or until spinach is wilted. Stir in cream, broth and salt. Bring to a gentle boil; cook 6-8 minutes or until slightly thickened.

3. Drain ravioli; add to squash mixture. Toss to coat. Sprinkle with walnuts.

HEARTY PORTOBELLO LINGUINE

PAIR IT!
All-Star Ice Cream Sandwiches, page 212 is a cool way to top off this sandwich.

CUBAN PANINI, 122

118

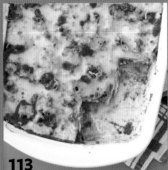

113

120

Carefree Weekend Dinners

Don't be tied to the kitchen on Saturday and Sunday. Let the **slow cooker** or **oven do the cooking**. For a **speedy meal,** look for one of the fast-cooking **grill or skillet dishes.**

CHICKEN & EGG NOODLE CASSEROLE, 115

**HONEY-GLAZED
PORK TENDERLOINS**

Honey-Glazed Pork Tenderloins

Honey, smoky chipotle pepper and soy sauce flavor this easy pork tenderloin. Serve it with veggies or rice for a satisfying meal.
—**DIANE COTTON** FRANKLIN, NC

PREP: 15 MIN. • **BAKE:** 20 MIN.
MAKES: 6 SERVINGS

- ½ **teaspoon garlic powder**
- ½ **teaspoon ground chipotle pepper**
- ½ **teaspoon pepper**
- 2 **pork tenderloins (1 pound each)**
- 1 **tablespoon canola oil**
- ½ **cup honey**
- 2 **tablespoons reduced-sodium soy sauce**
- 1 **tablespoon balsamic vinegar**
- 1 **teaspoon sesame oil**

1. Preheat oven to 350°. Combine the first three ingredients; rub over pork. In a large ovenproof skillet, brown pork in canola oil on all sides.

2. In a small bowl, combine the honey, soy sauce, vinegar and sesame oil; spoon over pork. Bake, uncovered, 20-25 minutes or until a thermometer reads 145°, basting occasionally with pan juices. Let stand 5 minutes before slicing.

TOP TIP

The U.S. Department of Agriculture's Food Safety Inspection Service recommends that pork roasts, chops and steaks be cooked to a temperature of 145° rather than 160°. With today's leaner cuts of pork the lower temperature internal will ensure a juicier product. Always let pork rest at least 5 minutes before slicing or serving.

Southwestern Turkey Bake

I make this as a way to get my nieces and husband to eat their vegetables. The creamy entree will fill you up.
—**CRYSTAL KOLADY** HENRIETTA, NY

PREP: 20 MIN. • **BAKE:** 25 MIN.
MAKES: 12 SERVINGS

- 2 **large onions, chopped**
- 2 **jalapeno peppers, seeded and chopped**
- 2 **tablespoons butter**
- 6 **cups cubed cooked turkey**
- 2 **cans (10¾ ounces each) condensed cream of chicken soup, undiluted**
- 2 **cups (16 ounces) sour cream**
- 1 **package (10 ounces) frozen chopped spinach, thawed and squeezed dry**
- 2 **cups (8 ounces) shredded Monterey Jack cheese**
- 1 **package (12½ ounces) nacho tortilla chips, crushed**
- 4 **green onions, sliced**

1. Preheat oven to 350°. In a Dutch oven, saute onions and jalapenos in butter until tender. Stir in turkey, soup, sour cream and spinach. In a greased 13x9-in. baking dish, layer half the turkey mixture, cheese and tortilla chips. Repeat layers.

2. Bake, uncovered, for 25-30 minutes or until bubbly. Let stand 5 minutes before serving. Sprinkle with green onions.

NOTE *Wear disposable gloves when cutting hot peppers; the oils can burn skin. Avoid touching your face.*

Oven-Fried Chicken Drumsticks

This fabulous oven-fried chicken uses Greek yogurt to create an amazing marinade that makes this chicken incredibly moist.
—**KIMBERLY WALLACE** DENNISON, OH

PREP: 20 MIN. + MARINATING
BAKE: 40 MIN. • **MAKES:** 4 SERVINGS

- 1 **cup fat-free plain Greek yogurt**
- 1 **tablespoon Dijon mustard**
- 2 **garlic cloves, minced**
- 8 **chicken drumsticks (4 ounces each), skin removed**
- ½ **cup whole wheat flour**
- 1½ **teaspoons paprika**
- 1 **teaspoon baking powder**
- 1 **teaspoon salt**
- 1 **teaspoon pepper**
  Olive oil-flavored cooking spray

1. In a large resealable plastic bag, combine yogurt, mustard and garlic. Add chicken; seal bag and turn to coat. Refrigerate 8 hours or overnight.

2. Preheat oven to 425°. In another plastic bag, mix flour, paprika, baking powder, salt and pepper. Remove chicken from marinade and add, one piece at a time, to flour mixture; close bag and shake to coat. Place on a wire rack over a baking sheet; spritz with cooking spray. Bake 40-45 minutes or until a thermometer reads 170°-175°.

SOUTHWESTERN TURKEY BAKE

Creamy Macaroni and Cheese

Here is the ultimate mac-and-cheese. It's creamy, thick and very rich, and it holds the wonderful cheddar flavor. Once you taste it, you will be hooked.
—**CINDY HARTLEY** CHESAPEAKE, VA

PREP: 20 MIN. • **BAKE:** 35 MIN.
MAKES: 6 SERVINGS

- 2 cups uncooked elbow macaroni
- ½ cup butter, cubed
- ½ cup all-purpose flour
- 1½ cups 2% milk
- 1 cup (8 ounces) sour cream
- 8 ounces process cheese (Velveeta), cubed
- ¼ cup grated Parmesan cheese
- ½ teaspoon salt
- ½ teaspoon ground mustard
- ½ teaspoon pepper
- 2 cups (8 ounces) shredded cheddar cheese

1. Cook macaroni according to package directions.
2. Meanwhile, preheat oven to 350°. In a large saucepan, melt butter. Stir in flour until smooth. Gradually add milk. Bring to a boil; cook and stir 2 minutes or until thickened. Reduce heat; stir in sour cream, process cheese, Parmesan cheese, salt, mustard and pepper until smooth and cheese is melted.
3. Drain the macaroni; toss with the cheddar cheese. Transfer to a greased 3-qt. baking dish. Stir in cream sauce.
4. Bake, uncovered, for 35-40 minutes or until golden brown and bubbly.

Baked Chicken Chimichangas

I developed this quick and easy recipe through trial and error. I used to garnish with sour cream, too, but eliminated it in order to cut calories. My friends all love it when I cook these, and they're much healthier than deep-fried chimichangas.
—**RICKEY MADDEN** CLINTON, SC

PREP: 20 MIN. • **BAKE:** 20 MIN.
MAKES: 6 SERVINGS

- 1½ cups cubed cooked chicken breast
- 1½ cups picante sauce, divided
- ½ cup shredded reduced-fat cheddar cheese
- ⅔ cup chopped green onions, divided
- 1 teaspoon ground cumin
- 1 teaspoon dried oregano
- 6 flour tortillas (8 inches), warmed
- 1 tablespoon butter, melted

1. Preheat oven to 375°. In a small bowl, combine chicken, ¾ cup picante sauce, cheese, ¼ cup green onions, cumin and oregano. Spoon ½ cup mixture down the center of each tortilla. Fold sides and ends over filling and roll up. Place seam side down in a 15x10x1-in. baking pan coated with cooking spray. Brush with butter.
2. Bake, uncovered, for 20-25 minutes or until heated through. Top with remaining picante sauce and onions.

FREEZER OPTION *Cover and freeze unbaked casserole up to 3 months. To use, thaw in the refrigerator overnight. Remove from the refrigerator 30 minutes before baking. Preheat oven to 375°. Bake according to directions.*

(5) INGREDIENTS

Cocoa-Crusted Beef Tenderloin

In my family, we enjoy having cooking competitions with secret ingredients and a 30-minute time limit. This tenderloin recipe earned me a sweet victory.
—**GINA MYERS** SPOKANE, WA

START TO FINISH: 30 MIN.
MAKES: 4 SERVINGS

- 4 beef tenderloin steaks (1½ inches thick and 6 ounces each)
- ½ teaspoon salt
- ½ teaspoon coarsely ground pepper
- 3 tablespoons baking cocoa
- 3 tablespoons finely ground coffee

1. Preheat broiler. Sprinkle steaks with salt and pepper. In a shallow bowl, mix cocoa and coffee. Dip steaks in cocoa mixture to coat all sides; shake off excess.
2. Place steaks on a rack of a broiler pan. Broil 3-4 in. from heat 9-11 minutes on each side or until meat reaches desired doneness (for medium-rare, a thermometer should read 145°; medium, 160°; well-done, 170°).

PAIR IT!
Favorite Mashed Sweet Potatoes, page 151, makes a tasty companion to the tenderloin steaks.

BAKED CHICKEN CHIMICHANGAS

COCOA-CRUSTED BEEF TENDERLOIN

Baked Ziti

I like to make this dish for family and friends. It's easy to prepare, and I can get creative with the sauce. For example, sometimes I might add my home-canned tomatoes, mushrooms or vegetables.

—ELAINE ANDERSON
NEW GALILEE, PA

PREP: 20 MIN. • **BAKE:** 45 MIN. + STANDING
MAKES: 6-8 SERVINGS

- 12 ounces uncooked ziti or small tube pasta
- 2 pounds ground beef
- 1 jar (24 ounces) spaghetti sauce
- 2 eggs, beaten
- 1 carton (15 ounces) ricotta cheese
- 2½ cups (10 ounces) shredded mozzarella cheese, divided
- ½ cup grated Parmesan cheese

1. Cook pasta according to the package directions.
2. Meanwhile, preheat oven to 350°. In a large skillet, cook beef over medium heat until no longer pink; drain. Stir in spaghetti sauce.
3. In a large bowl, combine eggs, ricotta cheese, 1½ cups mozzarella cheese and the Parmesan cheese. Drain pasta; add to cheese mixture and stir until blended.
4. Spoon a third of the meat sauce into a greased 13x9-in. baking dish; top with half of the pasta mixture. Repeat layers. Top with remaining meat sauce.
5. Cover and bake 40 minutes or until a thermometer reads 160°. Uncover; sprinkle with remaining mozzarella cheese. Bake 5-10 minutes longer or until cheese is melted. Let stand for 15 minutes before serving.

SLOW COOKER
Slow-Roasted Lemon Dill Chicken

This is a different, fresher-tasting meal than some of the heartier ones that are usually slow cooked. It goes perfectly with a side of noodles or a mixed green salad.

—LORI LOCKREY PICKERING, ON

PREP: 20 MIN.
COOK: 4 HOURS + STANDING
MAKES: 6 SERVINGS

- 2 medium onions, coarsely chopped
- 2 tablespoons butter, softened
- ¼ teaspoon grated lemon peel
- 1 broiler/fryer chicken (4 to 5 pounds)
- ¼ cup chicken stock
- 4 sprigs fresh parsley
- 4 fresh dill sprigs
- 3 tablespoons lemon juice
- 1 teaspoon salt
- 1 teaspoon paprika
- ½ teaspoon dried thyme
- ¼ teaspoon pepper

1. Place onions in bottom of a 6-qt. slow cooker. In a small bowl, mix butter and lemon peel.
2. Tuck wings under chicken; tie drumsticks together. With fingers, carefully loosen skin from chicken breast; rub butter mixture under the skin. Secure skin to underside of breast with toothpicks. Place chicken over onions, breast side up. Add stock, parsley and dill.
3. Drizzle lemon juice over the chicken; sprinkle with seasonings. Cook, covered, on low 4-5 hours (a thermometer inserted in thigh should read at least 175°).
4. Remove chicken from slow cooker; tent with foil. Let stand 15 minutes before carving.

Ginger Steak Fried Rice

When it's the end-of-the-week and you're ready to relax, this sensational dish comes together quickly with leftover rice. I learned a tip for the steak recently: Partially freeze it, and it will be easier to cut into thin slices.

—SIMONE GARZA EVANSVILLE, IN

START TO FINISH: 30 MIN.
MAKES: 4 SERVINGS

- 2 eggs, lightly beaten
- 2 teaspoons olive oil
- 1 beef top sirloin steak (¾ pound), cut into thin strips
- 4 tablespoons reduced-sodium soy sauce, divided
- 1 package (12 ounces) broccoli coleslaw mix
- 1 cup frozen peas
- 2 tablespoons grated fresh gingerroot
- 3 garlic cloves, minced
- 2 cups cooked brown rice
- 4 green onions, sliced

1. In a large nonstick skillet coated with cooking spray, cook and stir eggs over medium heat until no liquid egg remains, breaking up eggs into small pieces. Remove from pan; wipe skillet clean if necessary.
2. In the same pan, heat oil over medium-high heat. Add the beef; stir-fry 1-2 minutes or until no longer pink. Stir in 1 tablespoon soy sauce; remove from pan.
3. Add coleslaw mix, peas, ginger and garlic to the pan; cook and stir until coleslaw mix is crisp-tender. Add rice and remaining soy sauce, tossing to combine rice with vegetable mixture and heat through. Stir in cooked eggs, beef and green onions; heat through.

BEEF BRISKET IN BEER

Beef Brisket in Beer

One bite of my super-tender brisket, and you'll be in love! With its rich and satisfying gravy, it's ideal served with a side of mashed potatoes.

—**EUNICE STOEN** DECORAH, IA

PREP: 15 MIN. • **COOK:** 8 HOURS
MAKES: 6 SERVINGS

- 1 **fresh beef brisket (2½ to 3 pounds)**
- 2 **teaspoons liquid smoke, optional**
- 1 **teaspoon celery salt**
- ½ **teaspoon pepper**
- ¼ **teaspoon salt**
- 1 **large onion, sliced**
- 1 **can (12 ounces) beer or nonalcoholic beer**
- 2 **teaspoons Worcestershire sauce**
- 2 **tablespoons cornstarch**
- ¼ **cup cold water**

1. Cut brisket in half; rub with liquid smoke if desired, celery salt, pepper and salt. Place in a 3-qt. slow cooker. Top with the onion. Combine beer and Worcestershire sauce; pour over the meat. Cover and cook on low for 8-9 hours or until tender.

2. Remove the brisket and keep warm. Strain the cooking juices; transfer to a small saucepan. Mix the cornstarch and water until smooth; stir into juices. Bring to a boil; cook and stir 2 minutes or until thickened. Serve the gravy with the beef.

NOTE *This is a fresh beef brisket, not corned beef.*

SWAP IT
For a change use a full-body red wine instead of the beer.

**CHICKEN
ARTICHOKE CASSEROLE**

**CHICAGO-STYLE
BEEF ROLLS**

**TOMATO
BAGUETTE PIZZA**

Chicken Artichoke Casserole

With a flavor that's similar to artichoke dip, this rich and comforting chicken entree will warm you up on chilly nights.

—**AMY NUTONI** LA CRESCENT, MN

PREP: 20 MIN. • **BAKE:** 25 MIN.
MAKES: 6 SERVINGS

- 2 **cups uncooked bow tie pasta**
- 2 **cups cubed cooked chicken**
- 1 **can (14 ounces) water-packed artichoke hearts, rinsed, drained and chopped**
- 1 **can (10¾ ounces) condensed cream of chicken soup, undiluted**
- 1 **cup shredded Parmesan cheese**
- 1 **cup mayonnaise**
- ⅓ **cup 2% milk**
- 1 **garlic clove, minced**
- ½ **teaspoon onion powder**
- ½ **teaspoon pepper**
- 1 **cup onion and garlic salad croutons, coarsely crushed**

1. Preheat oven to 350°. Cook pasta according to the package directions. Meanwhile, in a large bowl, combine chicken, artichokes, soup, cheese, mayonnaise, milk, garlic, onion powder and pepper. Drain pasta; add to the chicken mixture.
2. Transfer to a greased 2-qt. baking dish. Sprinkle with the croutons. Bake, uncovered, 25-30 minutes or until heated through.

SLOW COOKER
Chicago-Style Beef Rolls

I have fond memories of eating these big, messy sandwiches at a neighbor's house when I was growing up. Freeze extras and save for another meal, too!

—**TRISHA KRUSE** EAGLE, ID

PREP: 20 MIN. • **COOK:** 8½ HOURS
MAKES: 16 SERVINGS

- 1 **boneless beef chuck roast (4 to 5 pounds)**
- 1 **tablespoon olive oil**
- 3 **cups beef broth**
- 1 **medium onion, chopped**
- 1 **package Italian salad dressing mix**
- 3 **garlic cloves, minced**
- 1 **tablespoon Italian seasoning**
- ½ **teaspoon crushed red pepper flakes**
- 16 **sourdough rolls, split**
  Sliced pepperoncini and pickled red pepper rings, optional

1. Brown roast in oil on all sides in a large skillet; drain. Transfer beef to a 5-qt. slow cooker. In a large bowl, mix broth, onion, dressing mix, garlic, Italian seasoning and pepper flakes; pour over roast.
2. Cover and cook on low 8-10 hours or until tender. Remove the meat; cool slightly. Skim fat from cooking juices. Shred beef with two forks and return to slow cooker; heat through. Place ½ cup on each roll, using a slotted spoon. Serve with pepperoncini and pepper rings if desired.

Tomato Baguette Pizza

When my tomatoes ripen all at once, I use them up in simple recipes like this one. Cheesy baguette pizzas, served with a salad, make an ideal lunch.

—**LORRAINE CALAND** SHUNIAH, ON

START TO FINISH: 25 MIN.
MAKES: 6 SERVINGS

- 3 **cups sliced fresh mushrooms**
- 2 **medium onions, sliced**
- 2 **teaspoons olive oil**
- 2 **garlic cloves, minced**
- ½ **teaspoon Italian seasoning**
- ¼ **teaspoon salt**
  Dash pepper
- 1 **French bread baguette (10½ ounces), halved lengthwise**
- 1½ **cups (6 ounces) shredded part-skim mozzarella cheese, divided**
- ¾ **cup thinly sliced fresh basil leaves, divided**
- 3 **medium tomatoes, sliced**

1. Preheat oven to 400°. In a large skillet, saute the mushrooms and onions in oil until tender. Add the garlic, Italian seasoning, salt and pepper; cook 1 minute longer.
2. Place baguette halves on a baking sheet; sprinkle with ¾ cup cheese. Top with ½ cup basil, mushroom mixture, tomatoes and remaining cheese.
3. Bake 10-15 minutes or until cheese is melted. Sprinkle with remaining basil. Cut each portion into three slices.

TOP TIP

Have cooked cubed chicken at the ready: When chicken parts are on sale, buy an extra package or two. Bake them in the oven then cool. Remove skin, bones and fat from chicken and cut meat into cubes or shred with two forks. Package one or two cups of meat in a resealable freezer bag, label, date and freeze. You'll have chicken for your favorite casseroles at your fingertips whenever you need it.

(5) INGREDIENTS
Glazed Roast Chicken

A few pantry items inspired this recipe, which I've since made for small weeknight meals or for big parties. The quince jelly comes from my boss, who grows the tasty fruit in his backyard.
—**VICTORIA MILLER** SAN RAMON, CA

PREP: 15 MIN.
BAKE: 1½ HOURS + STANDING
MAKES: 4 SERVINGS

- 1 cup white wine or chicken broth
- 1 cup apricot preserves or quince jelly
- 1 tablespoon stone-ground mustard
- 1 broiler/fryer chicken (3 to 4 pounds)
- ¾ teaspoon salt
- ½ teaspoon pepper

1. Preheat oven to 375°. In a small saucepan, bring wine to a boil; cook 3-4 minutes or until the wine is reduced by half. Stir in preserves and mustard. Reserve half of the glaze for basting.
2. Place chicken on a rack in a shallow roasting pan, breast side up. Sprinkle with salt and pepper. Tuck wings under chicken; tie drumsticks together. Pour the remaining glaze over chicken.
3. Roast 1½ to 1¾ hours or until a thermometer inserted in the thigh reads 170°-175°, basting occasionally with reserved glaze after 45 minutes. Remove chicken from oven; tent with foil. Let stand 15 minutes before carving.

SWAP IT
The marinade for the ribeyes will also be delicious on sirloin steaks.

Rustic Ribeyes

Since I usually have the ingredients on hand, these succulent ribeyes are a regular from my kitchen. But the tender meat also makes a lovely entree for more significant occasions or when I'm entertaining guests.
—**MARY SHIVERS** ADA, OK

PREP: 15 MIN. + MARINATING
BAKE: 5 MIN. • **MAKES:** 6 SERVINGS

- ¾ cup Worcestershire sauce
- 3 tablespoons lime juice
- 1 tablespoon brown sugar
- 1 tablespoon instant coffee granules
- ¾ teaspoon ground mustard
- ½ to ¾ teaspoon crushed red pepper flakes
- ¼ teaspoon smoked sweet paprika
- 3 beef ribeye steaks (1 inch thick and 1 pound each)
- 2 tablespoons canola oil
- 6 tablespoons unsalted butter

1. In a small bowl, combine the first seven ingredients. Set aside ¼ cup for sauce. Pour remaining marinade into a 2-gallon resealable plastic bag. Add the beef; seal bag and turn to coat. Refrigerate up to 8 hours. Drain and discard marinade.
2. Preheat oven to 375°. In a large nonstick skillet over medium-high heat, brown the beef in oil in batches. Transfer to a greased 15x10x1-in. baking pan. Bake, uncovered, 4-6 minutes or until meat reaches desired doneness (for medium-rare, a thermometer should read 145°; medium, 160°; well-done, 170°).
3. Meanwhile, in the same skillet, add butter and reserved marinade. Cook and stir over low heat until combined. Serve with steaks.

Pizza Roll-Up

This is a great, hearty dish for snacking or for dinner. It's also tasty made with ground turkey or Italian sausage instead of ground beef.
—**JANICE CHRISTOFFERSON** EAGLE RIVER, WI

PREP: 15 MIN. • **BAKE:** 25 MIN.
MAKES: 6 SERVINGS

- ½ pound lean ground beef (90% lean)
- 1 tube (13.8 ounces) refrigerated pizza crust
- 1 package (10 ounces) frozen chopped spinach, thawed and squeezed dry
- 1 jar (7 ounces) roasted sweet red peppers, drained and sliced
- 1 cup (4 ounces) shredded part-skim mozzarella cheese
- ½ teaspoon onion powder
- ½ teaspoon pepper
- ½ cup loosely packed basil leaves Cooking spray
- 1 tablespoon grated Parmesan cheese
- 1 can (8 ounces) pizza sauce, warmed

1. Preheat oven to 375°. In a small nonstick skillet, cook the beef over medium heat until meat is no longer pink; drain.
2. Unroll the dough into one long rectangle; top with spinach, beef, roasted peppers and mozzarella cheese. Sprinkle with the onion powder and pepper. Top with basil.
3. Roll up jelly-roll style, starting with a short side; tuck ends under and pinch seam to seal. Place, seam side down, on a baking sheet coated with cooking spray; spritz top and sides with additional cooking spray. Sprinkle with the Parmesan cheese.
4. Bake 25-30 minutes or until golden brown. Let stand 5 minutes. Cut into scant 1-in. slices. Serve with pizza sauce.

Sausage Ravioli Lasagna

You can easily alter this lasagna to please any palate—substitute ground beef or turkey for the sausage or use beef ravioli instead of cheese ravioli.

—NICOLE GAZZO BONDURANT, IA

PREP: 20 MIN. • **BAKE:** 35 MIN. + STANDING
MAKES: 8 SERVINGS

- 1 package (25 ounces) frozen cheese ravioli
- 1½ pounds bulk Italian sausage
- 1 container (15 ounces) ricotta cheese
- 1 egg, lightly beaten
- 1 teaspoon dried basil
- ½ teaspoon Italian seasoning
- 2 jars (one 26 ounces, one 14 ounces) spaghetti sauce
- 2 cups (8 ounces) shredded Italian cheese blend

1. Cook ravioli according to the package directions.

2. Meanwhile, preheat oven to 350°. In a large skillet, cook the sausage over medium heat until no longer pink; drain. In a small bowl, combine ricotta cheese, egg, basil and Italian seasoning; set aside. Drain ravioli.

3. Spoon 1⅓ cups spaghetti sauce into a greased 13x9-in. baking dish. Layer with half of the ravioli and sausage. Spoon ricotta mixture over sausage; top with 1⅓ cups sauce. Layer with remaining ravioli and sausage. Spread remaining sauce over top; sprinkle with the shredded cheese.

4. Cover and bake 30 minutes. Uncover and bake 5-10 minutes longer or until cheese is melted. Let stand 10 minutes before cutting.

PIZZA ROLL-UPS

SAUSAGE RAVIOLI LASAGNA

CARAMELIZED PORK TENDERLOIN

ROASTED CHICKEN & RED POTATOES

(5)INGREDIENTS
Caramelized Pork Tenderloin

They're a little bit savory and a little bit sweet, and best of all, they taste grilled even though you made it on the stovetop.
—**DEBI ARONE** FORT COLLINS, CO

START TO FINISH: 20 MIN.
MAKES: 4 SERVINGS

- 1 pork tenderloin (1 pound)
- ¼ cup packed brown sugar
- 4 garlic cloves, minced
- 1 tablespoon Montreal steak seasoning
- 2 tablespoons butter

1. Cut pork into four pieces and pound with a meat mallet to ¼-in. thickness. In a shallow bowl, mix brown sugar, garlic and steak seasoning. Dip pork in brown sugar mixture, patting to help coating adhere.
2. In a large skillet, heat butter over medium-high heat. Add pork; cook 2-3 minutes on each side or until tender.

Roasted Chicken & Red Potatoes

Pop this homey dinner in the oven for about an hour and enjoy! It's got plenty of flavor and appeal.
—**SHERRI MELOTIK** OAK CREEK, WI

PREP: 15 MIN. • **BAKE:** 55 MIN.
MAKES: 6 SERVINGS

- 2 pounds red potatoes, cut into 1-inch pieces
- 1 package (9 ounces) fresh spinach
- 1 large onion, cut into 1-inch pieces
- 2 tablespoons olive oil
- 4 garlic cloves, minced
- 1 teaspoon salt, divided
- 1 teaspoon dried thyme
- ¾ teaspoon pepper, divided
- 6 chicken leg quarters
- ¾ teaspoon paprika

1. Preheat oven to 375°. Place potatoes, spinach and onion in a greased shallow roasting pan. Add oil, garlic, ¾ teaspoon salt, thyme and ½ teaspoon pepper; toss to combine.

2. Arrange chicken over the vegetables; sprinkle with paprika and remaining salt and pepper. Roast 55-60 minutes or until a thermometer inserted in chicken reads 170°-175° and the potatoes are tender.

TOP TIP

The spiky side of a meat mallet is used for flattening and also tenderizing meat such as round steak. The spikes can tear more delicate cuts like pork tenderloin or chicken breast. For these cuts it is best to use the flat side of a meat mallet.

Chicken & Egg Noodle Casserole

After the fire at my friend's home, my heart broke for her family. Bringing over this casserole was the one thing I could think of to help her out in a tiny way and let her know I was thinking of her and her family.
—**LIN KRANKEL** OXFORD, MI

PREP: 20 MIN. • **BAKE:** 30 MIN.
MAKES: 8 SERVINGS

- 6 cups uncooked egg noodles (about 12 ounces)
- 2 cans (10¾ ounces each) condensed cream of chicken soup, undiluted
- 1 cup (8 ounces) sour cream
- ¾ cup 2% milk
- ¼ teaspoon salt
- ¼ teaspoon pepper
- 3 cups cubed cooked chicken breasts
- 1 cup crushed butter-flavored crackers (about 20)
- ¼ cup butter, melted

1. Preheat oven to 350°. Cook noodles according to package directions for al dente; drain.
2. In a large bowl, whisk the soup, sour cream, milk, salt and pepper until blended. Stir in the chicken and noodles.
3. Transfer to a greased 13x9-in. baking dish. In a small bowl, mix crushed crackers and butter; sprinkle over top. Bake 30-35 minutes or until bubbly.

Traditional Meat Loaf

Topped with a sweet sauce, this meat loaf tastes so good that you might want to double the recipe so everyone can have seconds. It also freezes well.
—**GAIL GRAHAM** MAPLE RIDGE, BC

PREP: 15 MIN.
BAKE: 1 HOUR + STANDING
MAKES: 6 SERVINGS

- 1 egg, lightly beaten
- ⅔ cup 2% milk
- 3 slices bread, crumbled
- 1 cup (4 ounces) shredded cheddar cheese
- 1 medium onion, chopped
- ½ cup finely shredded carrot
- 1 teaspoon salt
- ¼ teaspoon pepper
- 1½ pounds ground beef
- ¼ cup packed brown sugar
- ¼ cup ketchup
- 1 tablespoon prepared mustard

1. Preheat oven to 350°. In a large bowl, combine first eight ingredients. Crumble beef over mixture and mix well. Shape into a loaf. Place in a greased 9x5-in. loaf pan.
2. In a small bowl, combine the brown sugar, ketchup and mustard; spread over loaf. Bake for 60-75 minutes or until no pink remains and a thermometer reads 160°. Drain. Let stand for 10 minutes before slicing.

CHICKEN & EGG
NOODLE CASSEROLE

Bow Ties with Walnut-Herb Pesto

I can't resist having pasta at least once a week, but I also didn't want the fat and extra calories that come with it. So I created this healthier alternative, and now I sometimes have a second helping!
—**DIANE NEMITZ** LUDINGTON, MI

START TO FINISH: 20 MIN.
MAKES: 6 SERVINGS

- 4 **cups uncooked whole wheat bow tie pasta**
- 1 **cup fresh arugula**
- ½ **cup packed fresh parsley sprigs**
- ½ **cup loosely packed basil leaves**
- ¼ **cup grated Parmesan cheese**
- ½ **teaspoon salt**
- ⅛ **teaspoon crushed red pepper flakes**
- ¼ **cup chopped walnuts**
- ⅓ **cup olive oil**
- 1 **plum tomato, seeded and chopped**

1. Cook pasta according to the package directions.
2. Meanwhile, place the arugula, parsley, basil, cheese, salt and pepper flakes in a food processor; cover and pulse until chopped. Add the walnuts; cover and process until blended. While processing, gradually add the oil in a steady stream.
3. Drain the pasta, reserving 3 tablespoons cooking water. In a large bowl, toss pasta with pesto, tomato and reserved water.

---

⑤INGREDIENTS
Caribbean Grilled Ribeyes

With my father-in-law in mind, I created a steak with some zip that I hoped he would like. He loved it! You can serve it for casual suppers in the backyard or more elaborate parties.
—**DE'LAWRENCE REED** DURHAM, NC

PREP: 10 MIN. + MARINATING
GRILL: 10 MIN. • **MAKES:** 4 SERVINGS

- ½ **cup Dr. Pepper**
- 3 **tablespoons honey**
- ¼ **cup Caribbean jerk seasoning**
- 1½ **teaspoons chopped seeded habanero pepper**
- ½ **teaspoon salt**
- ½ **teaspoon pepper**
- 4 **beef ribeye steaks (¾ pound each)**

1. Place the first six ingredients in a blender; cover and process until blended. Pour into a large resealable plastic bag. Add the steaks; seal bag and turn to coat. Refrigerate at least 2 hours.
2. Drain and discard marinade. Grill steaks, covered, over medium heat or broil 3-4 in. from heat 4-6 minutes on each side or until meat reaches desired doneness (for medium-rare, a meat thermometer should read 145°; medium, 160°; well-done, 170°).
NOTE *Wear disposable gloves when cutting hot peppers; the oils can burn skin. Avoid touching your face.*

SLOW COOKER
Lip Smackin' Ribs

No matter what time of year you eat them, these ribs taste like summer. They're my feel-good food!
—**RON BYNAKER** LEBANON, PA

PREP: 20 MIN. • **COOK:** 6 HOURS
MAKES: 8 SERVINGS

- 3 **tablespoons butter**
- 3 **pounds boneless country-style pork ribs**

- 1 **can (15 ounces) tomato sauce**
- 1 **cup packed brown sugar**
- 1 **cup ketchup**
- ¼ **cup prepared mustard**
- 2 **tablespoons honey**
- 3 **teaspoons pepper**
- 2 **teaspoons dried savory**
- 1 **teaspoon salt**

In a large skillet, heat butter over medium heat. Brown ribs in batches; transfer to a 5-qt. slow cooker. Add remaining ingredients. Cook, covered, on low 6-8 hours or until meat is tender.

---

⑤INGREDIENTS
Maple Baked Salmon

This recipe is special because it comes from my mom, both my children like it and it's easy to prepare. I serve this recipe with rice and broccoli. The sauce tastes great on the rice.
—**DANIELLE ROTHE** GREENVILLE, NY

START TO FINISH: 30 MIN.
MAKES: 6 SERVINGS

- 6 **salmon fillets (6 ounces each)**
- ¼ **cup packed brown sugar**
- ¼ **cup maple syrup**
- 3 **tablespoons reduced-sodium soy sauce**
- 1 **tablespoon Dijon mustard**
- ¼ **teaspoon pepper**
- 4 **teaspoons sliced almonds, toasted, optional**

1. Preheat oven to 425°. Place the salmon fillets in a greased 13x9-in. baking dish. In a small bowl, combine the brown sugar, syrup, soy sauce, mustard and pepper. Pour over salmon.
2. Cover and bake 10 minutes. Uncover and bake 8-10 minutes longer or until fish flakes easily with fork. Sprinkle with almonds if desired.

CARIBBEAN
GRILLED RIBEYES

LIP SMACKIN' RIBS

MAPLE BAKED
SALMON

PORK AND ONION KABOBS

Pork and Onion Kabobs

A sweet and savory marinade brings out the best in pork, as these grilled kabobs prove. They're a super supper, easy to prepare and fun to serve to company. The pork is tasty grilled with onion wedges.

—MARY LOU WAYMAN
SALT LAKE CITY, UT

PREP: 15 MIN. + MARINATING
GRILL: 15 MIN. • **MAKES:** 6 SERVINGS

- ½ cup reduced-sodium soy sauce
- ¼ cup chili sauce
- ¼ cup honey
- 2 tablespoons olive oil
- 2 tablespoons finely chopped onion
- 2 teaspoons curry powder
- 2 pounds boneless pork, cut into 1-inch cubes
- 3 medium onions, cut into 1-inch wedges

1. In a small bowl, combine the first six ingredients. Remove half for basting; cover and refrigerate. Pour remaining marinade into a large resealable plastic bag. Add the pork; seal bag and turn to coat. Cover and refrigerate 3 hours or overnight.
2. Drain and discard marinade. On six metal or soaked wooden skewers, alternately thread pork and onions.
3. Grill, uncovered, over medium heat 5 minutes; turn. Baste with reserved marinade. Continue turning and basting 10-15 minutes longer or until meat is tender.

Grilled Bourbon Chops

My husband is a grill master and loves a good bourbon, making this recipe the perfect combination of both! Sometimes we use thicker chops. If you do, too, remember to cook them long enough to reach 145°.

—DONNA BRYAN
COLUMBIA FALLS, MT

START TO FINISH: 25 MIN.
MAKES: 4 SERVINGS

- ¼ cup bourbon or unsweetened apple juice
- 2 tablespoons brown sugar
- 2 tablespoons Dijon mustard
- 3 garlic cloves, minced
- 1 teaspoon onion powder
- ½ teaspoon salt
- ¼ teaspoon pepper
- 4 bone-in pork loin chops (½ inch thick and 8 ounces each)

1. In a small saucepan, mix bourbon, brown sugar, mustard and garlic; bring to a boil. Reduce heat; simmer, uncovered, for 2-3 minutes or until slightly thickened.
2. Mix onion powder, salt and pepper; sprinkle over pork chops. Grill, covered, over medium heat or broil 4 in. from heat 3-5 minutes on each side or until a thermometer reads 145°. Let stand 5 minutes before serving. Serve with sauce.

Chicken Marsala

A delicate wine sauce tops lightly breaded chicken for a truly elegant, restaurant-quality meal that will delight family and friends alike.

—CHER SCHWARTZ ELLISVILLE, MO

START TO FINISH: 30 MIN.
MAKES: 4 SERVINGS

- 4 boneless skinless chicken breast halves (4 ounces each)
- 2 tablespoons all-purpose flour
- 2 tablespoons olive oil
- 2 cups sliced fresh mushrooms
- 2 tablespoons butter
- ¾ cup marsala wine or chicken broth
- 2 tablespoons minced fresh parsley
- ¼ teaspoon dried rosemary, crushed
- 2 tablespoons grated Parmesan cheese, optional

1. Flatten chicken to ¼-in. thickness. Place flour in a large resealable plastic bag. Add chicken, two pieces at a time, and shake to coat.
2. In a large skillet over medium heat, cook chicken in oil for 3-5 minutes on each side or until a thermometer reads 165°. Remove and keep warm.
3. In the same skillet, saute the mushrooms in butter until tender. Add wine, parsley and rosemary. Bring to a boil; cook until liquid is reduced by half. Serve with the chicken; sprinkle with cheese if desired.

HOW TO

FLATTEN CHICKEN
Place boneless chicken breasts between two pieces of waxed paper or plastic wrap or in a resealable plastic bag. Starting in the center and working out to edges, pound lightly with the flat side of a meat mallet until the chicken is even in thickness.

GRILLED BOURBON CHOPS

Wiener Schnitzel

You may chill the veal for 30 minutes after coating it if desired, making the recipe more convenient while preparing other foods.

—**EMMA WEST** LEOMA, TN

START TO FINISH: 25 MIN.
MAKES: 4 SERVINGS

- 4 **veal cutlets (4 ounces each)**
- ¾ **teaspoon salt**
- ¾ **teaspoon pepper**
- ½ **cup all-purpose flour**
- 2 **eggs, lightly beaten**
- ¾ **cup dry bread crumbs**
- ¼ **cup butter**
- 4 **lemon slices**

1. Sprinkle veal with salt and pepper. Place the flour, eggs and bread crumbs in separate shallow bowls. Coat veal with flour, then dip in eggs and coat with crumbs.
2. In a large skillet over medium heat, cook veal in butter for 2-3 minutes on each side or until no longer pink. Serve with lemon.

SLOW COOKER

Cajun-Style Pot Roast

I often make this well-seasoned roast for dinner guests. It gives me time to visit and everyone always enjoys it, even my friend who's a chef.

—**GINGER MENZIES** OAK CREEK, CO

PREP: 15 MIN. • **COOK:** 6 HOURS
MAKES: 6 SERVINGS

- 1 **boneless beef chuck roast (2 to 3 pounds)**
- 2 **tablespoons Cajun seasoning**
- 1 **tablespoon olive oil**
- 2 **cans (10 ounces each) diced tomatoes and green chilies**
- 1 **medium sweet red pepper, chopped**
- 1½ **cups chopped celery**
- ¾ **cup chopped onion**
- ¼ **cup quick-cooking tapioca**
- 1½ **teaspoons minced garlic**
- 1 **teaspoon salt**
  Hot cooked rice

1. Cut roast in half; sprinkle with Cajun seasoning. In a large skillet, brown roast in oil on all sides. Transfer to a 5-qt. slow cooker. Combine tomatoes, red pepper, celery, onion, tapioca, garlic and salt; pour over roast.
2. Cover and cook on low for 6-8 hours or until meat is tender. Serve with rice.
FREEZE OPTION *Remove beef, vegetables and juices from slow cooker; cool slightly. Slice beef; transfer all to freezer containers. Freeze for up to 3 months. To use, thaw in the refrigerator overnight. Place in a Dutch oven; heat through. Thin with beef broth if necessary. Serve with rice.*

⑤ INGREDIENTS

Italian Crumb-Crusted Beef Roast

Italian-style panko crumbs and seasoning give this roast beef a special touch—it's an almost effortless weekend meal. That way, you can put your energy into relaxing.

—**MARIA REGAKIS** SAUGUS, MA

PREP: 10 MIN.
BAKE: 1¾ HOURS + STANDING
MAKES: 8 SERVINGS

- 1 **beef sirloin tip roast (3 pounds)**
- ¼ **teaspoon salt**
- ¾ **cup Italian-style panko (Japanese) bread crumbs**
- ¼ **cup mayonnaise**
- 3 **tablespoons dried minced onion**
- ½ **teaspoon Italian seasoning**
- ¼ **teaspoon pepper**

1. Preheat oven to 325°. Place roast on a rack in a shallow roasting pan; sprinkle with salt. In a small bowl, mix remaining ingredients; press onto top and sides of roast.
2. Roast 1¾ to 2¼ hours or until meat reaches desired doneness

(for medium-rare, a thermometer should read 145°; medium, 160°; well-done, 170°). Remove roast from oven; tent with foil. Let stand 10 minutes before slicing.

Savory Braised Chicken with Vegetables

Folks will think you worked all day on this masterpiece, but it can be your little secret how easy it is!

—**MICHELLE COLLINS** LAKE ORION, MI

PREP: 15 MIN. • **COOK:** 40 MIN.
MAKES: 6 SERVINGS

- ½ **cup seasoned bread crumbs**
- 6 **boneless skinless chicken breast halves (4 ounces each)**
- 2 **tablespoons olive oil**
- 1 **can (14½ ounces) beef broth**
- 2 **tablespoons tomato paste**
- 1 **teaspoon poultry seasoning**
- ½ **teaspoon salt**
- ½ **teaspoon pepper**
- 1 **pound fresh baby carrots**
- 1 **pound sliced fresh mushrooms**
- 2 **medium zucchini, sliced**
  Sliced French bread baguette, optional

1. Place bread crumbs in a shallow bowl. Dip chicken breasts in bread crumbs to coat both sides; shake off excess.
2. In a Dutch oven, heat oil over medium heat. Add the chicken in batches; cook 2-4 minutes on each side or until browned. Remove the chicken from pan.
3. Add broth, tomato paste and seasonings to same pan; cook over medium-high heat, stirring to loosen browned bits from pan. Add vegetables and chicken; bring to a boil. Reduce heat; simmer, covered, 25-30 minutes or until vegetables are tender and a thermometer inserted in chicken reads 165°. If desired, serve with baguette.

ITALIAN CRUMB-CRUSTED
BEEF ROAST

SAVORY BRAISED CHICKEN
WITH VEGETABLES

Cuban Panini

The Cuban sandwich is a twist on the traditional ham and cheese. It usually features ham, Swiss and pickles. For my version, I added smoked turkey.

—JANET SANDERS
PINE MOUNTAIN, GA

PREP: 20 MIN. • **COOK:** 5 MIN./BATCH
MAKES: 4 SERVINGS

- 2 **garlic cloves, minced**
- ½ **teaspoon olive oil**
- ½ **cup reduced-fat mayonnaise**
- 8 **slices artisan bread**
- 8 **thick slices deli smoked turkey**
- 4 **slices deli ham**
- 8 **slices Swiss cheese**
- 12 **dill pickle slices**
- 1 **cup fresh baby spinach**

1. In a small skillet, cook and stir garlic in oil over medium-high heat until tender. Cool.
2. Stir garlic into mayonnaise; spread over bread slices. Layer 4 slices of bread with turkey, ham, cheese, pickles and spinach; close sandwiches.
3. Cook on a panini maker or indoor grill 2-3 minutes or until browned and cheese is melted.

Mexi-Mac Skillet

My husband loves this recipe, and I love how simple it is to put together! Because you don't need to precook the noodles, you'll save time prepping this tasty dish.

—MAURANE RAMSEY
FORT WAYNE, IN

START TO FINISH: 30 MIN.
MAKES: 5 SERVINGS

- 1 **pound lean ground beef (90% lean)**
- 1 **large onion, chopped**
- 1 **can (14½ ounces) diced tomatoes, undrained**
- 1 **can (8 ounces) tomato sauce**
- 1 **cup fresh or frozen corn**
- ½ **cup water**
- 1¼ **teaspoons chili powder**
- 1 **teaspoon dried oregano**
- ½ **teaspoon salt**
- ⅔ **cup uncooked elbow macaroni**
- ⅔ **cup shredded reduced-fat cheddar cheese**

1. In a large nonstick skillet over medium-high heat, cook beef and onion until meat is no longer pink; drain. Stir in the tomatoes, tomato sauce, corn, water, chili powder, oregano and salt.
2. Bring to a boil; stir in macaroni. Reduce heat; cover and simmer 18-22 minutes or until macaroni is tender. Sprinkle with cheese.

Easy Curried Shrimp

I like to serve this dish with grapes or green veggies for added color. It's also nice with dried coconut or pineapple instead of apricots.

—DONA STONE CLEARWATER, FL

START TO FINISH: 20 MIN.
MAKES: 4 SERVINGS

- 1 **tablespoon butter**
- 2 **teaspoons curry powder**
- ¾ **teaspoon ground cumin**
- ¼ **teaspoon salt**
- ¼ **teaspoon garlic powder**
- ¼ **teaspoon ground coriander**
- ¼ **teaspoon ground cinnamon**
- 1 **cup light coconut milk**
- 1 **pound uncooked large shrimp, peeled and deveined**
- ⅓ **cup chopped dried apricots**
- 2 **cups hot cooked brown rice**

1. In a large skillet, melt butter. Add the curry, cumin, salt, garlic powder, coriander and cinnamon; cook over medium heat until lightly browned. Stir in coconut milk. Bring to a boil. Reduce heat; simmer, uncovered, 3-4 minutes or until thickened.
2. Add shrimp; cook and stir 2-4 minutes or until shrimp turn pink. Stir in the apricots; heat through. Serve with rice.

CUBAN PANINI

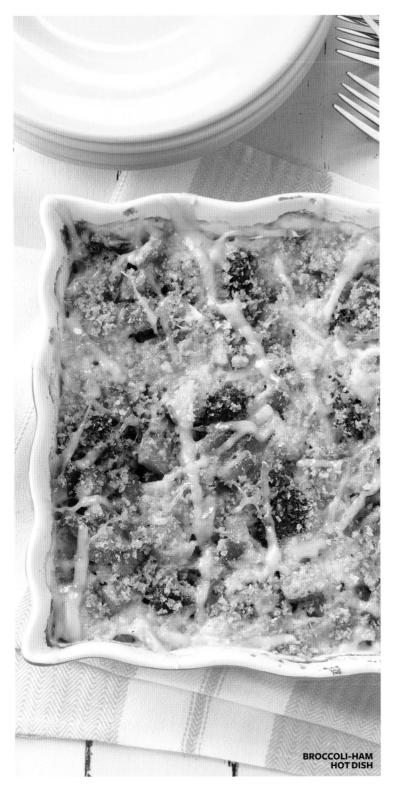

Broccoli-Ham Hot Dish

One of my best friends shared this recipe with me. My family enjoys it because it includes one of our favorite vegetables—broccoli. It's a delicious and colorful way to use up leftover ham.

—MARGARET ALLEN ABINGDON, VA

PREP: 20 MIN. • **BAKE:** 30 MIN.
MAKES: 8 SERVINGS

2 packages (10 ounces each) frozen cut broccoli
2 cups cooked rice
6 tablespoons butter, cubed
2 cups fresh bread crumbs (about 2½ slices)
1 medium onion, chopped
3 tablespoons all-purpose flour
1 teaspoon salt
¼ teaspoon pepper
3 cups milk
1½ pounds fully cooked ham, cubed
Shredded cheddar or Swiss cheese

1. Preheat oven to 350°. Cook broccoli according to package directions; drain. Spoon rice into a 13x9-in. baking pan. Place broccoli over rice.

2. Melt butter in a large skillet. Sprinkle 2 tablespoons of melted butter over the bread crumbs and set aside. In remaining butter, saute onion until soft. Add flour, salt and pepper, stirring constantly until blended; stir in milk. Bring to a boil; cook and stir 2 minutes or until thickened. Add ham.

3. Pour over rice and broccoli. Sprinkle with crumbs. Bake 30 minutes or until heated through. Sprinkle with cheese; let stand 5 minutes before serving.

BROCCOLI-HAM HOT DISH

EASY CITRUS HAM

HEARTY VEGETABLE
BEEF RAGOUT

TOMATO-BASIL
STEAK

Easy Citrus Ham

I created this recipe many years ago with items I already had on hand. The succulent ham has a mild citrus flavor. It was so popular at a church social that I knew I had a winner!

—SHEILA CHRISTENSEN
SAN MARCOS, CA

PREP: 15 MIN.
COOK: 4 HOURS + STANDING
MAKES: 10-12 SERVINGS

- 1 **boneless fully cooked ham (3 to 4 pounds)**
- ½ **cup packed dark brown sugar**
- 1 **can (12 ounces) lemon-lime soda, divided**
- 1 **medium navel orange, thinly sliced**
- 1 **medium lemon, thinly sliced**
- 1 **medium lime, thinly sliced**
- 1 **tablespoon chopped crystallized ginger**

1. Cut ham in half; place in a 5-qt. slow cooker. In a small bowl, combine brown sugar and ¼ cup soda; rub over ham. Top with orange, lemon and lime slices. Add candied ginger and remaining soda to the slow cooker.
2. Cover and cook on low 4-5 hours or until a thermometer reads 140°, basting the ham occasionally with cooking juices. Let stand 10 minutes before slicing.

Hearty Vegetable Beef Ragout

With this pasta ragout, I can have a hearty meal on the table in under 30 minutes. It's one my children gobble up.

—KIM VAN DUNK CALDWELL, NJ

START TO FINISH: 30 MIN.
MAKES: 8 SERVINGS

- 4 **cups uncooked whole wheat spiral pasta**
- 1 **pound lean ground beef (90% lean)**
- 1 **large onion, chopped**
- 3 **garlic cloves, minced**
- 2 **cans (14½ ounces each) Italian diced tomatoes, undrained**
- 1 **jar (24 ounces) meatless spaghetti sauce**
- 2 **cups finely chopped fresh kale**
- 1 **package (9 ounces) frozen peas, thawed**
- ¾ **teaspoon garlic powder**
- ¼ **teaspoon pepper**
  Grated Parmesan cheese, optional

1. Cook pasta according to the package directions; drain.
2. Meanwhile, in a Dutch oven, cook beef, onion and garlic over medium heat 6-8 minutes or until beef is no longer pink, breaking up beef into crumbles; drain.
3. Stir in tomatoes, spaghetti sauce, kale, peas, garlic powder and pepper. Bring to a boil. Reduce heat; simmer, uncovered, 8-10 minutes or until kale is tender. Stir pasta into sauce. If desired, serve with cheese.

Tomato-Basil Steak

I use basil and bell peppers from my herb and vegetable garden to make this dish. It's so easy to make and so rich and delicious.

—SHERYL LITTLE SHERWOOD, AR

PREP: 15 MIN. • **COOK:** 6 HOURS
MAKES: 4 SERVINGS

- 1¼ **pounds boneless beef shoulder top blade or flat iron steaks**
- ½ **pound whole fresh mushrooms, quartered**
- 1 **medium sweet yellow pepper, julienned**
- 1 **can (14½ ounces) stewed tomatoes, undrained**
- 1 **can (8 ounces) tomato sauce**
- 1 **envelope onion soup mix**
- 2 **tablespoons minced fresh basil**
  Hot cooked rice

1. Place steaks in a 4-qt. slow cooker. Add mushrooms and pepper. In a small bowl, mix tomatoes, tomato sauce, soup mix and basil; pour over top.
2. Cook, covered, on low 6-8 hours or until beef and vegetables are tender. Serve with rice.

Pineapple Shrimp Tacos

Taste the tropics with our cool and crispy take on shrimp tacos. Wrapping the shells in lettuce adds even more crunch, while keeping the tacos tidy after you take a bite.

—TASTE OF HOME TEST KITCHEN

START TO FINISH: 25 MIN.
MAKES: 4 SERVINGS

- 1 **pound uncooked large shrimp, peeled and deveined**
- 3 **teaspoons olive oil, divided**
- 1 **large sweet orange pepper, sliced**
- 1 **large sweet red pepper, sliced**
- 1 **small onion, halved and sliced**
- 1 **cup pineapple tidbits**
- 1 **envelope fajita seasoning mix**
- ⅓ **cup water**
- 8 **corn tortillas (6 inches), warmed**
- ½ **cup shredded cotija or mozzarella cheese**
- 8 **large romaine lettuce leaves**

1. Cook shrimp in 2 teaspoons oil in a large skillet over medium heat 4-6 minutes or until shrimp turn pink; remove and keep warm.
2. In the same skillet, saute the peppers, onion and pineapple in remaining oil until tender. Add seasoning mix and water. Bring to a boil; cook and stir 2 minutes.
3. Return shrimp to the skillet; heat through. Spoon onto tortillas; top with cheese. Wrap lettuce around tortillas to serve.

PAIR IT!
Garlic-Cheese Crescent Rolls, page 152, make a savory accompaniment to this juicy roast.

SALT-ENCRUSTED PRIME RIB, 128

158

132

159

Effortless Holidays

When you present your guests with these **impressive entrees and sides**, they'll think you've been slaving away for days in the kitchen. There's absolutely no reason to tell them how **easy these dishes** were to make.

LIGHTENED UP HASH BROWN CASSEROLE, 141

(5) INGREDIENTS | SLOW COOKER
Cherry Balsamic Pork Loin

After tasting a wonderful cherry topping for Brie from a local market, I knew I had to create one for pork. If you're really crazy about cherries, add even more to the slow cooker.

—SUSAN STETZEL GAINESVILLE, NY

PREP: 20 MIN.
COOK: 3 HOURS + STANDING
MAKES: 8 SERVINGS (1⅓ CUPS SAUCE)

- 1 boneless pork loin roast (3 to 4 pounds)
- 1 teaspoon salt
- ½ teaspoon pepper
- 1 tablespoon canola oil
- ¾ cup cherry preserves
- ½ cup dried cherries
- ⅓ cup balsamic vinegar
- ¼ cup packed brown sugar

1. Sprinkle roast with salt and pepper. In a large skillet, heat oil over medium-high heat. Brown roast on all sides.
2. Transfer to a 6-qt. slow cooker. In a small bowl, mix preserves, cherries, vinegar and brown sugar until blended; pour over roast. Cook, covered, on low 3-4 hours or until tender (a thermometer inserted into pork should read at least 145°).
3. Remove roast from slow cooker; tent with foil. Let stand 15 minutes before slicing. Skim the fat from cooking juices. Serve the pork with the sauce.

> ### SWAP IT
> For a classic pork and fruit pairing, use apricot preserves, chopped dried apricots and white balsamic vinegar for the cherries and vinegar.

(5) INGREDIENTS
Salt-Encrusted Prime Rib

Restaurants have nothing on this recipe. For a true meat lover, it's very easy and the results are fabulous!

—ROGER BOWLDS BAKERSFIELD, CA

PREP: 15 MIN.
BAKE: 2¼ HOURS + STANDING
MAKES: 10 SERVINGS

- 1 box (3 pounds) kosher salt (about 6 cups), divided
- 1 bone-in beef rib roast (6 to 8 pounds)
- 3 tablespoons Worcestershire sauce
- 2 tablespoons cracked black pepper
- 2 teaspoons garlic powder
- ½ cup water

1. Preheat oven to 450°. Line a shallow roasting pan with heavy-duty foil. Place 3 cups salt on foil, spreading evenly to form a ½-in. layer.
2. Brush the roast with Worcestershire sauce; sprinkle with pepper and garlic powder. Place roast on layer of salt, fat side up. In a small bowl, mix water and remaining salt (mixture should be just moist enough to pack). Beginning at the base of the roast, press salt mixture onto the sides and top of roast.
3. Roast 15 minutes. Reduce oven setting to 325°. Roast 2 to 2¼ hours or until a thermometer reaches 130° for medium-rare; 145° for medium. (Temperature of roast will continue to rise about 15° upon standing.) Let stand 20 minutes.
4. Remove and discard salt crust; brush away any remaining salt. Carve roast into slices.

Apple-Sage Roasted Turkey

Apple flavor gives this classic recipe a new spin that will appeal to even your pickiest eaters.

—SUZY HORVATH MILWAUKIE, OR

PREP: 20 MIN.
BAKE: 3½ HOURS + STANDING
MAKES: 14 SERVINGS

- ½ cup apple cider or juice
- ½ cup apple jelly
- ⅓ cup butter, cubed
TURKEY
- ⅓ cup minced fresh sage
- ¼ cup butter, softened
- 1 turkey (14 to 16 pounds)
- 2 tablespoons apple cider or juice
- 1½ teaspoons salt
- 1½ teaspoons pepper
- 2 large apples, cut into wedges
- 1 large onion, cut into wedges
- 8 fresh sage leaves

1. Preheat oven to 325°. In a small saucepan, combine apple cider, jelly and butter. Cook and stir until butter is melted. Remove from heat; set aside. Reserve 2 tablespoons for finishing.
2. In a small bowl, combine the minced sage and butter. With fingers, carefully loosen skin from the turkey breast; rub butter mixture under the skin. Brush turkey with apple cider. Sprinkle salt and pepper over turkey and inside cavity.
3. Place apples, onion and sage leaves inside the cavity. Tuck the wings under turkey; tie drumsticks together. Place breast side up on a rack in a roasting pan.
4. Bake, uncovered, 3½ to 4 hours or until a thermometer inserted into thigh reads 170°-175°, basting occasionally with cider mixture. Cover loosely with foil if turkey browns too quickly. Brush with reserved cider mixture. Cover and let stand 20 minutes before slicing.

**CHERRY BALSAMIC
PORK LOIN**

**SALT-ENCRUSTED
PRIME RIB**

**APPLE-SAGE
ROASTED TURKEY**

PRIME RIB WITH HORSERADISH SAUCE

MOIST & TENDER TURKEY BREAST

(5) INGREDIENTS SLOW COOKER

Moist & Tender Turkey Breast

This easy entree is sure to be popular in your home. Everyone will love the taste, and you'll love how quickly it comes together.

—HEIDI VAWDREY RIVERTON, UT

PREP: 10 MIN.
COOK: 4 HOURS • **MAKES:** 12 SERVINGS

- 1 bone-in turkey breast (6 to 7 pounds)
- ½ cup water
- 4 fresh rosemary sprigs
- 4 garlic cloves, peeled
- 1 tablespoon brown sugar
- ½ teaspoon coarsely ground pepper
- ¼ teaspoon salt

Place turkey breast and water in a 6-qt. slow cooker. Place rosemary and garlic around turkey. Combine the brown sugar, pepper and salt; sprinkle over turkey. Cover and cook on low 4-6 hours or until turkey is tender.

(5) INGREDIENTS

Prime Rib with Horseradish Sauce

We invite friends over for dinner to ring in the New Year. My menu featuring tender prime rib is festive yet simple to prepare. A pepper rub and mild horseradish sauce complement the beef's great flavor.

—PAULA ZSIRAY LOGAN, UT

PREP: 5 MIN.
BAKE: 3 HOURS + STANDING
MAKES: 6-8 SERVINGS

- 1 bone-in beef rib roast (4 to 6 pounds)
- 1 tablespoon olive oil
- 1 to 2 teaspoons coarsely ground pepper

HORSERADISH SAUCE

- 1 cup (8 ounces) sour cream
- 3 to 4 tablespoons prepared horseradish
- 1 teaspoon coarsely ground pepper
- ⅛ teaspoon Worcestershire sauce

1. Preheat oven to 450°. Brush roast with oil; rub with pepper. Place roast, fat side up, on a rack in a shallow roasting pan. Bake, uncovered, 15 minutes.

2. Reduce heat to 325°. Bake 2¾ hours or until meat reaches desired doneness (for medium-rare, a thermometer should read 145°; medium, 160°; well-done, 170°), basting with pan drippings every 30 minutes.

3. Let stand 10-15 minutes before slicing. In a small bowl, combine sauce ingredients. Serve with beef.

DID YOU KNOW?

The fumes from grating horseradish can cause your eyes and nose to burn. Horseradish sauce loses its heat as it ages. Refrigerate open containers up to 4 weeks or freeze up to 6 months.

(5)INGREDIENTS
Teriyaki Beef Tenderloin

A beautiful glaze coats this fantastic tenderloin. It's ideal for entertaining since it is so easy and so delicious. All you have to do is throw some ingredients together and let the marinade do all the work.

—LILY JULOW LAWRENCEVILLE, GA

PREP: 10 MIN. + MARINATING
BAKE: 45 MIN. + STANDING
MAKES: 8 SERVINGS

- 1 **cup sherry or reduced-sodium beef broth**
- ½ **cup reduced-sodium soy sauce**
- 1 **envelope onion soup mix**
- ¼ **cup packed brown sugar**
- 1 **beef tenderloin roast (2 pounds)**
- 2 **tablespoons water**

1. In a large bowl, combine the sherry, soy sauce, soup mix and brown sugar. Pour 1 cup into a large resealable plastic bag; add the tenderloin. Seal bag and turn to coat; refrigerate at least 5 hours or overnight. Cover and refrigerate remaining marinade.

2. Preheat oven to 425°. Drain and discard marinade. Place tenderloin on a rack in a shallow roasting pan. Bake, uncovered, 45-50 minutes or until meat reaches desired doneness (for medium-rare, a thermometer should read 145°; medium, 160°; well-done, 170°), basting often with ⅓ cup reserved marinade. Let stand 10-15 minutes.

3. Meanwhile, in a small saucepan, bring water and remaining marinade to a rolling boil 1 minute or until sauce is slightly reduced. Slice beef; serve with sauce.

Pan-Seared Lamb Chops

A trio of garlic, rosemary and mint enhances the flavor of these chops, along with the luxuriously flavorful sauce on top.

—MATTHEW LAWRENCE VASHON, WA

START TO FINISH: 30 MIN.
MAKES: 2 SERVINGS

- 3 **garlic cloves, minced**
- 2 **teaspoons minced fresh rosemary**
- 1 **teaspoon minced fresh mint**
- ¼ **teaspoon salt**
- ⅛ **teaspoon pepper**
- 4 **lamb loin chops (4 ounces each)**
- 1 **tablespoon butter**
- 1 **tablespoon olive oil**
- ¼ **cup white wine**
- ¼ **cup heavy whipping cream**

1. Combine first five ingredients; rub over chops. In a skillet over medium heat, cook chops in butter and oil 6-8 minutes on each side or until the meat reaches desired doneness (for medium-rare, a thermometer should read 145°; medium, 160°; well-done, 170°). Remove and keep warm.

2. Add wine to the same skillet, stirring to loosen browned bits from pan. Stir in cream; cook 1-2 minutes or until slightly thickened. Serve with chops.

TERIYAKI BEEF TENDERLOIN

Fig-Glazed Pork Tenderloin

I like to experiment with unique flavors and try to make the food look photo-worthy, too. But my husband's main concern is that the dish has to taste good. Here's a supper that is both eye appealing and delicious.
—**JEAN GOTTFRIED**
UPPER SANDUSKY, OH

START TO FINISH: 30 MIN.
MAKES: 4 SERVINGS

- 1 **pork tenderloin (1 pound),** cut into 8 slices
- ½ **teaspoon salt**
- ½ **teaspoon pepper**
- 1 **tablespoon olive oil**
- ⅓ **cup fig preserves**
- 3 **tablespoons apple juice**
- 2 **tablespoons cider vinegar**
- 1½ **teaspoons Worcestershire sauce**
- 1 **garlic clove, minced**
- ¾ **teaspoon curry powder**

1. Sprinkle pork with salt and pepper. In a large skillet, heat oil over medium-high heat. Brown pork on both sides; remove from the pan.
2. Add preserves, juice, vinegar, Worcestershire sauce, garlic and curry powder to same pan; bring to a boil. Return pork to pan. Reduce heat; simmer, covered, 5-7 minutes or until a thermometer inserted into pork reads 145°. Let stand 5 minutes before serving.

⑤ INGREDIENTS

Classic Beef Wellingtons

Perfect for holidays, this entree is also impressively easy. Find ready-made puff pastry sheets in the frozen food section.
—**KERRY DINGWALL** PONTE VEDRA, FL

PREP: 20 MIN. + CHILLING • **BAKE:** 25 MIN.
MAKES: 4 SERVINGS

- 4 **beef tenderloin steaks (6 ounces each)**
- ¾ **teaspoon salt, divided**
- ½ **teaspoon pepper, divided**
- 2 **tablespoons olive oil, divided**
- 1¾ **cups sliced fresh mushrooms**
- 1 **medium onion, chopped**
- 1 **package (17.3 ounces) frozen puff pastry, thawed**
- 1 **egg, lightly beaten**

1. Sprinkle the steaks with ½ teaspoon salt and ¼ teaspoon pepper. In a large skillet, brown steaks in 1 tablespoon oil for 2-3 minutes on each side. Remove from skillet and refrigerate until chilled.
2. In the same skillet, saute the mushrooms and onion in the remaining oil until tender. Stir in remaining salt and pepper; cool to room temperature.
3. Preheat oven to 425°. On a lightly floured surface, roll each puff pastry sheet into a 14x9½-in. rectangle. Cut into two 7-in. squares (use scraps to make decorative cutouts if desired). Place a steak in the center of each square; top with mushroom mixture. Lightly brush pastry edges with water. Bring opposite corners of pastry over steak; pinch seams to seal tightly.
4. Place in a greased 15x10x1-in. baking pan. Cut four small slits in top of pastry. Arrange cutouts over top if desired. Brush with egg.
5. Bake 25-30 minutes or until pastry is golden brown and meat reaches desired doneness (for medium-rare, a thermometer should read 145°; medium, 160°; well-done, 170°).

FIG-GLAZED PORK TENDERLOIN

PAIR IT!
Baked Broccolini, page 156, will make a simple but elegant side for the Wellingtons.

Savory Rubbed Roast Chicken

A blend of paprika, onion powder, garlic and cayenne go on the skin and inside the cavity to create a delicious, slightly spicy roast chicken. The aroma of this dish while it's cooking drives my family nuts.

—MARGARET COLE IMPERIAL, MO

PREP: 20 MIN.
BAKE: 2 HOURS + STANDING
MAKES: 8 SERVINGS

- 2 teaspoons paprika
- 1 teaspoon salt
- 1 teaspoon onion powder
- 1 teaspoon dried thyme
- 1 teaspoon white pepper
- 1 teaspoon cayenne pepper
- ¾ teaspoon garlic powder
- ½ teaspoon pepper
- 1 roasting chicken (6 to 7 pounds)
- 1 large onion, peeled and quartered

1. Preheat oven to 350°. In a small bowl, combine the seasonings; set aside. Place chicken breast side up on a rack in a shallow roasting pan; pat dry. Tuck wings under chicken; tie drumsticks together. Rub the seasoning mixture over the outside and inside of chicken. Place onion inside cavity.

2. Bake, uncovered, 2 to 2½ hours or until a thermometer inserted into thickest part of a thigh reads 170°-175°, basting occasionally with pan drippings. (Cover loosely with foil if chicken browns too quickly.) Cover and let stand for 15 minutes before carving.

CLASSIC BEEF WELLINGTONS

SAVORY RUBBED ROAST CHICKEN

Herb-Roasted Turkey

Made with everyday ingredients, this moist and tender turkey tastes absolutely extraordinary!

—TASTE OF HOME TEST KITCHEN

PREP: 20 MIN.
BAKE: 2 HOURS + STANDING
MAKES: 14 SERVINGS

- 1 tablespoon dried sage leaves
- 1 teaspoon dried thyme
- 1 teaspoon dried rosemary, crushed
- 1 teaspoon seasoned salt
- ½ teaspoon pepper
- 1 turkey (14 to 16 pounds)
- 2 tablespoons canola oil
- 1 tablespoon all-purpose flour
- 1 turkey-size oven roasting bag
- 2 celery ribs, sliced
- 1 medium onion, sliced

1. Preheat oven to 350°. In a small bowl, mix first five ingredients. Pat turkey dry; brush with the oil. Sprinkle herb mixture over skin of turkey. Skewer turkey openings; tie drumsticks together.
2. Place flour in oven bag; shake to coat. Place bag in a roasting pan; add celery and onion. Place the turkey, breast side up, over vegetables. Cut six ½-in. slits in top of bag; close bag with tie provided.
3. Bake 2 to 2½ hours or until a thermometer inserted into thigh reads 170°-175°. Remove turkey to a platter and keep warm. Let stand 15 minutes before carving. If desired, thicken pan drippings for gravy.

Lemon-Herb Leg of Lamb

This lamb recipe would be perfect for Easter or any other festive gathering.

—PATRICIA CRANDALL
INCHELIUM, WA

PREP: 10 MIN. + MARINATING
BAKE: 1¾ HOURS + STANDING
MAKES: 12 SERVINGS

- 2 teaspoons lemon juice
- 1½ teaspoons grated lemon peel
- 1 teaspoon garlic salt
- 1 teaspoon dried oregano
- 1 teaspoon dried thyme
- 1 teaspoon dried rosemary, crushed
- 1 teaspoon ground mustard
- 1 boneless leg of lamb (4 pounds), rolled and tied

1. In a small bowl, combine the first seven ingredients. Rub over leg of lamb. Cover and refrigerate overnight.
2. Preheat oven to 325°. Place lamb on a rack in a shallow roasting pan. Bake, uncovered, 1¾ to 2¼ hours or until meat reaches desired doneness (for medium-rare, a thermometer should read 145°; medium, 160°; well-done, 170°).
3. Let lamb stand 15 minutes before slicing.

⑤INGREDIENTS
Honey-Mustard Glazed Salmon

You won't need to fish for compliments from your dinner guests when you serve this spectacular salmon!

—TASTE OF HOME TEST KITCHEN

START TO FINISH: 20 MIN.
MAKES: 10 SERVINGS

- 10 salmon fillets (5 ounces each)
- ⅔ cup packed brown sugar
- 2 tablespoons Dijon mustard
- 2 tablespoons honey
- ½ teaspoon salt

1. Preheat broiler. Place fillets, skin side down, on a greased baking sheet. In a small bowl, combine brown sugar, mustard, honey and salt; spoon over salmon.
2. Broil 3-4 in. from heat 8-12 minutes or until fish flakes easily with a fork.

HERB-ROASTED TURKEY

Glazed Spiral-Sliced Ham

In my mind, few foods in a holiday spread are as tempting as a big baked ham. I always hope for leftovers so we can have ham sandwiches in the following days.

—**EDIE DESPAIN** LOGAN, UT

PREP: 10 MIN. • **BAKE:** 1 HOUR 35 MIN.
MAKES: 12 SERVINGS

- 1 spiral-sliced fully cooked bone-in ham (7 to 9 pounds)
- ½ cup pineapple preserves
- ½ cup seedless raspberry jam
- ¼ cup packed brown sugar
- ¼ teaspoon ground cloves

1. Preheat oven to 300°. Place ham directly on roasting pan, cut side down. Bake, covered with foil, 1¼ to 1¾ hours.

2. In a bowl, mix remaining ingredients. Spread over ham. Bake, uncovered, 20-30 minutes longer or until a thermometer reads 140° (do not overcook).

PAIR IT!
Lightened Up Hash Brown Casserole,
page 141,
is a classic that goes well with the ham.

**GLAZED SPIRAL-
SLICED HAM**

Herb-Crusted Rack of Lamb

For those who enjoy a main course of lamb, here's a quick and delicious treatment for it. The easy prep gives me the extra time I need to focus on other menu items.
—**CAROLYN SCHMELING**
BROOKFIELD, WI

PREP: 15 MIN. • **BAKE:** 30 MIN.+ STANDING
MAKES: 4 SERVINGS

- ½ cup fresh bread crumbs
- 2 tablespoons minced fresh parsley
- 1 tablespoon minced fresh thyme or 1 teaspoon dried thyme
- 1 garlic clove, minced
- 2 tablespoons olive oil
- 2 frenched racks of lamb (1½ pounds each)
- ¼ teaspoon salt
- ¼ teaspoon pepper
- 1 tablespoon Dijon mustard

1. Preheat oven to 375°. In a shallow dish, combine bread crumbs, parsley, thyme and garlic. Add oil and toss; set aside. Sprinkle lamb with salt and pepper. In a large skillet, brown meat on both sides. Brush mustard over top of meat, then roll in crumb mixture.
2. Place racks in a shallow baking pan side by side with bones interlaced resting against each other. Bake 30-40 minutes or until meat reaches desired doneness (for medium-rare, a thermometer should read 145°; medium, 160°; well-done, 170°). Let stand 10 minutes before slicing.

Roasted Cornish Hens with Vegetables

Roasting simply seasoned Cornish game hens and vegetables in one pan results in a full-flavored meal in one.
—**LILY JULOW** LAWRENCEVILLE, GA

PREP: 20 MIN. • **BAKE:** 1¼ HOURS
MAKES: 6 SERVINGS

- 6 medium potatoes, quartered
- 6 medium carrots, cut in half lengthwise and cut into chunks
- 1 large sweet onion, cut into wedges
- ½ cup butter, melted
- 2 teaspoons dried oregano
- 2 teaspoons dried rosemary, crushed
- 1½ teaspoons garlic salt
- 6 Cornish game hens (20 to 24 ounces each)
- 1 tablespoon olive oil
- ¼ teaspoon salt
- ¼ teaspoon pepper
- 6 bacon strips

1. Preheat oven to 350°. In a large bowl, combine first the seven ingredients. Transfer to a large shallow roasting pan.
2. Brush hens with oil; sprinkle with salt and pepper. Wrap a bacon strip around each hen; secure with a wooden toothpick. Tie legs together. Place over vegetables, breast side up.
3. Bake, uncovered, 1¼ to 1¾ hours or until a thermometer inserted into thigh reads 170°-175° and vegetables are tender. Remove hens to a serving platter; serve with vegetables.

SLOW COOKER
Brisket with Cranberry-Horseradish Gravy

Need a fix-it-and-forget-it entree for Christmas? Give this slow cooker specialty a try. I like to serve it with boiled red potatoes.
—**JEANNIE MANGAN** SPOKANE, WA

PREP: 15 MIN. • **COOK:** 6 HOURS
MAKES: 10 SERVINGS

- 1 teaspoon onion powder
- 1 teaspoon salt
- 1 teaspoon coarsely ground pepper
- ½ teaspoon ground allspice
- 1 fresh beef brisket (5 pounds)
- 1 can (14 ounces) whole-berry cranberry sauce
- ¾ cup horseradish sauce
- 2 teaspoons lemon juice
- 1 bay leaf
- 3 tablespoons cornstarch
- ¼ cup cold water

1. Combine the onion powder, salt, pepper and allspice; rub over brisket. Cut brisket in half; place in a 5-qt. slow cooker.
2. Combine the cranberry sauce, horseradish, lemon juice and bay leaf; pour over beef.
3. Cover and cook on low for 6-7 hours or until tender.
4. Remove brisket and keep warm. Strain cooking juices; discard bay leaf. Transfer 3 cups cooking juices to a small saucepan.
5. Combine cornstarch and cold water until smooth; stir into juices. Bring to a boil; cook and stir for 2 minutes or until thickened. Thinly slice beef across the grain; serve with gravy.
NOTE *This is a fresh beef brisket, not corned beef.*

ROASTED CORNISH HENS
WITH VEGETABLES

BRISKET WITH CRANBERRY-
HORSERADISH GRAVY

ORANGE-COCONUT FRENCH TOAST

CHOCOLATE PECAN WAFFLES

BANANA PANCAKE SNOWMEN

Orange-Coconut French Toast

You'll think you woke up in the tropics when you dive into this French toast breakfast. There's a bright, citrusy flavor and a wonderful blend of textures in every slice.

—CAROL GILLESPIE
CHAMBERSBURG, PA

PREP: 20 MIN. • **COOK:** 10 MIN./BATCH
MAKES: 4 SERVINGS

- 1 can (13.66 ounces) coconut milk
- 2 eggs
- ½ cup orange juice
- 1 teaspoon vanilla extract
- ½ teaspoon orange extract
- ½ teaspoon salt
- 1 cup flaked coconut, toasted, divided
- 8 slices white bakery bread (¾-inch thick)
- ½ cup macadamia nuts, chopped and toasted
  Maple syrup and orange slices, optional

1. In large bowl, whisk coconut milk, eggs, orange juice, extracts and salt. Stir in ½ cup coconut. Place bread slices in a 15x10x1-in. baking pan. Pour coconut milk mixture over bread; turn to coat. Let stand 10 minutes.
2. Toast bread on a greased hot griddle over medium heat 3-4 minutes on each side or until golden brown. Transfer to a serving platter. Sprinkle with the remaining coconut and macadamia nuts; keep warm. Serve with maple syrup and orange slices if desired.
NOTE *To toast coconut, spread in a 15x10x1-in. baking pan. Bake at 350° for 5-10 minutes or until golden brown, stirring frequently.*

Chocolate Pecan Waffles

Topped with fresh strawberries and chocolate whipped cream, these tender breakfast treats are rich and luscious enough to be served as dessert. They're sure to delight your family on Christmas morning.

—DIANE HALFERTY
CORPUS CHRISTI, TX

PREP: 15 MIN. • **BAKE:** 5 MIN./BATCH
MAKES: 20 WAFFLES

- ¾ cup semisweet chocolate chips
- ¾ cup butter, cubed
- 2 cups all-purpose flour
- ½ cup sugar
- 3 teaspoons baking powder
- ¾ teaspoon salt
- 3 eggs
- 1½ cups 2% milk
- 3 teaspoons vanilla extract
- ½ cup chopped pecans, toasted
  Chocolate whipped cream in a can and sliced fresh strawberries, optional

1. In a microwave, melt chocolate chips and butter; stir until smooth. Cool to room temperature.
2. In a large bowl, combine the flour, sugar, baking powder and salt. In another bowl, whisk the eggs, milk and vanilla; stir into dry ingredients until smooth. Stir in pecans and chocolate mixture (batter will be thick).
3. Bake in a preheated waffle iron according to the manufacturer's directions until golden brown. Garnish with whipped cream and strawberries if desired.

Banana Pancake Snowmen

Treat yourself to a weekend breakfast with yummy pancakes shaped like snowmen. Let little ones help decorate their characters with pretzels for arms and chocolate chips, raisins or cranberries for faces and buttons.

—PHYLLIS SCHMALZ KANSAS CITY, KS

PREP: 15 MIN. • **COOK:** 5 MIN./BATCH
MAKES: 7 SNOWMEN

- 1 cup complete buttermilk pancake mix
- ¾ cup water
- ⅓ cup mashed ripe banana
- 1 teaspoon confectioners' sugar
  Pretzel sticks, chocolate chips, halved banana slices and/or dried cranberries

1. In a small bowl, stir the pancake mix, water and banana just until moistened.
2. Pour ¼ cup batter onto a greased hot griddle, making three circles to form a snowman. Turn when bubbles form on top. Cook until the second side is golden brown. Transfer to a serving plate. Repeat with remaining batter.
3. Sprinkle with confectioners' sugar. Decorate the snowmen with pretzels, chocolate chips, banana and/or cranberries if desired.

TOP TIP

Consider breakfast an investment in your health. Not only does a nutrient-dense meal boost your vitamin and mineral intake, it can help you stay focused and energized all morning long. By fueling your body right, you may stop yourself from overindulging at the next meal.

So Easy Gazpacho

My daughter got this recipe from a friend and shared it with me. Now I serve it often as an appetizer. It certainly is the talk of the party.
—**LORNA SIRTOLI** CORTLAND, NY

PREP: 10 MIN. + CHILLING
MAKES: 5 SERVINGS

- 2 **cups tomato juice**
- 4 **medium tomatoes, peeled and finely chopped**
- ½ **cup chopped seeded peeled cucumber**
- ⅓ **cup finely chopped onion**
- ¼ **cup olive oil**
- ¼ **cup cider vinegar**
- 1 **teaspoon sugar**
- 1 **garlic clove, minced**
- ¼ **teaspoon salt**
- ¼ **teaspoon pepper**

In a large bowl, combine all the ingredients. Cover and refrigerate at least 4 hours or until chilled.

(5) INGREDIENTS

Sour Cream & Chive Biscuits

Chives add a nice, mild onion flavor to just about any dish, be it soup, dip, baked potato or buttery spread.
—**PRISCILLA GILBERT**
INDIAN HARBOUR BEACH, FL

START TO FINISH: 20 MIN.
MAKES: 16 BISCUITS

- 3 **cups biscuit/baking mix**
- 3 **tablespoons minced chives**
- ⅔ **cup water**
- ⅔ **cup sour cream**

1. Preheat oven to 450°. In a large bowl, combine biscuit mix and chives. Stir in water and sour cream just until moistened.
2. Drop by heaping tablespoonfuls onto a baking sheet coated with cooking spray. Bake 8-10 minutes or until the biscuits are lightly browned. Serve warm.

SO EASY
GAZPACHO

Lightened Up Hash Brown Casserole

As a side for brunch or dinner, this lightened-up casserole is just as good with eggs as it is with chicken. Kids love its cheesy flavor and crispy topping.
—**KELLY KIRBY** SHAWNIGAN LAKE, BC

PREP: 15 MIN. • **BAKE:** 40 MIN.
MAKES: 12 SERVINGS

- 1 package (30 ounces) frozen shredded hash brown potatoes, thawed
- 1 can (10¾ ounces) reduced-fat reduced-sodium condensed cream of chicken soup, undiluted
- 1 cup (4 ounces) shredded reduced-fat sharp cheddar cheese
- ⅔ cup reduced-fat sour cream
- 1 small onion, chopped
- ½ teaspoon salt
- ½ teaspoon pepper
- ¼ cup crushed cornflakes
- 1 tablespoon butter, melted

1. Preheat oven to 350°. In a large bowl, combine the first seven ingredients. Transfer to a 13x9-in. or 3-qt. baking dish coated with cooking spray.
2. In a small bowl, toss cornflakes with melted butter; sprinkle over top. Bake 40-45 minutes or until golden brown.

SLOW COOKER
Sausage Dressing

I first used this recipe on Thanksgiving when there was no room in the oven to bake dressing. The results were fantastic—very moist and flavorful. Everyone loved it. Even family members who don't usually eat dressing enjoyed it!
—**MARY KENDALL** APPLETON, WI

PREP: 20 MIN. • **COOK:** 4 HOURS
MAKES: 12 SERVINGS

- 1 pound bulk pork sausage
- 1 large onion, chopped
- 2 celery ribs, chopped

LIGHTENED UP HASH BROWN CASSEROLE

- 1 package (14 ounces) seasoned stuffing croutons
- 1 can (14½ ounces) chicken broth
- 1 large tart apple, chopped
- 1 cup chopped walnuts or pecans
- ½ cup egg substitute
- ¼ cup butter, melted
- 1½ teaspoons rubbed sage
- ½ teaspoon pepper

1. In a large skillet, cook the sausage, onion and celery over medium heat until meat is no longer pink; drain. Transfer to a greased 5-qt. slow cooker. Stir in the remaining ingredients.
2. Cover and cook on low for 4-5 hours or until a thermometer reads 160°.

Ginger Squash Soup

Guests always like the beautiful golden color and creamy consistency of this soup. A touch of ginger adds a spark to the mild squash flavor.
—**LAUREL LESLIE** SONORA, CA

PREP: 10 MIN. • **COOK:** 40 MIN.
MAKES: 6 SERVINGS

- 3 cups chicken broth
- 2 packages (10 ounces each) frozen cooked winter squash, thawed
- 1 cup unsweetened applesauce
- 3 tablespoons sugar
- 1 teaspoon ground ginger
- ½ teaspoon salt
- ½ cup heavy whipping cream, whipped

In a large saucepan, simmer broth and squash. Add the applesauce, sugar, ginger and salt. Bring to a boil. Reduce heat to low; stir in cream. Cook for 30 minutes or until soup reaches desired consistency, stirring occasionally.

Baked Creamy Spinach

Even folks not fond of spinach find this creamy casserole irresistible. It's a classic for our holidays.

—SUE DODD FRIENDSVILLE, TN

PREP: 10 MIN. • **BAKE:** 30 MIN.
MAKES: 6-8 SERVINGS

- 1   large onion, chopped
- 1   tablespoon butter
- 1   package (8 ounces) cream cheese, cubed
- ¼   cup 2% milk
- 1½   cups (6 ounces) shredded Parmesan cheese, divided
- ½   teaspoon cayenne pepper
- ¼   teaspoon salt
- ⅛   teaspoon pepper
- 2   packages (10 ounces each) frozen chopped spinach, thawed and squeezed dry

1. Preheat oven to 425°. In a large saucepan, saute onion in butter until tender. Add cream cheese and milk; stir until melted. Stir in 1 cup Parmesan cheese, cayenne, salt and pepper. Stir in spinach.
2. Transfer to a greased 1½-qt. baking dish. Sprinkle with the remaining Parmesan cheese. Bake, uncovered, 30-35 minutes or until hot and bubbly.

Creamy 'n' Fruity Gelatin Salad

I can remember looking forward to eating this pretty salad when I was a child. My grandmother served it during the holidays and on other special occasions and my mother did the same.

—ELAINE SCHMIT MIFFLINTOWN, PA

PREP: 15 MIN. + CHILLING
MAKES: 10 SERVINGS

- 2   packages (3 ounces each) orange gelatin

- 1   cup boiling water
- 1   pint orange or pineapple sherbet
- 1   can (11 ounces) mandarin oranges, drained
- 1   can (8 ounces) crushed pineapple, drained
- 1   cup miniature marshmallows
- 1   cup heavy whipping cream, whipped

1. In a large bowl, dissolve gelatin in boiling water. Add sherbet; stir until smooth. Stir in the oranges, pineapple and marshmallows. Fold in whipped cream.
2. Pour into a 6-cup serving bowl. Cover and refrigerate for 3-4 hours or until set.

Oyster Corn Chowder

Chock-full of mushrooms, corn and oysters, this robust soup comes together easily with a can of cream-style corn and a little half-and-half cream.

—LEWY OLFSON MADISON, WI

START TO FINISH: 20 MIN.
MAKES: 4 SERVINGS

- 2   cans (8 ounces each) whole oysters, undrained
- 1   can (14¾ ounces) cream-style corn
- 1   cup half-and-half cream
- 2   cans (4 ounces each) mushroom stems and pieces, drained
- 2   tablespoons butter
- ¼   teaspoon Worcestershire sauce
- ⅛   teaspoon pepper

In a large saucepan, combine all ingredients. Cook, uncovered, over medium-low heat until heated through (do not boil), stirring occasionally.

Mango Salsa

Mango adds an interesting twist to this healthy and colorful fruit salsa. I like it as an appetizer with chips, but it's also great served over salmon.

—MALA UDAYAMURTHY SAN JOSE, CA

START TO FINISH: 15 MIN.
MAKES: 2¼ CUPS

- 2   medium mangoes, peeled and finely chopped
- ¼   cup finely chopped red onion
- ¼   cup finely chopped green pepper
- ¼   cup finely chopped sweet red pepper
- 1   jalapeno pepper, chopped
- 3   tablespoons minced fresh cilantro
- 2   tablespoons cider vinegar
- 1   tablespoon sugar
- 1   tablespoon olive oil
- ½   teaspoon salt
- ½   teaspoon pepper
    Baked potato chips

In a bowl, mix first 11 ingredients; chill. Serve with chips.
NOTE *Wear disposable gloves when cutting hot peppers; the oils can burn skin. Avoid touching your face.*

> ## HOW TO

CUT A MANGO
Cut each side from mango, then score sides lengthwise and widthwise, without cutting through the skin. Push the skin up, turning the fruit out. Cut fruit off at the skin with a sharp knife.

OYSTER CORN
CHOWDER

MANGO
SALSA

Classic French Onion Soup

I make my signature soup in a French onion soup bowl complete with garlic croutons and gobs of melted Swiss.

—**LOU SANSEVERO** FERRON, UT

PREP: 20 MIN. • **COOK:** 2 HOURS
MAKES: 12 SERVINGS

- 5 **tablespoons olive oil, divided**
- 1 **tablespoon butter**
- 8 **cups thinly sliced onions (about 3 pounds)**
- 3 **garlic cloves, minced**
- ½ **cup port wine**
- 2 **cartons (32 ounces each) beef broth**
- ½ **teaspoon pepper**
- ¼ **teaspoon salt**
- 24 **slices French bread baguette (½ inch thick)**
- 2 **large garlic cloves, peeled and halved**
- ¾ **cup shredded Gruyere or Swiss cheese**

1. In a stockpot, heat 2 tablespoons oil and butter over medium heat. Add onions; cook and stir 10-13 minutes or until softened. Reduce heat to medium-low; cook 30-40 minutes or until deep golden brown, stirring occasionally. Add minced garlic; cook 2 minutes longer.
2. Stir in wine. Bring to a boil; cook until liquid is reduced by half. Add broth, pepper and salt; return to a boil. Reduce heat; simmer 1 hour, stirring occasionally.
3. Meanwhile, preheat oven to 400°. Place baguette slices on a baking sheet; brush both sides with remaining oil. Bake 3-5 minutes on each side or until toasted. Rub toasts with halved garlic.
4. To serve, place twelve 8-oz. broiler-safe bowls or ramekins on baking sheets. Place two toasts in each. Ladle with soup; top with cheese. Broil 4-in. from heat until cheese is melted.

NOTE *The soup can be made up to 3 days ahead. Just before serving, reheat soup, toast baguette slices and assemble and broil as directed.*

English Batter Buns

Since receiving this easy-to-prepare recipe from a dear friend, I've made these rolls often for the holidays.

—**GERALDINE WEST** OGDEN, UT

PREP: 15 MIN. + RISING • **BAKE:** 10 MIN.
MAKES: 1 DOZEN

- 2 **packages (¼ ounces each) active dry yeast**
- 1 **cup warm milk (110° to 115°)**
- ½ **cup shortening**
- 2 **tablespoons sugar**
- 1 **teaspoon salt**
- 2 **eggs**
- 3½ **cups all-purpose flour**
  Melted butter

1. In a large bowl, dissolve yeast in warm milk. Add shortening, sugar, salt, eggs and 2 cups flour; beat on medium speed 3 minutes. Stir in remaining flour until smooth. Cover and let rise in a warm place until doubled, about 30 minutes.
2. Stir batter vigorously for 25 strokes (dough will be slightly sticky). Spoon into greased muffin cups. Tap pans on counter to settle the batter. Cover and let rise until batter reaches tops of cups, about 20 minutes. Meanwhile, preheat oven to 400°.
3. Bake 10-15 minutes or until golden brown. Brush with butter.

CLASSIC FRENCH ONION SOUP

GRANDMA'S POULTRY DRESSING

Grandma's Poultry Dressing

Every family seems to have its own favorite dressing recipe which becomes a tradition, and this is ours. It came from Grandma, who passed it down to my mother. Now our children have carried it into their kitchens. This is truly a good old-fashioned recipe!

—**NORMA HOWLAND** JOLIET, IL

PREP: 20 MIN. • **BAKE:** 40 MIN.
MAKES: 6 CUPS (MAKES ENOUGH TO STUFF A MEDIUM-SIZE TURKEY)

- 1 **pound bulk pork sausage**
- 1 **cup milk**
- 7 **cups coarse dry bread crumbs**
- 1 **cup diced celery**
- 2 **eggs, lightly beaten**
- 2 **to 3 tablespoons minced fresh parsley**
- 2 **tablespoons diced onion**
- ½ **teaspoon salt or salt to taste**

1. Preheat oven to 350°. In a large skillet, brown sausage. Drain and discard drippings. Meanwhile, in a small saucepan, heat milk over medium heat until bubbles form around sides of pan. In a large bowl, combine sausage, milk and remaining ingredients.
2. Transfer to a greased 2-qt. baking dish. Cover and bake 40 minutes or until lightly browned.

PAIR IT!
Turkey and stuffing are a natural combination. Serve this with *Herb-Roasted Turkey, page 134.*

**ROASTED BRUSSELS SPROUTS
WITH HAZELNUTS**

**BUTTERY SWEET
POTATO CASSEROLE**

**ARUGULA SALAD
WITH SHAVED PARMESAN**

(5) INGREDIENTS
Roasted Brussels Sprouts with Hazelnuts

What I love about this recipe is the mix of Brussels sprouts and hazelnuts. This flavorful combo is festive enough for a special occasion yet homey and easy enough for every day.
—**GAIL PRATHER** HASTINGS, NE

START TO FINISH: 20 MIN.
MAKES: 4 SERVINGS

- 3 **tablespoons butter**
- ½ **to 1 teaspoon pepper**
- ½ **teaspoon salt**
- 1½ **pounds fresh Brussels sprouts, trimmed and quartered**
- ⅓ **cup chopped hazelnuts**

1. Preheat oven to 450°. In a small heavy saucepan, melt butter over medium heat. Heat 2-3 minutes or until golden brown, stirring constantly. Remove from heat; stir in pepper and salt.

2. Place Brussels sprouts and hazelnuts in a 15x10x1-in. baking pan coated with cooking spray. Drizzle with butter mixture; toss to coat. Roast 10-15 minutes or until Brussels sprouts are tender, stirring occasionally.

Buttery Sweet Potato Casserole

Whenever we get together as a family for major holidays, my kids, nieces and nephews beg me to make this dish. It goes together in minutes with canned sweet potatoes, which is ideal for the busy holiday season.
—**SUE MILLER** MARS, PA

PREP: 15 MIN. • **BAKE:** 20 MIN.
MAKES: 6-8 SERVINGS

- 2 **cans (15¾ ounces each) sweet potatoes, drained and mashed**
- ½ **cup sugar**
- 1 **egg**
- ¼ **cup butter, melted**
- ½ **teaspoon ground cinnamon Dash salt**

TOPPING
- 1 **cup coarsely crushed butter-flavored crackers (about 25 crackers)**
- ½ **cup packed brown sugar**
- ¼ **cup butter, melted**

1. Preheat oven to 350°. In a large bowl, combine first six ingredients. Transfer to a greased 8-in.-square baking dish. Combine topping ingredients; sprinkle over sweet potato mixture.

2. Bake, uncovered, for 20-25 minutes or until a thermometer reads 160°.

Arugula Salad with Shaved Parmesan

A mother deserves a beautiful salad that combines her favorite flavors, like fresh peppery arugula, golden raisins, crunchy almonds and shredded Parmesan. I put this simple salad together for my mom, and the whole family ended up loving it!
—**NICOLE RASH** BOISE, ID

START TO FINISH: 15 MIN.
MAKES: 4 SERVINGS

- 6 **cups fresh arugula**
- ¼ **cup golden raisins**
- ¼ **cup sliced almonds, toasted**
- 3 **tablespoons olive oil**
- 1 **tablespoon lemon juice**
- ¼ **teaspoon salt**
- ¼ **teaspoon freshly ground pepper**
- ⅓ **cup shaved Parmesan cheese**

In a bowl, combine the arugula, raisins and almonds. Drizzle with oil and lemon juice. Sprinkle with salt and pepper; toss to coat. Divide among four plates; top with cheese.
NOTE *To toast nuts, spread in a 15x10x1-in. baking pan. Bake at 350° for 5-10 minutes or until lightly browned, stirring occasionally. Or, spread in a dry nonstick skillet and heat over low heat until lightly browned, stirring occasionally.*

Squash and Mushroom Medley

Bring a taste of summer to your holiday table with zucchini and summer squash.
—**HEATHER ESPOSITO** ROME, NY

START TO FINISH: 20 MIN.
MAKES: 5 SERVINGS

- 1 **large yellow summer squash, chopped**
- 1 **large zucchini, chopped**
- 1 **medium onion, chopped**
- 2 **teaspoons butter**
- 1 **can (7 ounces) mushroom stems and pieces, drained**
- 2 **garlic cloves, minced**
- ¼ **teaspoon salt**
- ⅛ **teaspoon pepper**

In a large skillet, saute the squash, zucchini and onion in butter until tender. Add the mushrooms, garlic, salt and pepper; saute 2-3 minutes longer or until heated through.

TOP TIP

Summer squash have edible thin skins and soft seeds. Zucchini, pattypan and yellow are the most common varieties. Choose firm summer squash with brightly colored skin that's free from spots and bruises. Generally, smaller-size squash are more tender. Refrigerate in a plastic bag for up to five days.

CHEESE 'N' GRITS CASSEROLE

Cheese 'n' Grits Casserole

Grits are a staple in Southern cooking. Serve this as a brunch item with bacon and eggs or as a side dish for dinner.

—**JENNIFER WALLIS** GOLDSBORO, NC

PREP: 10 MIN. • **BAKE:** 30 MIN. + STANDING
MAKES: 8 SERVINGS

- 4 cups water
- 1 cup uncooked old-fashioned grits
- ½ teaspoon salt
- ½ cup 2% milk
- ¼ cup butter, melted
- 2 eggs, lightly beaten
- 1 cup (4 ounces) shredded cheddar cheese
- 1 tablespoon Worcestershire sauce
- ⅛ teaspoon cayenne pepper
- ⅛ teaspoon paprika

1. Preheat oven to 350°. In a large saucepan, bring water to a boil. Slowly stir in grits and salt. Reduce heat; cover and simmer 5-7 minutes or until thickened. Cool slightly. Gradually whisk in milk, butter and eggs. Stir in the cheese, Worcestershire sauce and cayenne.
2. Transfer to a greased 2-qt. baking dish. Sprinkle with paprika. Bake, uncovered, 30-35 minutes or until bubbly. Let stand 10 minutes before serving.

⑤ INGREDIENTS
Effortless Broccoli Soup

This soup is easy to make, tastes good and is very good for you. Nice and thick, it easily serves as a meal.

—**BETTY VAUGHN** ELKHART, IN

START TO FINISH: 30 MIN.
MAKES: 4 SERVINGS

- ½ cup chopped onion
- ¼ cup butter
- 4 cups chopped fresh broccoli
- 2 cans (14½ ounces each) reduced-sodium chicken broth
- 1 teaspoon garlic powder
- ½ teaspoon pepper
- ¼ teaspoon salt
  Sour cream, optional

1. In a large saucepan, saute onion in butter until tender. Add broccoli, broth and seasonings. Bring to a boil. Reduce heat; cover and simmer 10-12 minutes or until broccoli is tender. Cool slightly.
2. In a blender, cover and process soup until smooth. Return to the pan and heat through. Garnish servings with sour cream.

Creamed Potatoes and Peas

New potatoes and peas are treated to a creamy sauce for this special side.

—**JANE UPHOFF** CUNNINGHAM, KS

START TO FINISH: 25 MIN.
MAKES: 12 SERVINGS

- 2 pounds small red potatoes, quartered
- 3 cups fresh or frozen peas
- 1 cup water
- 2 tablespoons chopped onion
- 2 tablespoons butter
- 3 tablespoons plus 1 teaspoon all-purpose flour
- 1½ teaspoons salt
- ¼ teaspoon pepper
- 2 cups 2% milk
- 1 cup half-and-half cream

1. Place potatoes in a large saucepan and cover with water. Bring to a boil. Reduce heat; cover and simmer 8-12 minutes or until tender. Drain.
2. Meanwhile, place peas and water in a saucepan. Bring to a boil. Reduce heat; cover and simmer 3-5 minutes or until tender. Drain.
3. In a saucepan, saute onion in butter until tender. Stir in flour, salt and pepper until blended; gradually add milk and cream. Bring to a boil; cook and stir 2 minutes or until thickened. Stir in the potatoes and peas; heat through.

Spicy Garlic Shrimp

Zesty, spicy and simple, these garlicky shrimp are perfect for a party. For more fire, substitute minced fresh hot chili peppers for the red pepper flakes.

—**JASMIN BARON** LIVONIA, NY

START TO FINISH: 25 MIN.
MAKES: ABOUT 2½ DOZEN

- **1 pound uncooked medium shrimp**
- **3 garlic cloves, minced**
- **½ teaspoon crushed red pepper flakes**
- **3 tablespoons butter**
- **½ cup white wine**

1. Peel and devein shrimp, leaving tails on.

2. In a large skillet over medium heat, cook garlic and pepper flakes in butter for 1 minute. Add shrimp; cook and stir until shrimp turn pink. Remove from the pan and set aside. Add the wine to the pan; cook until liquid is reduced by half. Return the shrimp to the skillet and heat through.

SWAP IT

If you don't have crushed red pepper flakes in your pantry, use about 2 tablespoons of chopped jalapeno pepper.

CREAMED
POTATOES AND PEAS

SPICY GARLIC
SHRIMP

CHERRY-BRANDY BAKED BRIE

MASHED POTATOES WITH GARLIC-OLIVE OIL

Cherry-Brandy Baked Brie

You won't believe how fast and easy this is to prepare and it's delicious! If you like, you can substitute dried cranberries or apricots, chopped, for the cherries.

—**KEVIN PHEBUS** KATY, TX

START TO FINISH: 20 MIN.
MAKES: 8 SERVINGS

- 1 round (8 ounces) Brie cheese
- ½ cup dried cherries
- ½ cup chopped walnuts
- ¼ cup packed brown sugar
- ¼ cup brandy or unsweetened apple juice
  French bread baguette, sliced and toasted or assorted crackers

1. Preheat oven to 350°. Place cheese in a 9-in. pie plate. Combine cherries, walnuts, brown sugar and brandy; spoon over cheese.
2. Bake 15-20 minutes or until cheese is softened. Serve with baguette.

Mashed Potatoes with Garlic-Olive Oil

Garlic mashed potatoes are high on our love it list. To intensify the taste, I combine garlic and olive oil in the food processor and drizzle it on top of the potatoes.

—**EMORY DOTY** JASPER, GA

START TO FINISH: 30 MIN.
MAKES: 12 SERVINGS (¾ CUP EACH)

- 4 pounds red potatoes, quartered
- ½ cup olive oil
- 2 garlic cloves
- ⅔ cup heavy whipping cream
- ¼ cup butter, softened
- 2 teaspoons salt
- ½ teaspoon pepper
- ⅔ to ¾ cup whole milk
- 3 green onions, chopped
- ¾ cup grated Parmesan cheese, optional

1. Place potatoes in a Dutch oven; add water to cover. Bring to a boil. Reduce heat; cook, uncovered, for 15-20 minutes or until tender.

Meanwhile, place oil and garlic in a small food processor; process until blended.
2. Drain potatoes; return to pan. Mash potatoes, gradually adding cream, butter, salt, pepper and enough milk to reach desired consistency. Stir in green onions. Serve with garlic olive oil and, if desired, cheese.
NOTE *For food safety purposes, prepare garlic olive oil just before serving; do not store leftover oil mixture.*

DID YOU KNOW?

Brie is a soft cheese made from cow's milk, and it's named for the Brie region of France. The cheese is pale yellow with a grayish-white edible rind. The interior is spreadable at room temperature. Use Brie for cheese trays, or melted on sandwiches and in soups or fondues.

Spinach Pear Salad with Chocolate Vinaigrette

Tangy from balsamic vinegar and mellowed with chocolate, this light vinaigrette stays well blended.
—**TASTE OF HOME** TEST KITCHEN

START TO FINISH: 15 MIN.
MAKES: 4 SERVINGS

- 1 ounce milk chocolate, chopped
- 3 tablespoons balsamic vinegar
- 3 tablespoons canola oil
- 1 teaspoon honey
- ¼ teaspoon salt
- ⅛ teaspoon pepper
- 1 package (6 ounces) fresh baby spinach
- 1 large pear, sliced
- 3 tablespoons dried cranberries
- 2 tablespoons sliced almonds, toasted

1. In a microwave, melt chocolate; stir until smooth. Whisk in the vinegar, oil, honey, salt and pepper; set aside.

2. Divide spinach among four salad plates. Top with pear, cranberries and almonds. Drizzle with dressing.

(5) INGREDIENTS
Favorite Mashed Sweet Potatoes

My family likes this because pumpkin pie spice enhances the flavor of the sweet potatoes. I like that it can be made a day ahead.
—**SENJA MERRILL** SANDY, UT

START TO FINISH: 20 MIN.
MAKES: 8 SERVINGS

- 6 medium sweet potatoes, peeled and cubed

- 3 tablespoons orange juice
- 2 tablespoons brown sugar
- 2 tablespoons maple syrup
- ¼ teaspoon pumpkin pie spice

Place potatoes in a Dutch oven and cover with water. Bring to a boil. Reduce heat; cover and cook for 10-15 minutes or until tender. Drain. Mash potatoes with remaining ingredients.

Walnut Rice

Walnuts give a crunchy pop to this rice dish that also contains flavorful sesame seeds and healthy broccoli.
—**VERA WHISNER** ELKTON, MD

START TO FINISH: 20 MIN.
MAKES: 4 SERVINGS

- ⅔ cup chopped walnuts
- ⅓ cup chopped onion
- 1 tablespoon sesame seeds
- ¼ teaspoon salt
- ¼ teaspoon garlic powder
- 3 tablespoons butter
- 1½ cups hot water
- 2 tablespoons soy sauce
- 1½ cups frozen broccoli florets
- 1 cup uncooked instant rice

In a large skillet, saute the walnuts, onion, sesame seeds, salt and garlic powder in butter until onion is tender and sesame seeds are golden brown. Add water and soy sauce; bring to a boil. Stir in broccoli and rice. Cover and remove from the heat. Let stand 5 minutes or until rice is tender.

SPINACH PEAR SALAD WITH CHOCOLATE VINAIGRETTE

(5) INGREDIENTS
Garlic-Cheese Crescent Rolls

Here's a recipe that just couldn't be much quicker or easier and is sure to add a nice touch to any dinner. The garlic and Parmesan flavors really come through. Enjoy!

—**LORI ABAD** EAST HAVEN, CT

START TO FINISH: 20 MIN.
MAKES: 8 SERVINGS

- 1 **tube (8 ounces) refrigerated crescent rolls**
- 3 **tablespoons butter, melted**
- 1½ **teaspoons garlic powder**
- 1 **teaspoon dried oregano**
- 2 **tablespoons grated Parmesan cheese**

1. Preheat oven to 375°. Separate crescent dough into eight triangles. Roll up from the wide end and place point side down 2 in. apart on an ungreased baking sheet. Curve ends to form a crescent.
2. Combine butter, garlic powder and oregano; brush over rolls. Sprinkle with cheese.
3. Bake 10-12 minutes or until golden brown. Serve warm.

Cranberry Broccoli Salad

Since our home state is a top producer of cranberries, I've nicknamed this tasty recipe "Wisconsin Salad." It features sweetened dried cranberries, which our family produces from the fresh crop we harvest every fall.

—**CHERYL URBAN**
WISCONSIN RAPIDS, WI

START TO FINISH: 15 MIN.
MAKES: 6 SERVINGS

- 4 **cups fresh broccoli florets**
- ½ to ¾ **cup thinly sliced red onion**
- 1 **cup dried cranberries**
- ⅓ **cup crumbled cooked bacon**
- ½ **cup mayonnaise**
- ½ **cup half-and-half cream**
- 3 **tablespoons sugar**

In a salad bowl, combine broccoli, onion, cranberries and bacon. In a bowl, combine mayonnaise, cream and sugar until smooth. Pour over broccoli mixture and toss to coat. Refrigerate until serving.

(5) INGREDIENTS
Pancetta-Wrapped Shrimp with Honey-Lime Glaze

Every year during the holidays my family requests these shrimp appetizers. We're all familiar with bacon-wrapped shrimp bites, but my version uses pancetta and a honey-lime cilantro glaze.

—**JENN TIDWELL** FAIR OAKS, CA

START TO FINISH: 25 MIN.
MAKES: 1½ DOZEN

- 6 **thin slices pancetta**
- 18 **uncooked large shrimp, peeled and deveined**
- ¼ **cup honey**
- 2 **tablespoons lime juice**
- 1 **teaspoon hot water**
- 1 **tablespoon minced fresh cilantro**

1. Preheat oven to 375°. Cut each slice of pancetta into three strips. Wrap one strip around each shrimp; secure with a toothpick. Place in a foil-lined 15x10x1-in. baking pan. In a small bowl, whisk honey, lime juice and water until blended; reserve 2 tablespoons for brushing cooked shrimp.
2. Brush half the remaining honey mixture over the shrimp. Bake 5 minutes. Turn the shrimp; brush with remaining half of the honey mixture. Bake 4-6 minutes longer or until pancetta is crisp and the shrimp turns pink.
3. Remove from oven; brush with reserved 2 tablespoons honey mixture. Sprinkle with cilantro.

Buttered Poppy Seed Noodles

Mom's delicious fried noodles are absolute comfort food. Mom would roll out the dough, and we kids got to cut the long noodles and hang them up to dry. To make it easier, I use packaged noodles.

—**SHIRLEY JOAN HELFENBEIN**
LAPEER, MI

START TO FINISH: 25 MIN.
MAKES: 8 SERVINGS

- 1 **package (16 ounces) egg noodles**
- 1 **medium onion, chopped**
- 3 **tablespoons butter**
- 2 **green onions, chopped**
- 2 **tablespoons poppy seeds**
  Salt and pepper to taste
- 1 **tablespoon minced fresh parsley**

1. Cook noodles according to package directions. In a large heavy skillet, saute onion in butter until onion begins to brown. Drain noodles; add to skillet. Cook and stir until noodles begin to brown.
2. Add the green onions, poppy seeds, salt and pepper; cook and stir 1 minute longer. Sprinkle with parsley.

PAIR IT!
Rolls always are a welcome companion to roasts. Serve these with *Teriyaki Beef Tenderloin, page 131.*

GARLIC-CHEESE
CRESCENT ROLLS

CRANBERRY
BROCCOLI SALAD

PANCETTA-WRAPPED SHRIMP
WITH HONEY-LIME GLAZE

**CHRISTMAS TORTELLINI
& SPINACH SOUP**

Christmas Tortellini & Spinach Soup

I made this soup for the first time in the summer, but when I saw its bright red and green colors, the first thought that occurred to me was this would make a perfect first course for Christmas dinner.
—**MARIETTA SLATER** JUSTIN, TX

START TO FINISH: 25 MIN.
MAKES: 6 SERVINGS

- 2 **cans (14½ ounces each) vegetable broth**
- 1 **package (9 ounces) refrigerated cheese tortellini or tortellini of your choice**
- 1 **can (15 ounces) white kidney or cannellini beans, rinsed and drained**
- 1 **can (14½ ounces) Italian diced tomatoes, undrained**
- ¼ **teaspoon salt**
- ⅛ **teaspoon pepper**
- 3 **cups fresh baby spinach**
- 3 **tablespoons minced fresh basil**
- ¼ **cup shredded Asiago cheese**

1. In a large saucepan, bring broth to a boil. Add the tortellini; reduce heat. Simmer, uncovered, for 5 minutes. Stir in beans, tomatoes, salt and pepper; return to a simmer. Cook 4-5 minutes longer or until tortellini are tender.
2. Stir in spinach and basil; cook until spinach is wilted. Top servings with cheese.

Swiss Beer Bread

This recipe isn't greasy like other cheese breads I have tried. It won't last long after you serve it!

—**DEBI WALLACE** CHESTERTOWN, NY

PREP: 15 MIN. • **BAKE:** 50 MIN. + COOLING
MAKES: 1 LOAF (12 SLICES)

- 4 **ounces Jarlsberg or Swiss cheese**
- 3 **cups all-purpose flour**
- 3 **tablespoons sugar**
- 3 **teaspoons baking powder**
- 1½ **teaspoons salt**
- ½ **teaspoon pepper**
- 1 **bottle (12 ounces) beer or nonalcoholic beer**
- 2 **tablespoons butter, melted**

Preheat oven to 375°. Divide cheese in half. Cut half of cheese into ¼-in. cubes; shred remaining cheese. In a large bowl, mix flour, sugar, baking powder, salt and pepper. Stir the beer into dry ingredients just until moistened. Fold in shredded and cubed cheese.

1. Transfer to a greased 8x4-in. loaf pan. Drizzle with butter. Bake 50-60 minutes or until a toothpick inserted near the center comes out clean. Cool 10 minutes before removing from pan to a wire rack.

Broccoli Rice Casserole

When I was little, serving this dish was the only way my mother could get me to eat broccoli.

—**JENNIFER FULLER**
BALLSTON SPA, NY

PREP: 15 MIN. • **BAKE:** 30 MIN.
MAKES: 8 SERVINGS

- 1½ **cups water**
- ½ **cup butter, cubed**
- 1 **tablespoon dried minced onion**
- 2 **cups uncooked instant rice**
- 1 **package (16 ounces) frozen chopped broccoli, thawed**
- 1 **can (10¾ ounces) condensed cream of mushroom soup, undiluted**
- 1 **jar (8 ounces) process cheese sauce**

1. Preheat oven to 350°. In a large saucepan, bring water, butter and onion to a boil. Stir in rice. Remove from heat; cover and let stand for 5 minutes or until water is absorbed.
2. Stir in broccoli, soup and cheese sauce. Transfer to a greased 2-qt. baking dish. Bake, uncovered, 30-35 minutes or until bubbly.

⑤INGREDIENTS
Confetti Corn

This easy dish has tender corn paired with the crunch of water chestnuts, red peppers and carrots.

—**GLENDA WATTS** CHARLESTON, IL

START TO FINISH: 15 MIN.
MAKES: 4 SERVINGS

- ¼ **cup chopped carrot**
- 1 **tablespoon olive oil**
- 2¾ **cups fresh or frozen corn, thawed**
- ¼ **cup chopped water chestnuts**
- ¼ **cup chopped sweet red pepper**
- 1 **teaspoon dried parsley flakes**

In a large skillet, saute carrot in oil until crisp-tender. Stir in the corn, water chestnuts, red pepper and parsley; heat through.

SWISS BEER BREAD

HOW TO

REMOVE CORN KERNELS
Stand one end of the cob on a cutting board. Starting at the top, run a sharp knife down the cob, cutting deeply to remove whole kernels. One medium cob yields ⅓ to ½ cup kernels.

⑤ INGREDIENTS
Crab Rangoon Tartlets

Serve up crab rangoon without all the hassle! These savory bites don't take long to make if company drops over unexpectedly.

—DONNA MARIE RYAN
TOPSFIELD, MA

START TO FINISH: 25 MIN.
MAKES: 2½ DOZEN

- 1 carton (8 ounces) whipped cream cheese
- 3 sour cream onion dip
- ⅔ cup fresh crabmeat
- 2 packages (1.9 ounces each) frozen miniature phyllo tart shells
  Sweet-and-sour sauce, optional

1. Preheat oven to 400°. In a small bowl, beat cream cheese and onion dip until blended; stir in crab. Arrange tart shells on an ungreased baking sheet. Fill with crab mixture.

2. Bake 11-13 minutes or until golden brown and heated through. If desired, serve with sweet-and-sour sauce.

⑤ INGREDIENTS
Marinated Mushrooms and Cheese

I like to serve these savory mushrooms alongside sliced baguettes and crackers.

—KIM MARIE VAN RHEENEN
MENDOTA, IL

PREP: 10 MIN. + MARINATING
MAKES: 12-14 SERVINGS

- ½ cup sun-dried tomatoes (not packed in oil), julienned
- 1 cup boiling water
- ½ cup olive oil
- ½ cup white wine vinegar
- 2 garlic cloves, minced
- ½ teaspoon salt
- ½ pound sliced fresh mushrooms
- 8 ounces Monterey Jack cheese, cubed

1. In a small bowl, combine the tomatoes and water. Let stand 5 minutes; drain.

2. In a large resealable plastic bag, combine the oil, vinegar, garlic and salt; add the tomatoes, mushrooms and cheese. Seal bag and toss to coat. Refrigerate for at least 4 hours before serving. Drain and discard marinade.

Cheese & Herb Potato Fans

On top of tasting great, this is a downright fun way to make and serve potatoes. The fresh herbs, butter and cheeses are just what a potato needs.

—SUSAN CURRY WEST HILLS, CA

PREP: 15 MIN. • **BAKE:** 55 MIN.
MAKES: 8 SERVINGS

- 8 medium potatoes
- ½ cup butter, melted
- 2 teaspoons salt
- ½ teaspoon pepper
- ⅔ cup shredded cheddar cheese
- ⅓ cup shredded Parmesan cheese
- 2 tablespoons each minced fresh chives, sage and thyme

1. Preheat oven to 425°. With a sharp knife, cut each potato into ⅛-in. slices, leaving slices attached at the bottom; fan potatoes slightly and place in a greased 13x9-in. baking dish. In a small bowl, mix butter, salt and pepper; drizzle over potatoes.

2. Bake 50-55 minutes or until potatoes are tender. In a small bowl, toss cheeses with herbs; sprinkle over potatoes. Bake about 5 minutes longer or until cheese is melted.

Honey-Thyme Butternut Squash

This golden, honey-sweetened squash can easily pass as a potato dish. A hearty, pretty side for special autumn meals.

—BIANCA NOISEUX BRISTOL, CT

START TO FINISH: 30 MIN.
MAKES: 10 SERVINGS

- 1 large butternut squash (about 5 pounds), peeled and cubed
- ¼ cup butter, cubed
- 3 tablespoons half-and-half cream
- 2 tablespoons honey
- 2 teaspoons dried parsley flakes
- ½ teaspoon salt
- ⅛ teaspoon dried thyme
- ⅛ teaspoon coarsely ground pepper

1. In a saucepan, bring 1 in. of water to a boil. Add squash; cover and cook 10-15 minutes or until tender.

2. Drain. Mash squash with the remaining ingredients.

⑤ INGREDIENTS
Baked Broccolini

Broccoli is my favorite vegetable, but I heard about Broccolini and wanted to try it out. This is really tasty.

—KATIE HELLIWELL HINSDALE, IL

START TO FINISH: 15 MIN.
MAKES: 4 SERVINGS

- ¾ pound Broccolini or broccoli spears
- 2 tablespoons lemon juice
- 2 tablespoons olive oil
- ½ teaspoon salt
- ⅛ teaspoon pepper

1. Preheat oven to 425°. Place Broccolini in a greased 15x10x1-in. baking pan. Combine lemon juice, oil, salt and pepper; drizzle over Broccolini and toss to coat.

2. Bake, uncovered, 10-15 minutes or until the Broccolini is tender, stirring occasionally.

CHEESE & HERB
POTATO FANS

HONEY-THYME
BUTTERNUT SQUASH

⑤ INGREDIENTS
Garlic Knots

These novel knots are handy because they can be made ahead of time.
—**JANE PASCHKE** UNIVERSITY PARK, FL

START TO FINISH: 30 MIN.
MAKES: 2½ DOZEN

- 1 **tube (12 ounces) refrigerated buttermilk biscuits**
- ¼ **cup canola oil**
- 3 **tablespoons grated Parmesan cheese**
- 1 **teaspoon garlic powder**
- 1 **teaspoon dried oregano**
- 1 **teaspoon dried parsley flakes**

1. Preheat oven to 400°. Cut each biscuit into thirds. Roll each piece into a 3-in. rope and tie into a knot; tuck ends under. Place 2 in. apart on a greased baking sheet. Bake 8-10 minutes or until golden brown.
2. In a large bowl, combine the remaining ingredients; add the warm knots and gently toss to coat.

Corn Bread Dressing

I revised a main-dish casserole to make this unique stuffing side dish. I've often delivered it, along with pork or chicken, to friends who are just out of the hospital.
—**MARYBETH THOMPSON** THURMONT, MD

START TO FINISH: 30 MIN.
MAKES: 4-6 SERVINGS

- 1 **package (8 ounces) corn bread stuffing cubes**
- 1 **medium onion, finely chopped**
- 1 **celery rib, finely chopped**
- 1 **can (8¼ ounces) cream-style corn**
- 1 **cup water**
- 1 **tablespoon butter, melted**
- 1 **tablespoon spicy brown mustard**

Preheat oven to 375°. In a large bowl, combine stuffing, onion, celery, corn and water. Spoon into a greased 8-in.-square baking dish.

Combine butter and mustard; drizzle over stuffing. Bake, uncovered, 20 minutes or until heated through.

⑤ INGREDIENTS
Balsamic Asiago Salad

You can toss this tasty salad together in minutes. Simply drizzle bottled dressing over the colorful blend of greens, tomato and peppers, add a quick sprinkle of garlic-seasoned cheese and serve.
—*TASTE OF HOME* **TEST KITCHEN**

START TO FINISH: 20 MIN.
MAKES: 6 SERVINGS

- 6 **cups torn mixed salad greens**
- 3 **plum tomatoes, cut into wedges**
- 1½ **cups chopped sweet yellow pepper**
- ⅓ **cup balsamic vinaigrette**
- 6 **tablespoons shredded mozzarella and Asiago cheese with roasted garlic**

In a small serving bowl, combine the salad greens, tomato and yellow pepper. Drizzle with vinaigrette and toss to coat. Sprinkle with cheese.

GARLIC KNOTS

CHRISTMAS RICE

Christmas Rice

My family has enjoyed this delicious rice dish for many years. With chopped red and green peppers, it's both fresh-tasting and festive-looking. It's the perfect light side dish for a big holiday meal.

—CHERE BELL
COLORADO SPRINGS, CO

START TO FINISH: 20 MIN.
MAKES: 6 SERVINGS

- ½ cup finely chopped onion
- 3 celery ribs, finely chopped
- ½ medium sweet red pepper, chopped
- ½ medium green pepper, chopped
- 1 tablespoon butter
- 2 cups chicken broth
- 2 cups uncooked instant rice
- ½ teaspoon salt, optional
- ¼ teaspoon pepper

1. In a skillet, saute the onion, celery and peppers in butter over medium heat for 2 minutes or until crisp-tender. Remove from heat; set aside.

2. In a saucepan, bring broth to a full boil. Remove from the heat. Quickly stir in rice, celery mixture, salt if desired and pepper. Cover and let stand for 6-7 minutes. Stir before serving.

SWAP IT
Use chopped red onion for the regular onion.

SWEET AND SAVORY STUFFING

ITALIAN STUFFED MUSHROOMS

MINTY SUGAR SNAP PEAS

Sweet and Savory Stuffing

Thanks to bacon, apple and sage, this stuffing bursts with delightful flavors. Make it for the holidays, but you'll be tempted to have it during the week, too!

—SHARON FERRANTE
MIFFLINTOWN, PA

PREP: 20 MIN. • **BAKE:** 30 MIN.
MAKES: 7 CUPS

- ½ **pound bacon strips, diced**
- ½ **cup chopped sweet onion**
- 5 **cups unseasoned stuffing cubes**
- 1 **large tart apple, finely chopped**
- 2 **tablespoons minced fresh parsley**
- 1 **teaspoon rubbed sage**
- ½ **teaspoon salt**
- ½ **teaspoon pepper**
- 1¼ to 1¾ **cups chicken broth**

1. Preheat oven to 350°. In a large skillet, cook bacon and onion over medium heat until bacon is crisp. Transfer to a large bowl. Add the stuffing cubes, apple, parsley, sage, salt and pepper. Stir in enough broth to reach desired moistness.

2. Transfer to a greased 8-in.-square baking dish. Bake, uncovered, 30-35 minutes or until golden brown.

Italian Stuffed Mushrooms

I use this delicious recipe that I got from my brother for special occasions. These appealing bites get hearty flavor from the ham, bacon and cheese.

—VIRGINIA SLATER
WEST SUNBURY, PA

START TO FINISH: 30 MIN.
MAKES: 15 SERVINGS

- 4 **bacon strips, diced**
- 30 **large fresh mushrooms**
- 1 **cup onion and garlic salad croutons, crushed**
- 1 **cup (4 ounces) shredded part-skim mozzarella cheese**
- 1 **medium tomato, finely chopped**
- ¼ **pound ground fully cooked ham**
- ¼ **cup grated Parmesan cheese**
- 2 **tablespoons minced fresh parsley**
- 1½ **teaspoons minced fresh oregano or ½ teaspoon dried oregano**

1. Preheat oven to 425°. In a large skillet, cook the bacon over medium heat until crisp. Using a slotted spoon, remove the bacon to paper towels; drain, reserving 1 tablespoon drippings.

2. Remove the stems from the mushrooms; set caps aside. Finely chop half of the stems (save the remaining for another use). Add chopped stems to drippings with bacon; saute 2-3 minutes. Remove from heat. Stir in the remaining ingredients.

3. Firmly stuff crouton mixture into the mushroom caps. Place in a greased 15x10x1-in. baking pan. Bake 12-15 minutes or until the mushrooms are tender.

⑤INGREDIENTS
Minty Sugar Snap Peas

Fresh mint is great on cooked sugar snap peas. Mint is also nice on green beans or carrots.

—ALICE KALDAHL RAY, ND

START TO FINISH: 10 MIN.
MAKES: 4 SERVINGS

- 3 **cups fresh sugar snap peas, trimmed**
- ¼ **teaspoon sugar**
- 2 to 3 **tablespoons minced fresh mint**
- 2 **tablespoons butter**

In a large skillet, bring 1 in. of water, peas and sugar to a boil. Reduce heat; cover and simmer for 4-5 minutes or until crisp-tender; drain. Stir in mint and butter.

Zesty Roasted Vegetables

Even picky eaters will devour these tangy veggies. With only 15 minutes of prep, they leave you plenty of hands-free time.

—TASTE OF HOME ONLINE COMMUNITY

PREP: 15 MIN. • **COOK:** 30 MIN.
MAKES: 9 SERVINGS

- 1 **pound medium fresh mushrooms**
- 3 **cups fresh baby carrots, cut in half lengthwise**
- 2 **medium green peppers, cut into 1-inch strips**
- 2 **medium onions, cut into wedges**
- ⅔ **cup Italian salad dressing**
- ½ **cup plus 2 tablespoons grated Parmesan cheese, divided**
- ¼ **teaspoon salt**
- ¼ **teaspoon pepper**

1. Preheat oven to at 425°. In a large bowl, combine mushrooms, carrots, peppers, onions, salad dressing, ½ cup cheese, salt and pepper. Transfer to an ungreased 15x10x1-in. baking pan.

2. Bake, uncovered, 30-40 minutes or until tender; stir once. Sprinkle with remaining cheese.

(5) INGREDIENTS
Sweet Candied Carrots

These tender, vibrant carrots have a buttery glaze and a mild sweetness. It sure makes carrots seem special.
—**P. LAUREN FAY-NERI** SYRACUSE, NY

START TO FINISH: 30 MIN.
MAKES: 8 SERVINGS

- 2 **pounds carrots, cut into sticks**
- ¼ **cup butter**
- ¼ **cup packed brown sugar**
- ¼ **teaspoon salt**
- ⅛ **teaspoon white pepper**

1. Place carrots in a large saucepan; add 1 in. of water. Bring to a boil. Reduce heat; cover and simmer 8-10 minutes or until crisp-tender. Drain and set aside.
2. In the same pan, combine butter, brown sugar, salt and pepper; cook and stir until butter is melted. Return carrots to the pan; cook and stir over medium heat 5 minutes or until glazed.

(5) INGREDIENTS
Caesar Orzo with Asparagus

My teenage sons love this creamy side dish so much, they'll eat it regardless of which vegetables I use.
—**KAREN HOYLE** EXCELSIOR, MN

START TO FINISH: 25 MIN.
MAKES: 12 SERVINGS

- 2 **cans (14½ ounces each) reduced-sodium chicken broth**
- 2 **cups water**
- 2 **cups uncooked orzo pasta**
- 2 **pounds fresh asparagus, trimmed and cut into 2-inch pieces**
- ⅔ **cup fat-free creamy Caesar salad dressing**
- ⅔ **cup shredded Parmesan cheese**

In a saucepan, bring broth and water to a boil. Add orzo; cook and stir 3 minutes. Add asparagus. Cook, uncovered, over medium heat 6-8 minutes or until orzo and asparagus are tender, stirring frequently; drain. Stir in salad dressing and cheese; toss to coat.

Blue Cheese & Berry Tossed Salad

The sweet tang of blueberries complements the sharpness of blue cheese in this breezy side. Topped with pecans, it could pass for a fancy restaurant's signature salad.
—**RACHAEL ZAVALA** PLEASANT HILL, CA

START TO FINISH: 10 MIN.
MAKES: 9 SERVINGS

- 1 **package (5 ounces) spring mix salad greens**
- 1 **cup (4 ounces) crumbled blue cheese**
- 1 **cup fresh blueberries**
- 1 **cup pecan halves, toasted**
- **VINAIGRETTE**
- ½ **cup olive oil**
- 2 **tablespoons champagne vinegar or white wine vinegar**
- 2 **tablespoons raspberry vinegar**
- ⅛ **teaspoon pepper**
- **Dash salt**

1. In a salad bowl, combine the salad greens, cheese, blueberries and pecans.
2. In a small bowl, whisk the vinaigrette ingredients. Drizzle over salad and toss to coat. Serve immediately.

SWEET CANDIED CARROTS

Squash au Gratin

This is a fabulous dish that has an awesome aroma while baking. Tart apples add a fruity flavor.

—DEB WILLIAMS PEORIA, AZ

PREP: 20 MIN. • **BAKE:** 45 MIN.
MAKES: 9 SERVINGS

- 5½ **cups thinly sliced peeled butternut squash**
- ½ **teaspoon salt**
- ¼ **teaspoon pepper**
- ⅛ **teaspoon ground nutmeg**
- 2 **tablespoons olive oil, divided**
- 1 **cup heavy whipping cream**
- 2 **medium tart apples, peeled and thinly sliced**
- 1 **cup (4 ounces) crumbled Gorgonzola cheese**

1. Preheat oven to 325°. In a large bowl, combine squash, salt, pepper, nutmeg and 1 tablespoon oil; toss to coat. Transfer to a greased 11x7-in. baking dish; pour cream over top.
2. Cover and bake 30 minutes. In a small bowl, toss the apples in remaining oil. Spoon over squash.
3. Bake, uncovered, 25-30 minutes or until squash is tender. Sprinkle with cheese; bake 3-5 minutes longer or until cheese is melted.

PAIR IT!
Moist & Tender Turkey Breast, page 130, and Squash au Gratin make a winning holiday pairing.

BLUE CHEESE & BERRY TOSSED SALAD

SQUASH AU GRATIN

PAIR IT!
This will be great alongside *Provolone-Stuffed Pork Chops with Tarragon Vinaigrette,* page 66.

LEMON PARMESAN ORZO, 202

179

175

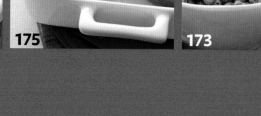
173

All the Extras

A side dish or two makes a meal **feel complete and more balanced.** These no-fuss veggies, pastas, soups and salads will **round out meals** in no time.

DILLED NEW POTATOES, 169

(5) INGREDIENTS
Crispy Ranch Fries

Would you like fries with that? Coming right up is an express recipe for Crispy Ranch Fries with a zippy not-so-secret sauce.

—**PHYLLIS SCHMALZ** KANSAS CITY, KS

START TO FINISH: 20 MIN.
MAKES: 6 SERVINGS

- 1 **package (26 ounces) frozen French-fried potatoes**
- 1 **envelope ranch dip mix, divided**
- ½ **cup mayonnaise**
- ½ **cup ketchup**

1. Preheat oven to 450°. Arrange French fries in a single layer in a greased 15x10x1-in. baking pan. Sprinkle with 2 tablespoons dip mix; toss lightly to coat. Bake 15-20 minutes or until potatoes are lightly browned.
2. Meanwhile, in a small bowl, combine mayonnaise, ketchup and remaining dip mix. Serve with fries.

Herbed Potato Soup

Rosemary and thyme add just the right amount of seasoning to this creamy, satisfying soup.

—**JO CROUCH** EAST ALTON, IL

START TO FINISH: 30 MIN.
MAKES: 5 SERVINGS

- 3 **medium potatoes, peeled and diced**
- 2 **cups water**
- 1 **large onion, chopped**
- ¼ **cup butter, cubed**
- ¼ **cup all-purpose flour**
- 1 **teaspoon salt**
- ½ **teaspoon dried thyme**
- ¼ **teaspoon dried rosemary, crushed**
- ¼ **teaspoon pepper**
- 1½ **cups 2% milk**

1. Place potatoes and water in a large saucepan. Bring to a boil. Reduce heat; cover and simmer 15-20 minutes or until tender.
2. Meanwhile, in another large saucepan, saute onion in butter until tender. Stir in flour, salt, thyme,

rosemary and pepper until blended. Gradually add milk. Bring to a boil; cook and stir 2 minutes or until thickened. Add potatoes with cooking liquid; heat through.

(5) INGREDIENTS
Three-Cheese Creamed Spinach

Parmesan, mozzarella and cream cheese make this dish wonderful.

—**KATHY VAZQUEZ** AMARILLO, TX

START TO FINISH: 20 MIN.
MAKES: 6 SERVINGS

- 2 **packages (10 ounces each) frozen chopped spinach, thawed and squeezed dry**
- 1½ **cups spreadable chive and onion cream cheese**
- 1 **cup grated Parmesan cheese**
- 1 **cup (4 ounces) shredded part-skim mozzarella cheese**
- ¼ **cup butter, cubed**
- ¼ **teaspoon pepper**

In a large saucepan, combine all ingredients. Cook and stir over medium heat 8-10 minutes or until blended and heated through.

(5) INGREDIENTS
Bacon-Tomato Salad

We love this colorful salad that tastes like a piled-high BLT without the time or effort.

—**DENISE THURMAN** COLUMBIA, MO

START TO FINISH: 15 MIN.
MAKES: 6 SERVINGS

- 1 **package (9 ounces) iceberg lettuce blend**
- 2 **cups grape tomatoes, halved**
- ¾ **cup coleslaw salad dressing**
- ¾ **cup shredded cheddar cheese**
- 12 **bacon strips, cooked and crumbled**

In a large bowl, toss together the lettuce blend and the tomatoes. Drizzle with dressing; sprinkle with cheese and bacon.

HERBED POTATO SOUP

THREE-CHEESE CREAMED SPINACH

BACON-TOMATO SALAD

DILLED NEW
POTATOES

WINTER
SALAD

HONEY MUSTARD
COLESLAW

Dilled New Potatoes

With six kids at home, I try to grow as much of our own food as possible, and our big potato patch means easy and affordable meals for much of the year. For this fresh and tasty side dish, I season red potatoes with homegrown dill.

—JENNIFER FERRIS BRONSON, MI

START TO FINISH: 25 MIN.
MAKES: 8 SERVINGS

- 2 **pounds baby red potatoes (1¾ inch wide, about 24)**
- ¼ **cup butter, melted**
- 2 **tablespoons snipped fresh dill**
- 1 **tablespoon lemon juice**
- 1 **teaspoon salt**
- ½ **teaspoon pepper**

1. Place potatoes in a Dutch oven; add water to cover. Bring to a boil. Reduce heat; cook, uncovered, 15-20 minutes or until tender.
2. Drain; return to pan. Mix remaining ingredients; drizzle over potatoes and toss to coat.

Winter Salad

I make this salad for special dinners. Everyone loves the combination of flavors and interesting textures of the pears, walnuts, greens and Gorgonzola cheese. It's nice for winter when other fruits aren't readily available.

—LYNN GANSER OAKLAND, CA

START TO FINISH: 20 MIN.
MAKES: 6 SERVINGS

- 1 **garlic clove, peeled and halved**
- 2 **tablespoons lemon juice**
- 2 **tablespoons honey**
- ⅛ **teaspoon salt**
- 2 **medium ripe pears, thinly sliced**
- 8 **cups torn mixed salad greens**
- ½ **cup chopped walnuts, toasted**
- ⅓ **cup crumbled Gorgonzola cheese**

Rub garlic clove over the bottom and sides of a large salad bowl; discard garlic. In the bowl, combine lemon juice, honey and salt. Add pears; gently toss to coat. Add the greens, walnuts and cheese; toss to coat.

Honey Mustard Coleslaw

I switched up a family coleslaw recipe—using packaged shredded cabbage is a real time-saver. And now there's very little cleanup!

—REBECCA ANDERSON MELISSA, TX

START TO FINISH: 10 MIN.
MAKES: 5 SERVINGS

- 1 **package (14 ounces) coleslaw mix**
- ½ **cup mayonnaise**
- 2 **tablespoons honey**
- 1 **tablespoon cider vinegar**
- 1 **tablespoon spicy brown mustard**
- ½ **teaspoon lemon-pepper seasoning**
- ⅛ **teaspoon celery seed**

Place coleslaw mix in a large bowl. Combine the remaining ingredients. Pour over coleslaw mix and toss to coat. Serve immediately or chill until serving.

Vegetable Rice Medley

When my kids were toddlers, I created this recipe. The veggies and rice were small enough for them to pick up with their fingers.

—COLEEN MARTIN BROOKFIELD, WI

START TO FINISH: 20 MIN.
MAKES: 4-6 SERVINGS

- 1 **cup uncooked long grain rice**
- 2¼ **cups water**
- 2 **to 3 tablespoons onion or vegetable soup mix**
- ¼ **teaspoon salt**
- 2 **cups frozen corn, peas or mixed vegetables**

In a large saucepan, combine the rice, water, soup mix and salt; bring to a boil. Add the vegetables; return to a boil. Reduce heat; cover and simmer for 15 minutes. Cook until rice and vegetables are tender.

Maple-Pecan Brussels Sprouts

I found this recipe in the local paper. It puts a holiday-worthy twist on basic Brussels sprouts. Double it for a memorable Thanksgiving side dish.

—MAUREEN BAISDEN CANAL WINCHESTER, OH

START TO FINISH: 20 MIN.
MAKES: 4 SERVINGS

- 1 **pound fresh Brussels sprouts, halved**
- 2 **tablespoons butter**
- 1½ **teaspoons cider vinegar**
- 1½ **teaspoons maple syrup**
- ½ **teaspoon salt**
- ¼ **teaspoon pepper**
- ⅓ **cup chopped pecans, toasted**

Saute Brussels sprouts in butter in a large skillet 8-10 minutes until tender. Add vinegar, syrup, salt and pepper; cook and stir for 1 minute longer. Sprinkle with pecans.

DID YOU KNOW?

The sap from maple trees is mostly water, which evaporates during boiling in the process of making maple syrup and maple sugar. The sap is collected for about a month at late winter or early spring. The first sap from the trees produces a sweet, light amber syrup with a slight maple flavor. The last sap produces a darker syrup with a more intense maple flavor.

GLAZED
SNAP PEAS

CHEESE
FRIES

(5) INGREDIENTS

Glazed Snap Peas

For me, veggies are a must-have at
with every meal, and this recipe is
perfect for busy days. The naturally
sweet taste of the snap peas makes
this a nice side dish on any table.
—**IDA TUEY** KOKOMO, IN

START TO FINISH: 20 MIN.
MAKES: 10 SERVINGS

- 2 **packages (24 ounces each)
  frozen sugar snap peas**
- ¼ **cup honey**
- 2 **tablespoons butter**
- 1 **teaspoon salt**
- ¼ **teaspoon crushed red pepper
  flakes**
- ¼ **cup real bacon bits**

Cook peas according to package
directions; drain. Stir in the honey,
butter, salt and pepper flakes.
Sprinkle with bacon.

SWAP IT
Substitute frozen
sweet potato fries for
the steak fries.

Cheese Fries

I came up with this recipe after
my daughter had cheese fries at a
restaurant and couldn't stop talking
about them. She loves that I can fix
them so quickly at home.
—**MELISSA TATUM** GREENSBORO, NC

START TO FINISH: 20 MIN.
MAKES: 8 TO 10 SERVINGS

- 1 **package (28 ounces) frozen
  steak fries**
- 1 **can (10¾ ounces) condensed
  cheddar cheese soup,
  undiluted**
- ¼ **cup 2% milk**
- ½ **teaspoon garlic powder**
- ¼ **teaspoon onion powder
  Paprika**

1. Preheat oven to 450°. Arrange
steak fries in a single layer in two
greased 15x10x1-in. baking pans.
Bake 15-18 minutes or until tender
and golden brown.
2. Meanwhile, in a small saucepan,
combine the soup, milk, garlic
powder and onion powder; heat
through. Drizzle over the fries;
sprinkle with paprika.

Thymed Zucchini Saute

Simple and flavorful, this side is a
tasty and healthy way to use up all
those zucchini that are taking over
your garden. It's ready in no time!
—**BOBBY TAYLOR** ULSTER PARK, NY

START TO FINISH: 15 MIN.
MAKES: 4 SERVINGS

- 1 **tablespoon olive oil**
- 1 **pound medium zucchini,
  quartered lengthwise and
  halved**
- ¼ **cup finely chopped onion**
- ½ **vegetable bouillon cube,
  crushed**
- 2 **tablespoons minced fresh
  parsley**
- 1 **teaspoon minced fresh thyme
  or ¼ teaspoon dried thyme**

In a large skillet, heat oil over
medium-high heat. Add zucchini,
onion and bouillon; cook and stir
4-5 minutes or until zucchini is
crisp-tender. Sprinkle with herbs.
NOTE *This recipe was prepared with
Knorr vegetable bouillon.*

THYMED
ZUCCHINI SAUTE

CREAMY HAM &
CORN SOUP

Creamy Ham & Corn Soup

Here's a quick and easy soup that really hits the spot on a cold winter night (and yes, we do occasionally have those in Arizona). I like to serve it with a salad and homemade bread.
—**AUDREY THIBODEAU** GILBERT, AZ

START TO FINISH: 30 MIN.
MAKES: 7 SERVINGS

- 2 **cans (14½ ounces each) chicken broth**
- 2 **cups fresh or frozen corn**
- 1 **cup half-and-half cream**
- ⅓ **cup chopped onion**
- ⅓ **cup chopped sweet red pepper**
- ¼ **cup plus 3 tablespoons all-purpose flour**
- ½ **cup cold water**
- ½ **teaspoon salt**
- ¼ **teaspoon pepper**
- 1 **cup diced fully cooked ham**
  Snipped fresh dill, optional

1. Combine the broth, corn, cream, onion and red pepper in a large saucepan. Bring to a boil. Combine the flour, water, salt and pepper until smooth; gradually stir into pan. Bring to a boil; cook and stir 2 minutes or until thickened. Stir in ham.

2. Reduce heat; cover and simmer 10-15 minutes or until vegetables are tender. Garnish servings with dill if desired.

TOP TIP

Add a little eye appeal to soups with some simple garnishes. Depending on the type of soup, add croutons, chopped fresh herbs, a sprinkle of nuts, sliced green onions, slivers of fresh vegetables, shredded cheese, a dollop of sour cream or some crumbled bacon.

Sunny Strawberry & Cantaloupe Salad

My little ones absolutely love this salad and ask me to make it all the time. Fruit and cheese taste delish together and the kids like to bite into the crunchy sunflower seeds.

—AYSHA SCHURMAN AMMON, ID

START TO FINISH: 15 MIN.
MAKES: 4 SERVINGS

- 1 cup sliced fresh strawberries
- 1 cup cubed cantaloupe
- ½ cup (about 2 ounces) cubed part-skim mozzarella cheese
- 2 tablespoons raspberry vinaigrette
- ½ cup fresh raspberries
- 1 tablespoon sunflower kernels
  Thinly sliced fresh mint leaves, optional

In a large bowl, combine the strawberries, cantaloupe and cheese. Drizzle with vinaigrette and toss to coat. Just before serving, gently stir in raspberries; top with sunflower kernels. If desired, sprinkle with mint.

Dill & Chive Peas

Growing my own vegetables and herbs helps keep things fresh in the kitchen. This side is a breeze to make.

—TANNA RICHARD CEDAR RAPIDS, IA

START TO FINISH: 10 MIN.
MAKES: 4 SERVINGS

- 1 package (16 ounces) frozen peas
- ¼ cup snipped fresh dill
- 2 tablespoons minced fresh chives
- 1 tablespoon butter
- 1 teaspoon lemon-pepper seasoning
- ¼ teaspoon kosher salt

Cook peas according to package directions. Stir in remaining ingredients; serve immediately.

SUNNY STRAWBERRY & CANTALOUPE SALAD

DILL & CHIVE PEAS

Easy Sauteed Spinach

Spinach doesn't have to be bland—dress up the everyday veggie with garlic, onion, a lick of sherry and a sprinkling of pine nuts.

—TASTE OF HOME TEST KITCHEN

START TO FINISH: 20 MIN.
MAKES: 4 SERVINGS

- 1 small onion, finely chopped
- 1 garlic clove, minced
- 2 packages (6 ounces each) fresh baby spinach
- 3 tablespoons sherry or reduced-sodium chicken broth
- ¼ teaspoon salt
- ⅛ teaspoon pepper
- 1 tablespoon pine nuts

In a large nonstick skillet coated with cooking spray, saute onion until tender. Add garlic; cook 1 minute longer. Stir in spinach, sherry, salt and pepper; cook and stir 4-5 minutes or until spinach is wilted. Sprinkle with pine nuts.

Spanish Rice

This rice recipe has been in our family for years. It's handy when you're in a hurry for a side dish to complement almost any main dish, not just Tex-Mex fare. Made with vegetable broth, it's ideal to serve to your friends who are vegetarians.

—SHARON DONAT KALISPELL, MT

START TO FINISH: 30 MIN.
MAKES: 6 SERVINGS

- 1 can (14½ ounces) vegetable broth
- 1 can (14½ ounces) stewed tomatoes
- 1 cup uncooked long grain rice
- 1 teaspoon olive oil
- 1 teaspoon chili powder
- ¼ teaspoon dried oregano
- ¼ teaspoon garlic salt

In a large saucepan, combine all ingredients. Bring to a boil. Reduce heat; cover and simmer 20-25 minutes or until rice is tender and liquid is absorbed.

Mushroom & Zucchini Pesto Saute

With pesto and a handful of other ingredients, you can make a quick but delicious side dish. It goes together easily on the stove.

—BENJAMIN SMITH BEAUMONT, TX

START TO FINISH: 10 MIN.
MAKES: 4 SERVINGS

- 2 teaspoons olive oil
- ½ pound sliced fresh mushrooms
- 1 small onion, chopped
- 2 medium zucchini, cut into ¼ inch slices
- 3 tablespoons prepared pesto
- ¼ teaspoon lemon-pepper seasoning

In a large skillet, heat oil over medium-high heat. Add the mushrooms and onion; cook and stir 2 minutes. Add zucchini; cook and stir until vegetables are tender. Stir in pesto and lemon-pepper.

Balsamic Broiled Asparagus

My simple asparagus dish is a tasty side that goes well with pasta or with grilled steak, pork or chicken.

—HOLLY BAUER WEST BEND, WI

START TO FINISH: 15 MIN.
MAKES: 4 SERVINGS

- 1 pound fresh asparagus, trimmed
- 3 tablespoons balsamic vinegar
- 2 tablespoons olive oil
- ½ teaspoon salt
- ¼ teaspoon pepper

1. Place the asparagus in an ungreased 15x10x1-in. baking pan. In a small bowl, combine vinegar, oil, salt and pepper. Brush half of the mixture over asparagus.
2. Broil 4 in. from heat 8-10 minutes or until tender, stirring occasionally. Brush with the remaining mixture.

EASY SAUTEED SPINACH

COCONUT ACORN SQUASH

Coconut Acorn Squash

Save yourself some time in the kitchen and toss the squash in the microwave for a truly fast dish. Sometimes squash can be a bit tasteless. I conquer this by adding a bit of mango chutney and coconut—they really makes the flavor pop.

—**DEIRDRE COX** KANSAS CITY, MO

START TO FINISH: 20 MIN.
MAKES: 4 SERVINGS

- 2 **small acorn squash**
- ¼ **cup mango chutney**
- ¼ **cup flaked coconut**
- 3 **tablespoons butter, melted**
- ¼ **teaspoon salt**
- ⅛ **teaspoon pepper**

1. Cut each squash in half; remove and discard seeds. Place squash in a microwave-safe dish, cut side down. Microwave, covered, on high 10-12 minutes or until tender.
2. Turn squash cut side up. Mix the chutney, coconut and melted butter; spoon into centers of the squash. Sprinkle with salt and pepper. Microwave, covered, on high for 2-3 minutes or until heated through.
NOTE *This recipe was tested in a 1,100-watt microwave.*

PAIR IT!
Cola BBQ Chicken,
page 83, goes well
with this squash.

Sweet Potato Biscuits

Just four ingredients make these tender biscuits. I modified my grandma's recipe to make it shorter and quicker.

—PAM BOUILLION RAYNE, LA

START TO FINISH: 25 MIN.
MAKES: ABOUT 1 DOZEN

- 2½ cups biscuit/baking mix
- 1½ cups canned sweet potatoes
- 6 tablespoons milk
- ⅓ cup butter, melted

1. Preheat oven to 425°. Place biscuit mix in a large bowl. In a small bowl, mash sweet potatoes; stir in milk and butter. Stir into the biscuit mix just until moistened.
2. Drop by heaping tablespoonfuls 2 in. apart onto a greased baking sheet. Bake 8-10 minutes or until golden brown. Serve warm.

Lemon-Feta Angel Hair

Serve my pasta side with any light chicken or fish dish. For an easy entree, toss the pasta with asparagus and chopped cooked chicken or shrimp.

—MELISSA JUST MINNEAPOLIS, MN

START TO FINISH: 20 MIN.
MAKES: 4 SERVINGS

- 8 ounces uncooked angel hair pasta
- 2 garlic cloves, minced
- 2 tablespoons olive oil

- 1 package (4 ounces) crumbled feta cheese
- 2 teaspoons grated lemon peel
- ½ teaspoon dried oregano
- ½ teaspoon salt
- ½ teaspoon pepper

1. Cook pasta according to the package directions.
2. In a large skillet, saute garlic in oil 1 minute. Drain pasta; stir into skillet. Add remaining ingredients; toss to coat.

Apple Salad with Maple-Mustard Vinaigrette

This seasonal salad will be a hit at any gathering. It's also easy for weeknights; just halve the recipe.

—BETH DAUENHAUER PUEBLO, CO

START TO FINISH: 15 MIN.
MAKES: 12 SERVINGS (1 CUP EACH)

- ¼ cup thawed frozen apple juice concentrate
- 2 tablespoons cider vinegar
- 2 tablespoons canola oil
- 2 tablespoons spicy brown mustard
- 2 tablespoons maple syrup
- ¼ teaspoon salt
- ⅛ teaspoon pepper

SALAD
- 9 cups torn mixed salad greens
- 2 large tart apples, chopped
- 1 small red onion, thinly sliced
- ⅓ cup chopped walnuts, toasted

1. In a small bowl, whisk the first seven ingredients.
2. In a large bowl, combine salad greens, apples, onion and walnuts. Drizzle with the vinaigrette; toss to coat.
NOTE *To toast nuts, spread in a 15x10x1-in. baking pan. Bake at 350° for 5-10 minutes or until lightly browned, stirring occasionally. Or, spread in a dry nonstick skillet and heat over low heat until lightly browned, stirring occasionally.*

Spinach Rice

I like to serve this Greek-style rice dish alongside steaks with mushrooms. The elegant meal can be doubled for guests.

—JEANETTE CAKOUROS BRUNSWICK, ME

START TO FINISH: 20 MIN.
MAKES: 2 SERVINGS

- ½ cup chopped onion
- 2 tablespoons olive oil
- 2 cups torn baby spinach
- ¾ cup water
- 1 tablespoon dried parsley flakes
- ½ cup uncooked instant rice
- ¼ to ½ teaspoon salt
- ⅛ teaspoon pepper

In a saucepan, saute onion in oil until tender. Add spinach, water and parsley. Bring to a boil. Stir in rice, salt and pepper. Cover and remove from heat; let stand 7-10 minutes or until rice is tender and liquid is absorbed.

Poached Corn

Here's a comforting side dish that is sure to remind you of your mom's cooking. The corn tastes fresh off the cob.

—DONNA SASSER HINDS MILWAUKIE, OR

START TO FINISH: 20 MIN.
MAKES: 6 SERVINGS

- 5 cups fresh or frozen corn
- 2 cups milk
- 4 teaspoons sugar
- 1 tablespoon butter
- ¾ teaspoon salt
- ½ teaspoon pepper

In a large saucepan, combine all ingredients. Cook over low heat 10-12 minutes or until corn is tender, stirring frequently. Serve with a slotted spoon.

**POACHED
CORN**

**OH-SO-GOOD
CHICKEN SOUP**

PAIR IT!
Soup and a
sandwich is such
a natural combo.
Try with *Buffalo
Turkey Burgers,*
page 83.

Oh-So-Good Chicken Soup

I came up with this soup one weekend when my wife and I were hungry for something better than the standard fare. It turned out fantastic.

—**CHRIS DALTON** MUNDELEIN, IL

START TO FINISH: 30 MIN.
MAKES: 6 SERVINGS

- 4 cans (14½ ounces each) reduced-sodium chicken broth
- 2 cups uncooked bow tie pasta
- 1 tablespoon olive oil
- 1 pound boneless skinless chicken breasts, cut into ½-inch strips
- 4 green onions, chopped
- 1 pound fresh asparagus, cut into 1-inch pieces
- 1½ cups sliced fresh shiitake mushrooms
- 1 garlic clove, minced
- ⅛ teaspoon pepper
- 6 tablespoons shredded Parmesan cheese

1. In a large saucepan, bring broth to a boil. Stir in pasta; return to a boil. Reduce heat; simmer, covered, 8-10 minutes or until pasta is tender, stirring occasionally.
2. In a large skillet, heat oil over medium-high heat. Add chicken and green onions; cook and stir 5 minutes. Add the asparagus, mushrooms and garlic; cook and stir 2-3 minutes or until chicken is no longer pink and asparagus is crisp-tender. Sprinkle with pepper.
3. Add chicken mixture to pasta mixture; heat through. Sprinkle with cheese.
FREEZE OPTION *Before adding cheese, cool soup. Freeze soup and cheese separately in freezer containers. To use, partially thaw in refrigerator overnight. Heat soup through in a saucepan, stirring occasionally and adding a little broth if necessary. Sprinkle with cheese.*

Zesty Corn and Beans

When you're in the mood for Mexican food, reach for this recipe. The tomato, corn and bean mixture can also be refrigerated and eaten as a relish without the rice.

—*TASTE OF HOME* **TEST KITCHEN**

START TO FINISH: 25 MIN.
MAKES: 6 SERVINGS

- 1 can (14½ ounces) Cajun or Mexican diced tomatoes, undrained
- 2 cups frozen corn
- 1 cup canned black beans, rinsed and drained
- ¼ teaspoon dried oregano
- ¼ teaspoon chili powder
  Hot cooked rice

In a large saucepan, combine the tomatoes, corn, beans, oregano and chili powder. Cook over medium heat 6-8 minutes or until the corn is tender, stirring occasionally. Serve with rice.

(5) INGREDIENTS
Balsamic Vegetable Salad

Looking for a refreshing and colorful salad? Look no further. This mixture has a tang from balsamic vinegar and is so simple to prepare.

—**EMILY PALUSZAK** SPARTANBURG, SC

START TO FINISH: 10 MIN.
MAKES: 6 SERVINGS

- 3 large tomatoes, cut into wedges
- 3 medium cucumbers, peeled, halved and sliced
- ½ cup olive oil
- ¼ cup balsamic vinegar
- 3 tablespoons water
- 1 envelope Italian salad dressing mix

In a salad bowl, combine tomatoes and cucumbers. In a small bowl, whisk oil, vinegar, water and the dressing mix. Pour over vegetables and toss to coat.

BALSAMIC VEGETABLE SALAD

Emerald Rice

Half-and-half cream and cheddar cheese give this uncomplicated rice dish its down-home flavor.

—**SUE CALL** BEECH GROVE, IN

START TO FINISH: 30 MIN.
MAKES: 8 SERVINGS

 3 cups cooked rice
 1 package (10 ounces) frozen chopped spinach, thawed and squeezed dry
 1 cup (4 ounces) shredded cheddar cheese
 1 cup half-and-half cream
 ½ cup chopped onion
 1 tablespoon butter
 1 teaspoon salt

Preheat oven to 350°. In a bowl, combine all ingredients. Transfer to a greased 1½-qt. baking dish. Cover and bake 25-35 minutes or until heated through.

⑤ INGREDIENTS
Orzo with Parmesan & Basil

Dried basil adds its rich herb flavor to this creamy and delicious skillet pasta dish. Orzo is a rice-shaped pasta that cooks quickly.

—**ANNA CHANEY** ANTIGO, WI

START TO FINISH: 20 MIN.
MAKES: 4 SERVINGS

 1 cup uncooked orzo pasta
 2 tablespoons butter
 1 can (14½ ounces) chicken broth
 ½ cup grated Parmesan cheese
 2 teaspoons dried basil
 ⅛ teaspoon pepper

1. In a large skillet, saute the orzo in butter 3-5 minutes or until lightly browned.
2. Stir in broth. Bring to a boil. Reduce heat; cover and simmer 10-15 minutes or until liquid is absorbed and orzo is tender. Stir in the cheese, basil and pepper.

⑤ INGREDIENTS
Chive Smashed Potatoes

No need to peel the potatoes—in fact, this is the only way we make mashed potatoes anymore. Mixing in the flavored cream cheese is a delightful twist.

—**BEVERLY NORRIS** EVANSTON, WY

START TO FINISH: 30 MIN.
MAKES: 12 SERVINGS (⅔ CUP EACH)

 4 pounds red potatoes, quartered
 2 teaspoons chicken bouillon granules
 1 carton (8 ounces) spreadable chive and onion cream cheese
 ½ cup half-and-half cream
 ¼ cup butter, cubed
 1 teaspoon salt
 ¼ teaspoon pepper

1. Place potatoes and bouillon in a Dutch oven and cover with 8 cups water. Bring to a boil. Reduce heat; cover and cook 15-20 minutes or until tender.
2. Drain and return potatoes to pan. Mash with cream cheese, cream, butter, salt and pepper.

Cheese & Garlic Biscuits

My biscuits won the division Best Quick Bread at my county fair. One of the judges liked it so much, she asked for the recipe! These buttery, savory biscuits go with just about anything.

—**GLORIA JARRETT, TALL PINES FARM** LOVELAND, OH

START TO FINISH: 20 MIN.
MAKES: 2½ DOZEN

 2½ cups biscuit/baking mix
 ¾ cup shredded sharp cheddar cheese
 1 teaspoon garlic powder
 1 teaspoon ranch salad dressing mix
 1 cup buttermilk
TOPPING
 ½ cup butter, melted
 1 tablespoon minced chives

 ½ teaspoon garlic powder
 ½ teaspoon ranch salad dressing mix
 ¼ teaspoon pepper

1. Preheat oven to 450°. In a large bowl, combine baking mix, cheese, garlic powder and salad dressing mix. Stir in buttermilk just until moistened. Drop by tablespoonfuls onto greased baking sheets.
2. Bake 6-8 minutes or until golden brown. Meanwhile, combine topping ingredients. Brush over biscuits. Serve warm.

⑤ INGREDIENTS
Fresh Asparagus with Pecans

This is one of my family's favorite special occasion dishes. We all love the fresh taste of asparagus and we know it's nutritious, too!

—**JENNIFER CLARK** BLACKSBURG, VA

PREP: 15 MIN. + MARINATING
MAKES: 4 SERVINGS

 1 pound fresh asparagus, trimmed
 ¼ cup cider vinegar
 ¼ cup reduced-sodium soy sauce
 2 tablespoons sugar
 2 tablespoons olive oil
 3 tablespoons chopped pecans, toasted

1. In a large skillet, bring 3 cups water to a boil. Add asparagus; cover and boil 3 minutes. Drain and immediately place asparagus in ice water. Drain and pat dry.
2. In a large resealable plastic bag, combine vinegar, soy sauce, sugar and oil. Add the asparagus; seal bag and turn to coat. Refrigerate up to 3 hours.
3. Drain and discard marinade. Sprinkle asparagus with pecans.

CHIVE SMASHED
POTATOES

CHEESE & GARLIC
BISCUITS

FRESH ASPARAGUS
WITH PECANS

BROCCOLI-CHICKEN RICE SOUP

Broccoli-Chicken Rice Soup

I transformed leftover chicken and rice into this tasty soup. It even passed the company test.

—**KAREN REED** MIDDLETOWN, OH

START TO FINISH: 30 MIN.
MAKES: 6 SERVINGS (2½ QUARTS)

- 4 **cups whole milk**
- 2 **cans (14½ ounces each) chicken broth**
- 1 **envelope ranch salad dressing mix**
- 2 **cups fresh broccoli florets**
- ½ **pound process cheese (Velveeta), cubed**
- 3 **cups cooked rice**
- 2 **cups cubed cooked chicken**

In a Dutch oven, combine milk, broth and dressing mix; bring to a boil. Add the broccoli; cook, uncovered, 3-5 minutes or until tender. Stir in process cheese until melted. Add rice and chicken; heat through, stirring occasionally.

⑤ INGREDIENTS

Almond Rice

A side of fragrant almond rice perfectly complements most any type of meat—steaks, chicken or fish.

—**TONYA BURKHARD** DAVIS, IL

START TO FINISH: 10 MIN.
MAKES: 4 SERVINGS

- 1½ **cups water**
- 1½ **cups uncooked instant rice**
- 1 **tablespoon butter**
- ½ **cup slivered almonds, toasted**
- ¼ **teaspoon salt**
- ¼ **teaspoon pepper**
- 1 **tablespoon minced fresh parsley**

In a saucepan, bring the water, rice and butter to a boil. Remove from heat. Cover; let stand 5 minutes or until water is absorbed. Stir in the almonds, salt and pepper. Sprinkle with parsley.

(5) INGREDIENTS
Green Beans with Shallots

My recipe starts with a package of frozen green beans. It's a simple solution for rounding out any meal.
—**LINDA RABBITT** CHARLES CITY, IA

START TO FINISH: 15 MIN.
MAKES: 4 SERVINGS

- 1 package (12 ounces) frozen Steamfresh whole green beans
- 1¾ cups sliced fresh mushrooms
- 2 shallots, chopped
- 1 tablespoon olive oil
- ½ teaspoon salt
- ½ teaspoon dill weed
- ½ teaspoon pepper

1. Cook green beans according to package directions.
2. Meanwhile, in a large skillet, saute mushrooms and shallots in oil until tender. Remove from the heat. Add green beans, salt, dill and pepper; toss to coat.

Pasta with Garlic Oil

My family is Italian, and they can't get enough of this garlic-, mushroom- and herb-loaded dish. Don't rinse the pasta in water after you drain it, or the sauce won't stick.
—**PAM VITTORI** CHICAGO HEIGHTS, IL

START TO FINISH: 20 MIN.
MAKES: 5 SERVINGS

- 8 ounces uncooked spaghetti
- 2 garlic cloves, minced
- ⅓ cup olive oil
- ½ cup jarred sliced mushrooms
- ¼ cup sliced ripe olives
- 2 to 3 teaspoons minced fresh basil
- 2 to 3 teaspoons minced fresh parsley
- ⅛ teaspoon garlic salt
- ⅛ to ¼ teaspoon pepper
- Shredded Parmesan cheese, optional

1. Cook spaghetti according to package directions.
2. Meanwhile, in a large skillet, saute garlic in oil. Stir in the mushrooms, olives, basil, parsley, garlic salt and pepper. Cook for 5 minutes.
3. Drain spaghetti; place in a serving bowl. Pour sauce over pasta; toss to coat. If desired, sprinkle with Parmesan cheese.

(5) INGREDIENTS
Garlic Poppy Seed Spirals

This is a fast, easy way to dress up plain crescent rolls. Adjust the seasoning to your family's taste...or use a little powdered ranch dressing mix as an alternative.
—**STACEY SCHERER** MACOMB, MI

START TO FINISH: 25 MIN.
MAKES: 10 SERVINGS

- 3 tablespoons butter, melted
- 1 teaspoon garlic powder
- 1 teaspoon dried minced onion
- ½ teaspoon poppy seeds
- 1 tube (8 ounces) refrigerated crescent rolls

1. Preheat oven to 350°. In a small bowl, combine the butter, garlic powder, onion and poppy seeds; set aside. Remove the crescent dough from tube; do not unroll. Cut dough into 10 slices; dip one side into the butter mixture.
2. Place buttered side up in an ungreased 9-in. round baking pan. Brush with remaining butter mixture. Bake 14-16 minutes or until golden brown. Serve warm.

GREEN BEANS WITH SHALLOTS

SKILLET SCALLOPED POTATOES

LIME-BUTTERED BROCCOLI

Skillet Scalloped Potatoes

I use the produce from my husband's potato patch to make this side dish.
—**LORI LEE DANIELS** BEVERLY, WV

START TO FINISH: 30 MIN.
MAKES: 4 SERVINGS

- 1 tablespoon butter
- 1 pound small red potatoes, thinly sliced (about 3 cups)
- 1 tablespoon dried minced onion
- ¾ cup chicken broth
- ½ cup half-and-half cream
- ¾ teaspoon salt
- ¼ teaspoon pepper
- 1 cup (4 ounces) shredded cheddar cheese

1. In a nonstick skillet, heat butter over medium heat. Add potatoes and onion; cook and stir 5 minutes.
2. Stir in broth, cream, salt and pepper. Bring to a boil. Reduce heat; simmer, covered, 10-12 minutes or until potatoes are tender. Sprinkle with cheese; cook, covered, 2-3 minutes longer or until cheese is melted.

---

⑤ INGREDIENTS

Lime-Buttered Broccoli

My family got tired of having broccoli the same way every time I made it, so I tried this recipe. The simple butter sauce turns the tender florets into something special.
—**DENISE ALBERS** FREEBURG, IL

START TO FINISH: 20 MIN.
MAKES: 8 SERVINGS

- 8 cups fresh broccoli florets
- 3 tablespoons butter, melted
- 1 tablespoon lime juice
- ¼ teaspoon salt
- ¼ teaspoon pepper

1. Place the broccoli in a steamer basket; place in a large saucepan over 1 in. of water. Bring to a boil; cover and steam 3-4 minutes or until crisp-tender.
2. Meanwhile, in a small bowl, combine remaining ingredients. Drizzle the butter mixture over the broccoli; toss to coat.

Basil Tortellini Soup

For a fast meal, I keep the ingredients on hand for this delicious soup.
—**JAYNE DWYER-REFF** FORT WAYNE, IN

START TO FINISH: 20 MIN.
MAKES: 6 SERVINGS

- 4½ cups chicken broth
- 1 package (9 ounces) refrigerated cheese tortellini
- 1 can (15 ounces) white kidney or cannellini beans, rinsed and drained
- 1 cup chopped fresh tomato
- ⅓ to ½ cup shredded fresh basil
- 1 to 2 tablespoons balsamic vinegar
- ¼ teaspoon salt
- ⅛ to ¼ teaspoon pepper
- ⅓ cup shredded Parmesan cheese

1. In a large saucepan, bring broth to a boil. Add tortellini; cook 7-9 minutes or until tender.
2. Stir in beans, tomato and basil. Reduce heat; simmer, uncovered, 5 minutes. Add vinegar, salt and pepper. Serve with cheese.

BASIL TORTELLINI SOUP

Green Grape Salad

Here's a salad that is convenient and easy to make at any time of the year. The flavors and textures of the fruits combine with the crunchiness of the nuts to become a tasty salad that will be requested often.

—**MARJORIE GREEN**
SOUTH HAVEN, MI

START TO FINISH: 10 MIN.
MAKES: 4 SERVINGS

- 2 **cups green grapes, halved**
- 2 **large firm bananas, sliced**
- 1 **cup chopped walnuts**
- ½ **cup blue cheese salad dressing**
- 6 **tablespoons mayonnaise**
- 4 **teaspoons honey**

In a small bowl, combine grapes, banana and walnuts. In a small bowl, whisk the salad dressing, mayonnaise and honey; pour over grape mixture and toss to coat. Chill until serving.

---

⑤ INGREDIENTS

Speedy Stuffed Potatoes

My stuffed potatoes are always a hit when I serve them. The garlic adds a delicious note to this simple recipe.

—**MARIE HATTRUP** SPARKS, NV

START TO FINISH: 30 MIN.
MAKES: 8 SERVINGS

- 4 **large baking potatoes**
- 3 **tablespoons butter, softened**
- ⅔ **cup sour cream**
- ½ **teaspoon minced garlic**
- ¾ **teaspoon salt**
- ¼ **teaspoon pepper**
- ½ **cup shredded cheddar cheese**

1. Scrub and pierce the potatoes; place on a microwave-safe plate. Microwave, uncovered, on high 10-12 minutes or until tender, turning once.
2. When cool enough to handle, cut potatoes in half lengthwise. Scoop out pulp, leaving a thin shell. In a

large bowl, mash the pulp with butter. Stir in sour cream, garlic, salt and pepper. Spoon into the potato shells.
3. Place on a microwave-safe plate. Sprinkle with cheese. Microwave, uncovered, on high 1-2 minutes or until heated through.
NOTE *This recipe was tested in a 1,100-watt microwave.*

---

⑤ INGREDIENTS

Green Bean & Corn Medley

A colorful side option, this veggie dish helps any entree look even better. Use fresh veggies in the summer or frozen beans and corn in the winter, as suggested below. Either way, it's a winner!

—**KIMBERLY STINE** MILFORD, PA

START TO FINISH: 15 MIN.
MAKES: 4 SERVINGS

- 3 **cups frozen cut green beans, thawed**
- 1 **package (10 ounces) frozen corn, thawed**
- 2 **tablespoons butter**
- 1 **teaspoon canola oil**
- 1½ **teaspoons dried thyme**
- ¼ **teaspoon salt**
  Dash pepper

In a large skillet, saute beans and corn in butter and oil until tender. Stir in the thyme, salt and pepper.

GREEN GRAPE SALAD

CHEESY SUN CRISPS

Cheesy Sun Crisps

The two-cheese flavor of these crisps makes them perfect for snacking.

—MARY DETWEILER
FARMINGTON, OH

PREP: 10 MIN. + CHILLING • **BAKE:** 10 MIN.
MAKES: 32 SERVINGS

- 2 cups (8 ounces) shredded cheddar cheese
- ½ cup grated Parmesan cheese
- ½ cup butter, softened
- 3 tablespoons water
- 1 cup all-purpose flour
- ¼ teaspoon salt
- 1 cup quick-cooking oats
- ⅔ cup roasted salted sunflower kernels

1. In a bowl, combine cheddar and Parmesan cheeses, butter and water until well mixed. Combine the flour and salt; add to cheese mixture. Stir in oats and sunflower kernels. Knead dough until it holds together. Shape into a 12-in. roll. Cover with plastic wrap; chill for 4 hours or overnight.

2. Preheat oven to 400°. Remove the dough from the refrigerator 10 minutes before cutting into ⅛-in. slices. Place on greased foil-lined baking sheets. Bake 8-10 minutes or until edges are golden. Slide crackers and foil off baking sheets to wire racks to cool.

PAIR IT!
These crisps will add a delightful crunch to a menu with *Easy Citrus Ham, page 125.*

EASY GRILLED SQUASH

Easy Grilled Squash

Excellent alongside grilled steak or chicken, this is one of the best ways to prepare butternut squash. As a bonus, butternut squash is full of vitamin A.

—ESTHER HORST MONTEREY, TN

START TO FINISH: 20 MIN.
MAKES: 4 SERVINGS

- 3 **tablespoons olive oil**
- 2 **garlic cloves, minced**
- ¼ **teaspoon salt**
- ¼ **teaspoon pepper**
- 1 **small butternut squash, peeled and cut lengthwise into ½-inch slices**

1. In a small bowl, combine the oil, garlic, salt and pepper. Brush over squash slices.
2. Grill squash, covered, over medium heat or broil 4 in. from heat 4-5 minutes on each side or until tender.

Parmesan-Basil Breadsticks

Round out any Italian meal with these breadsticks hot from the oven.

—MARY RELYEA CANASTOTA, NY

START TO FINISH: 15 MIN.
MAKES: 1 DOZEN

- 1 **tube (11 ounces) refrigerated breadsticks**
- 1 **egg**
- 1 **tablespoon 2% milk**
- ⅓ **cup grated Parmesan cheese**
- ½ **teaspoon dried basil**

1. Preheat oven to 375°. Unroll and separate breadsticks. Twist each breadstick two to three times; place on a greased baking sheet. Whisk egg and milk in a bowl; brush over breadsticks. Mix cheese and basil; sprinkle over tops.
2. Bake 10-12 minutes or until golden brown. Serve warm.

Green Peas with Onion

Just a hint of garlic boosts the flavor in my versatile side dish.

—LORRAINE STROMBERG TAYLOR, TX

START TO FINISH: 20 MIN.
MAKES: 5 SERVINGS

- 1 **medium onion, sliced**
- 1 **teaspoon minced garlic**
- 2 **tablespoons butter**
- 1 **package (16 ounces) frozen peas**
- 3 **tablespoons water**
- ½ **teaspoon salt**
- ¼ **teaspoon pepper**

In a large skillet, saute onion and garlic in butter until tender. Add peas and water. Bring to a boil. Reduce heat; cover and simmer 4-5 minutes or until peas are tender. Season with salt and pepper.

Zesty Crouton Salad

It takes no time at all to prepare the few ingredients for this recipe. And everyone loves the resulting combination of tastes and textures. The salad pairs well with everything from grilled entrees to pasta.

—VALERIE SMITH ASTON, PA

START TO FINISH: 10 MIN.
MAKES: 5 SERVINGS

- 2 **cups grape tomatoes, halved**
- 1½ **cups salad croutons**
- 4 **pieces string cheese, cut into ½-inch pieces**
- 8 **fresh basil leaves, thinly sliced**
- 2 **tablespoons red wine vinegar**
- 1 **tablespoon olive oil**
- ½ **teaspoon minced garlic**

In a large bowl, combine all the ingredients.

ZESTY CROUTON SALAD

Steakhouse Mushrooms

I got this recipe from a friend back in nursing school. Whenever my husband is cooking meat on the grill, you can bet I'll be in the kitchen preparing these mushrooms.

—KENDA BURGETT RATTAN, OK

START TO FINISH: 20 MIN.
MAKES: 4 SERVINGS

- ¼ cup butter, cubed
- 1 pound medium fresh mushrooms
- 2 teaspoons dried basil
- ½ teaspoon dried oregano
- ½ teaspoon seasoned salt
- ¼ teaspoon garlic powder
- 1 teaspoon browning sauce, optional

In a large skillet, heat butter over medium-high heat. Add the mushrooms; cook and stir until tender. Stir in seasonings and, if desired, browning sauce. Reduce heat to medium; cook, covered, 3-5 minutes to allow flavors to blend.

Kielbasa Chili

If you love chili dogs, you'll enjoy this recipe! This combines the flavors of a chili dog in one bowl! I make it when I need a hot, hearty meal in a hurry.

—AUDRA L. DUVALL
CANOGA PARK, CA

START TO FINISH: 20 MIN.
MAKES: 7 SERVINGS

- 1 pound smoked kielbasa or Polish sausage, halved and sliced
- 2 cans (14½ ounces each) diced tomatoes, undrained
- 1 can (15 ounces) chili with beans
- 1 can (8¾ ounces) whole kernel corn, drained
- 1 can (2¼ ounces) sliced ripe olives, drained

In a Dutch oven coated with cooking spray, saute kielbasa until browned. Stir in the remaining ingredients. Bring to a boil. Reduce heat; simmer, uncovered, 4-5 minutes or until the chili is heated through.

Romaine & Orange Salad with Lime Dressing

Three ingredients plus a dressing equals a delightful salad for special occasions. I first had it at a friend's wedding, and it has since become a family favorite.

—LINDA PALLOTTO MANTUA, OH

START TO FINISH: 15 MIN.
MAKES: 6 SERVINGS

- 2 tablespoons olive oil
- 1 tablespoon lime juice
- 1 small garlic clove, minced
- ¾ teaspoon sugar
- ⅛ teaspoon salt
- ⅛ teaspoon grated lime peel
- 6 cups torn romaine
- ½ cup sliced red onion
- 1 can (11 ounces) mandarin oranges, drained

In a small bowl, whisk the first six ingredients. In a large bowl, mix the romaine and onion. Drizzle with the dressing; toss to coat. Top with the mandarin oranges. Serve immediately.

STEAKHOUSE MUSHROOMS

KIELBASA
CHILI

ROMAINE & ORANGE SALAD
WITH LIME DRESSING

**COOL AS A
CUCUMBER SOUP**

(5) INGREDIENTS

Cool as a Cucumber Soup

Chilled soup is a wonderful appetizer or side on a hot summer day. In this version, bright bursts of dill provide a pleasant contrast to the milder flavor of cucumber.

—**DEIRDRE COX** KANSAS CITY, MO

PREP: 15 MIN. + STANDING
MAKES: 7 SERVINGS

   1   pound cucumbers, peeled,
        seeded and sliced
  ½   teaspoon salt
1½   cups fat-free plain yogurt
   1   green onion, coarsely chopped
   1   garlic clove, minced
4½   teaspoons snipped fresh dill
        Additional chopped green
           onion and snipped fresh dill

1. In a colander set over a bowl, toss cucumbers with salt. Let stand 30 minutes. Squeeze and pat dry.
2. Place cucumbers, yogurt, onion and garlic in a food processor; cover and process until smooth. Stir in dill. Serve immediately in chilled bowls. Garnish with the additional onion and dill.

HOW TO

SEED A CUCUMBER

You can quickly seed a cucumber with a spoon. Peel or score cucumber if desired. With a sharp knife, cut lengthwise in half. Using a teaspoon, run the tip under the seeds to loosen and remove.

Special Occasion Salad

This simple salad consistently gets rave reviews. Feel free to change the types of lettuce and dried fruit and even substitute candied pecans for almonds or walnut.

—JEAN FOLLMER LAFAYETTE, CA

START TO FINISH: 20 MIN.
MAKES: 16 SERVINGS (¾ CUP EACH)

- 1 package (6 ounces) fresh baby spinach
- 1 package (5 ounces) fresh arugula or additional baby spinach
- ½ cup dried cherries
- ⅓ cup sliced almonds, toasted
- ¼ cup olive oil
- ¼ cup balsamic vinegar
- ½ teaspoon salt
- ¼ teaspoon pepper
- 1 cup crumbled goat cheese

In a salad bowl, combine the spinach, arugula, cherries and almonds. Combine the oil, vinegar, salt and pepper; drizzle over salad and toss to coat. Sprinkle with goat cheese. Serve immediately.

Rosemary Rice

My full-flavored rice makes a lovely side for a wide variety of main dishes. It's also an easy recipe to double for when you have a few guests.

—SUZANNE MCKINLEY LYONS, GA

START TO FINISH: 30 MIN.
MAKES: 2 SERVINGS

- 1 cup water
- ½ cup uncooked long grain rice
- 1½ teaspoons chopped green onions
- 1 teaspoon reduced-sodium beef bouillon granules
- ½ teaspoon minced fresh rosemary or ⅛ teaspoon dried rosemary, crushed
- ½ teaspoon butter
- ¼ teaspoon dried marjoram
- ¼ teaspoon dried thyme
- ⅛ teaspoon salt

1. In a small saucepan, combine all the ingredients. Bring to a boil. Reduce heat; cover and simmer 15-18 minutes or until the liquid is absorbed and rice is tender.
2. Remove from heat; let stand for 5 minutes. Fluff with a fork before serving.

Cauliflower with Buttered Crumbs

Add home-style flavor and interest to steamed cauliflower with a few ingredients you probably have in your kitchen. Serve this side with a variety of entrees, like baked chicken, grilled steaks, fish or even a burger.

—TASTE OF HOME TEST KITCHEN

START TO FINISH: 20 MIN.
MAKES: 6 SERVINGS

- 1 large head cauliflower, broken into florets
- ⅓ cup butter, cubed
- 1 tablespoon lemon juice
- ¼ cup dry bread crumbs
- ¼ cup grated Parmesan cheese
- 2 tablespoons minced fresh parsley
- ⅛ teaspoon salt
- ⅛ teaspoon pepper

1. Place 1 in. of water in a large saucepan; add cauliflower. Bring to a boil. Reduce heat; cover and simmer 10-12 minutes or until crisp-tender.
2. Meanwhile, in a small heavy saucepan, cook the butter over medium heat 5 minutes or until golden brown, stirring frequently. Remove from heat; stir in the lemon juice.
3. In a small bowl, combine the bread crumbs, cheese, parsley, salt and pepper; stir in 3 tablespoons browned butter.
4. Drain the cauliflower and transfer to a serving dish. Drizzle with the remaining browned butter; sprinkle with the bread crumb mixture.

CAULIFLOWER WITH BUTTERED CRUMBS

(5) INGREDIENTS

In-a-Flash Beans

No one will guess this recipe begins in a can. The chopped onion and green pepper lend a little crunch while barbecue sauce brings lots of home-cooked flavor.

—**LINDA COLEMAN** CEDAR RAPIDS, IA

START TO FINISH: 10 MIN.
MAKES: 4 SERVINGS

- 1 **can (15¾ ounces) pork and beans**
- ½ **cup barbecue sauce**
- ½ **cup chopped onion**
- ¼ **cup chopped green pepper, optional**

In a large saucepan, combine the beans, barbecue sauce, onion and, if desired, green pepper. Cook and stir over medium heat until beans are heated through.

(5) INGREDIENTS

Super-Simple Garlic Broccoli

My kids love broccoli, especially with lots of garlic. This recipe shines on special occasions, but it's so quick that I usually fix it once a week in our home. Everyone gobbles it up.

—**CARAMIA SOMMERS** OSWEGO, NY

START TO FINISH: 20 MIN.
MAKES: 12 SERVINGS (¾ CUP EACH)

- 13 **cups fresh broccoli florets (about 2½ pounds)**
- 3 **tablespoons olive oil**
- 5 **garlic cloves, minced**
- ¾ **teaspoon Italian seasoning**
- ¼ **teaspoon salt**

In a Dutch oven, bring ½ in. of water to a boil. Add broccoli; cover and cook 3-5 minutes or until crisp-tender; drain. Combine the remaining ingredients. Add to broccoli; toss to combine.

(5) INGREDIENTS

Chunky Garlic Mashed Potatoes

I like to dress up these mashed spuds with a whole bulb of roasted garlic. It may seem like overkill, but once the dish is cooked, any harshness mellows out and you're left with sweet and delicate garlic flavor.

—**JACKIE GREGSTON** HALLSVILLE, TX

START TO FINISH: 30 MIN.
MAKES: 9 SERVINGS

- 3 **pounds Yukon Gold potatoes, cut into quarters**
- 1 **whole garlic bulb, cloves separated and peeled**
- ½ **cup butter, cubed**
- ½ **cup half-and-half cream**
- 2 **tablespoons prepared horseradish**
- ¾ **teaspoon salt**
- ¾ **teaspoon pepper**
  Fresh thyme leaves, optional

1. Place potatoes and garlic cloves in a large saucepan; cover with water. Bring to a boil. Reduce heat; cover and cook 15-20 minutes or until potatoes are tender.
2. Meanwhile, in a small saucepan, heat butter and cream; keep warm. Drain potatoes and garlic; return to pan. Add horseradish, salt, pepper and butter mixture; mash to reach desired consistency. Garnish with thyme if desired.

DID YOU KNOW?

Yellow potatoes are a popular choice for mashing because of their buttery flavor and creamy texture. Russets are another good choice for mashing since their high starch content makes the fluffiest mashed potatoes.

IN-A-FLASH
BEANS

CHUNKY GARLIC MASHED POTATOES

SUPER-SIMPLE GARLIC BROCCOLI

QUINOA TABBOULEH

Quinoa Tabbouleh

When my mom and sister developed several food allergies, we had to modify many recipes. I substituted quinoa for couscous in this tabbouleh.
—**JENNIFER KLANN** CORBETT, OR

PREP: 35 MIN. + CHILLING
MAKES: 8 SERVINGS

- 2 cups water
- 1 cup quinoa, rinsed
- 1 can (15 ounces) black beans, rinsed and drained
- 1 small cucumber, peeled and chopped
- 1 small sweet red pepper, chopped
- ⅓ cup minced fresh parsley
- ¼ cup lemon juice
- 2 tablespoons olive oil
- ½ teaspoon salt
- ½ teaspoon pepper

1. In a large saucepan, bring water to a boil. Add quinoa. Reduce heat; cover and simmer 12-15 minutes or until liquid is absorbed. Remove from the heat; fluff with a fork. Transfer to a bowl; cool completely.
2. Add the beans, cucumber, red pepper and parsley. In a small bowl, whisk the lemon juice, olive oil, salt and pepper; drizzle over salad and toss to coat. Refrigerate the salad until chilled.
NOTE *Look for quinoa in the cereal, rice or organic food aisle.*

⑤ INGREDIENTS

Hearty Cannellini & Sausage Soup

Is there anything better than a soup full of smoked sausage, creamy cannellini beans and hearty cabbage? I don't think so!
—**PAULINE WHITE** EL CAJON, CA

START TO FINISH: 30 MIN.
MAKES: 6 SERVINGS

- 12 ounces beef summer or smoked sausage, cut into ½-inch pieces
- 4½ cups vegetable broth
- 2 cans (15 ounces each) cannellini or white kidney beans, rinsed and drained
- 4 cups coarsely chopped Chinese or napa cabbage
- 3 green onions, chopped
- ¼ teaspoon salt
- ¼ teaspoon pepper

1. In a large saucepan, cook and stir sausage over medium heat until lightly browned; drain.
2. Add the remaining ingredients; bring to a boil. Reduce the heat; simmer 5-10 minutes or until the cabbage is tender and the flavors are blended.

Harvard Beets

This recipe makes a vibrant, pretty accompaniment to any meal and has a bright flavor. Even those who normally shy away from beets will enjoy these.
—**JEAN ANN PERKINS** NEWBURYPORT, MD

START TO FINISH: 15 MIN.
MAKES: 4-6 SERVINGS

- 1 can (16 ounces) sliced beets
- ¼ cup sugar
- 1½ teaspoons cornstarch
- 2 tablespoons cider vinegar
- 2 tablespoons orange juice
- 1 tablespoon grated orange peel

1. Drain the beets, reserving 2 tablespoons juice; set beets and juice aside.
2. In a saucepan, combine the sugar and cornstarch. Add vinegar, orange juice and beet juice; bring to a boil. Reduce heat and simmer 3-4 minutes or until thickened. Add beets and orange peel; heat through.

HARVARD
BEETS

YELLOW SQUASH
AND PEPPERS

SEASONED
BROCCOLI SPEARS

(5) INGREDIENTS
Yellow Squash and Peppers

Here's a veggie side dish that is sure to perk up any dinner without a lot of fuss. It's also a wonderfully delicious way to use the fresh yellow squash and peppers from the garden.
—ANNA STODOLAK VOLANT, PA

START TO FINISH: 20 MIN.
MAKES: 4 SERVINGS

- 3 cups sliced yellow summer squash
- ½ cup sliced onion
- ½ cup each julienned green and sweet red peppers
- 1 tablespoon canola oil
- ¼ cup water
- 1½ teaspoons minced garlic
- ¼ teaspoon salt
- ¼ teaspoon pepper

1. In a large skillet, saute squash, onion and peppers in oil 4-5 minutes or until crisp-tender. Add the remaining ingredients. Reduce heat to medium.

2. Cook, uncovered, 3-4 minutes or until the vegetables are tender, stirring occasionally. Serve with a slotted spoon.

Seasoned Broccoli Spears

Add a few simple herbs to basic broccoli for an easy, nutritious, microwave-fast vegetable dish.
—MELISSA JUST MINNEAPOLIS, MN

START TO FINISH: 15 MIN.
MAKES: 5 SERVINGS

- 5 cups frozen broccoli florets, thawed
- 1 tablespoon butter, melted
- 2 garlic cloves, minced
- ¼ teaspoon onion salt
- ¼ teaspoon dried basil
- ¼ teaspoon dried thyme
- ⅛ teaspoon pepper

Place the broccoli in a large microwave-safe bowl. Combine the remaining ingredients. Pour over broccoli; toss to coat. Cover and microwave on high 3-4 minutes or until tender.
NOTE *This recipe was tested in a 1,100-watt microwave.*

Colorful Couscous

We love it when sides pop with color, like the red and green pepper in this fluffy couscous. It's a welcome switch from potatoes or rice.
—*TASTE OF HOME* TEST KITCHEN

START TO FINISH: 25 MIN.
MAKES: 6 SERVINGS

- ⅓ cup each finely chopped onion, green pepper and sweet red pepper
- 2 garlic cloves, minced
- 2 tablespoons olive oil
- 1 can (14½ ounces) chicken broth
- ¼ cup water
- ½ teaspoon salt
- ¼ teaspoon pepper
- 1 package (10 ounces) couscous

In a large saucepan, saute onion, peppers and garlic in olive oil 2-3 minutes or until tender. Stir in broth, water, salt and pepper. Bring to a boil. Stir in couscous. Cover and remove from heat; let stand 5 minutes. Fluff with a fork.

Sesame Snap Peas

With their fresh taste, these snap peas make an ideal partner for most any entree. Sweet red pepper adds flavorful accents.

—TASTE OF HOME TEST KITCHEN

START TO FINISH: 15 MIN.
MAKES: 8 SERVINGS

- 1½ **pounds fresh sugar snap peas**
- 1 **small sweet red pepper, chopped**
- 2 **tablespoons butter**
- 1 **tablespoon sesame seeds, toasted**
- 1 **tablespoon reduced-sodium soy sauce**
- ⅛ **teaspoon pepper**

In a large nonstick skillet, saute peas and red pepper in butter until crisp-tender. Stir in the remaining ingredients; heat through.

SESAME SNAP PEAS

Hot Dog Potato Soup

You can use leftover meatballs instead of hot dogs in this yummy soup.

—JEANNIE KLUGH LANCASTER, PA

START TO FINISH: 15 MIN.
MAKES: 5 SERVINGS

- 2 **cans (18.8 ounces each) ready-to-serve chunky baked potato with cheddar and bacon bits soup**
- 4 **hot dogs, halved lengthwise and sliced**
- 1 **cup (4 ounces) shredded cheddar-Monterey Jack cheese**
- 1 **cup frozen corn**
- 1 **cup milk**

In a large microwave-safe bowl, combine the ingredients. Cover and microwave on high for 8-10 minutes or until heated through, stirring every 2 minutes.
NOTE *This recipe was tested in a 1,100-watt microwave.*

HOT DOG POTATO SOUP

FABULOUS
GREEN BEANS

COUNTRY
SAUSAGE SOUP

AVOCADO-TOMATO
SALAD

Fabulous Green Beans

Butter sauce makes any veggie more interesting. My family loves it over green beans. I've used the easy sauce recipe over sugar snap peas as well.
—**LORI DANIELS** BEVERLY, WV

START TO FINISH: 20 MIN.
MAKES: 4 SERVINGS

- 1 pound fresh green beans, trimmed
- ¼ cup butter, cubed
- 1 tablespoon olive oil
- ½ teaspoon salt
- ½ teaspoon Italian seasoning
- ½ teaspoon lemon juice
- ¼ teaspoon grated lemon peel

1. Place the beans in a steamer basket; place in a large saucepan over 1 in. of water. Bring to a boil; cover and steam 8-10 minutes or until crisp-tender.
2. Meanwhile, in a saucepan, heat the remaining ingredients until butter is melted. Transfer beans to a serving bowl; drizzle with butter mixture and toss to coat.

Country Sausage Soup

Savory pork sausage, beans and tomatoes make this a soup I fall back on time and again. It's perfect when I can't decide what to have for supper.
—**GRACE MEYER** GALVA, KS

START TO FINISH: 20 MIN.
MAKES: 4 SERVINGS

- ¾ pound bulk pork sausage
- 1 can (14½ ounces) diced tomatoes, undrained
- 1 can (14½ ounces) chicken broth
- 1 teaspoon dried thyme
- ¾ to 1 teaspoon dried rosemary, crushed
- ¼ teaspoon pepper
- 1 can (15½ ounces) great northern beans, rinsed and drained

- 1 can (15 ounces) garbanzo beans or chickpeas, rinsed and drained

In a large saucepan, cook sausage over medium heat until no longer pink; drain. Stir in the tomatoes, broth, thyme, rosemary and pepper. Bring to a boil. Stir in the beans; heat through.

Avocado-Tomato Salad

My mother came up with this salad when she had too many ripe avocados and tomatoes on hand. It's a lovely way to use them up.
—**JENNIFER REID** FARMINGTON, ME

START TO FINISH: 10 MIN.
MAKES: 4 SERVINGS

- 2 medium ripe avocados, peeled and cubed
- 2 cups grape tomatoes
- ¼ cup thinly sliced red onion
- ¼ cup reduced-fat Italian salad dressing
- 1 tablespoon lime juice
- 1 teaspoon sugar
- ½ teaspoon chili powder
- ¼ teaspoon salt
- ¼ teaspoon pepper

In a large bowl, combine avocados, tomatoes and onion. In a small bowl, whisk the remaining ingredients. Pour over avocado mixture; toss gently to coat.

(5) INGREDIENTS
Pesto Breadsticks

Whether you serve these cheese-dusted breadsticks with soup, salad or even a pasta supper, the cute twists add fun to any menu.
—*TASTE OF HOME* **TEST KITCHEN**

START TO FINISH: 20 MIN.
MAKES: 1 DOZEN

- 1 tube (11 ounces) refrigerated breadsticks
- 2 tablespoons prepared pesto

- ¼ teaspoon garlic pepper blend
- 1 tablespoon butter, melted
- 2 tablespoons shredded Parmesan cheese

1. Preheat oven to 375°. Unroll and separate breadsticks; place on an ungreased baking sheet. Combine pesto and garlic pepper; brush over breadsticks. Twist each breadstick three times.
2. Brush with butter; sprinkle with cheese. Bake 10-13 minutes or until golden brown. Serve warm.

(5) INGREDIENTS
Spiced-Up Sweet Potato Fries

A little salt, a little spice and a whole lot of sweetness turn these fries into a winner!
—**DEBRA HUMPHRIES** CHANHASSEN, MN

START TO FINISH: 30 MIN.
MAKES: 4 SERVINGS

- 3 medium sweet potatoes, peeled and cut into 1-inch wedges (about 1½ pounds)
- 2 tablespoons olive oil
- 1 teaspoon Cajun seasoning
- ½ teaspoon kosher salt
- ½ teaspoon coarsely ground pepper

1. Preheat oven to 425°. In a large bowl, combine potatoes and oil; toss to coat. Sprinkle with the seasonings; toss to combine. Arrange in a single layer on a greased 15x10x1-in. baking pan.
2. Bake, uncovered, 20-25 minutes or until tender and lightly browned, turning occasionally.

SWAP IT
Try Creole or Italian seasoning for the Cajun seasoning.

⑤INGREDIENTS
Lemon Parmesan Orzo

A splash of lemon and a dash of chopped parsley help make this orzo one of my family's most requested springtime sides. It's fantastic with chicken, pork and fish, or it can stand on its own as a light lunch.

—**LESLIE PALMER** SWAMPSCOTT, MA

START TO FINISH: 20 MIN.
MAKES: 4 SERVINGS

- 1 cup uncooked whole wheat orzo pasta
- 1 tablespoon olive oil
- ¼ cup grated Parmesan cheese
- 2 tablespoons minced fresh parsley
- ½ teaspoon grated lemon peel
- ¼ teaspoon salt
- ¼ teaspoon pepper

Cook orzo according to package directions; drain. Transfer to a small bowl; drizzle with oil. Stir in remaining ingredients.

⑤INGREDIENTS
Pineapple-Glazed Carrots

These pretty and versatile carrots are ready in just 10 minutes and pair up with a variety of meats for holiday meal magic!

—**ANNA STODOLAK** VOLANT, PA

START TO FINISH: 10 MIN.
MAKES: 4 SERVINGS

- 1 pound fresh baby carrots
- 2 tablespoons water
- ¼ cup pineapple preserves
- 2 tablespoons sugar
- 2 tablespoons butter
- ¼ teaspoon salt
- 1 tablespoon minced fresh parsley

1. Place carrots and water in a microwave-safe bowl. Cover and microwave on high 4-6 minutes or until crisp-tender. Drain and keep warm.

2. In another microwave-safe bowl, combine the preserves, sugar, butter and salt; cook on high 1-2 minutes or until preserves are melted. Pour over carrots; toss to coat. Sprinkle with parsley.
NOTE *This recipe was tested in a 1,100-watt microwave.*

⑤INGREDIENTS
Garlic Corn on the Cob

Every summer we look forward to fresh corn on the cob. I make it extra special by jazzing it up with garlic.

—**HEATHER CARROLL** COLORADO SPRINGS, CO

START TO FINISH: 15 MIN.
MAKES: 4 SERVINGS

- 4 garlic cloves, minced
- 4 teaspoons olive oil
- 4 medium ears sweet corn, husks removed
- 1 teaspoon sugar

1. In a small bowl, combine garlic and oil; brush over corn. Sprinkle with sugar. Place each on a double thickness of heavy-duty foil (about 14 in. x 12 in.). Fold foil over corn and seal tightly.

2. Grill corn, covered, over medium heat 10-15 minutes or until tender, turning occasionally. Open foil carefully to allow steam to escape.

LEMON PARMESAN ORZO

HOW TO

PEEL GARLIC
Using the blade of a chef's knife, crush each garlic clove. Peel away skin. Chop or mince as directed in the recipe.

CANDY BAR
APPLE SALAD

⑤ INGREDIENTS

Candy Bar Apple Salad

For a real people-pleasing dish, turn to my creamy, sweet salad with crisp apple crunch. It makes a lot—which is good, because it will go fast!
—**CYNDI FYNAARDT** OSKALOOSA, IA

START TO FINISH: 15 MIN.
MAKES: 12 SERVINGS (¾ CUP EACH)

1½ cups cold 2% milk
1 package (3.4 ounces) instant vanilla pudding mix
1 carton (8 ounces) frozen whipped topping, thawed
4 large apples, chopped (about 6 cups)
4 Snickers candy bars (1.86 ounces each), cut into ½-inch pieces

In a large bowl, whisk milk and pudding mix 2 minutes. Let stand 2 minutes or until soft-set. Fold in whipped topping. Fold in apples and candy bars. Chill until serving.

⑤ INGREDIENTS

Herbed Egg Noodles

A seasoned butter sauce pleasantly coats tender noodles, making this perfect alongside Swedish meatballs or any other meaty entree.
—**TASTE OF HOME** TEST KITCHEN

START TO FINISH: 20 MIN.
MAKES: 4 SERVINGS

8 ounces uncooked wide egg noodles
3 tablespoons butter
1 garlic clove, minced
¼ teaspoon salt
¼ teaspoon dill weed
¼ teaspoon dried thyme

Cook noodles according to package directions. Meanwhile, in a large skillet, melt butter. Stir in the garlic, salt, dill and thyme. Drain noodles and add to butter mixture; toss to coat.

PAIR IT!
This will make a
fun dessert for
*Salisbury Steak
Deluxe, page 61.*

DOUBLE-CHOCOLATE TOFFEE ICEBOX CAKE, 220

211

218

212

Sweet Endings

A simple dessert is a **delightful way** to **end a meal**. While these are all **quick to fix,** some are ready to **eat immediately** and others require some chilling and should be **made the night before.**

APPLE-CINNAMON MINI PIES, 223

ORANGE-DRIZZLED
GRAPE TARTLETS

Orange-Drizzled Grape Tartlets

Sugar cookie dough and cream cheese make it easy to build these crunchy, tangy tartlets.
—**JULIE STERCHI** CAMPBELLSVILLE, KY

START TO FINISH: 20 MIN.
MAKES: 1 DOZEN

- 1 tube (16½ ounces) refrigerated sugar cookie dough
- 1 package (8 ounces) cream cheese, softened
- ½ cup confectioners' sugar
- ½ teaspoon vanilla extract
- ¾ cup seedless red grapes, halved
- ¾ cup green grapes, halved
- ¼ cup orange marmalade

1. Preheat oven to 350°. Cut cookie dough into twelve slices, about ¾ in. thick. On ungreased baking sheets, pat each slice to form ½-in.-thick circles. Bake 10-12 minutes or until golden brown. Remove to wire racks to cool completely.
2. Meanwhile, in a small bowl, beat cream cheese, confectioners' sugar and vanilla until blended. Spread over cookie crusts. Top with grapes.
3. In a microwave-safe dish, microwave marmalade, covered, on high 15-20 seconds or until warmed. Drizzle over grapes.

SWAP IT
Use an assortment of fresh berries for the grapes.

Glazed Pear Shortcakes

Family and friends will savor every last crumb of this lickety-split dessert. The pound cake absorbs the apricot taste and the warm sweetness of the pears.

—FRAN THOMAS
SAINT JAMES CITY, FL

START TO FINISH: 10 MIN.
MAKES: 4 SERVINGS

- 2   medium pears, sliced
- 2   tablespoons butter
- 4   teaspoons apricot spreadable fruit
- 8   thin slices pound cake
- 4   teaspoons chopped walnuts
- 4   tablespoons whipped topping

1. In a small skillet, saute pears in butter until tender. Remove from heat; stir in spreadable fruit.
2. Place cake slices on four dessert dishes; top with pear mixture, walnuts and whipped topping.

Blueberry-Rhubarb Crisp

Microwaving this recipe produces a crisp that's just as good as when it's baked in the oven. It is simply unbeatable warmed with a scoop of vanilla ice cream.

—LORRI CAMPBELL MANKATO, MN

START TO FINISH: 25 MIN.
MAKES: 6 SERVINGS

- 2½   cups diced fresh or frozen rhubarb, thawed
- ⅓   cup sugar
- 2   tablespoons all-purpose flour
- 1   can (21 ounces) blueberry pie filling

TOPPING
- ¾   cup all-purpose flour
- ¾   cup old-fashioned oats
- ⅓   cup packed brown sugar
- ¾   teaspoon ground cinnamon
- ½   cup cold butter, cubed

1. In a 2-qt. microwave-safe dish, combine the rhubarb, sugar and flour. Cover and microwave on high 3 minutes; stir. Add pie filling.
2. In a small bowl, combine flour, oats, brown sugar and cinnamon. Cut in the butter until mixture is crumbly; sprinkle over the filling. Cover and cook 4-5 minutes longer or until bubbly and the rhubarb is tender. Serve warm.

NOTES *If using frozen rhubarb, measure rhubarb while still frozen, then thaw completely. Drain in a colander, but do not press liquid out. This recipe was tested in a 1,100-watt microwave.*

No-Bake Cherry Dessert

I adapted this recipe from one given to me by my first best friend, Sandy, in 1966. I often made it for my kids. Now when they visit, they'll ask for it because they still love it.

—JUDY HARRIS MCRAE, GA

START TO FINISH: 15 MIN.
MAKES: 4 SERVINGS

- ⅔   cup graham cracker crumbs
- 2   tablespoons brown sugar
- 2   tablespoons butter, melted
- 4   ounces cream cheese, softened
- 1   tablespoon confectioners' sugar
- 1   cup whipped topping
- 1¼   cups cherry pie filling

1. In a small bowl, combine the cracker crumbs, brown sugar and butter; press into an ungreased 9x5-in. loaf pan.
2. In a large bowl, beat cream cheese and confectioners' sugar until smooth; fold in whipped topping. Spread over crust. Top with pie filling. Chill until serving.

GLAZED PEAR SHORTCAKES

Blueberry Shortcake Sundaes

These sundaes offer a summery conclusion to any meal. If you need time in the kitchen, just purchase blueberry pie filling and thin it out with a little orange juice.
—**AGNES WARD** STRATFORD, ON

START TO FINISH: 20 MIN.
MAKES: 4 SERVINGS

- ⅓ cup sugar
- 1½ teaspoons cornstarch
- ¼ teaspoon ground cinnamon
- 3 tablespoons water
- 1½ cups fresh or frozen blueberries
- 4 slices pound cake
- 4 scoops vanilla ice cream

1. In a small saucepan, combine sugar, cornstarch and cinnamon. Stir in water and blueberries until blended. Bring to a boil; cook and stir 2-4 minutes or until thickened.
2. Place cake slices on four dessert plates. Top each with ice cream and blueberry sauce.

Chocolate Scotcheroos

One of my students gave me a copy of this recipe. It has become one of my family's all-time favorites, and it's so easy to make.
—**LOIS MAYS** COVINGTON, PA

PREP: 25 MIN. + CHILLING
MAKES: 2 DOZEN

- 1 cup sugar
- 1 cup light corn syrup
- 1 cup creamy peanut butter
- 6 cups crisp rice cereal
- ¾ cup butterscotch chips
- ¾ cup semisweet chocolate chips
- ¾ teaspoon shortening

1. In a large saucepan, bring sugar and corn syrup to a boil. Cook and stir until sugar is dissolved; stir in peanut butter.
2. Remove from the heat. Add cereal and mix well. Press into a greased 13x9-in. pan.
3. In a microwave-safe bowl, melt chips and shortening; stir until smooth. Spread over cereal mixture. Cover and refrigerate for at least 1 hour before cutting.

Butterscotch-Toffee Cheesecake Bars

I took a cheesecake bar recipe and added a new flavor combo to transform it! The butterscotch and toffee really taste divine here.
—**PAMELA SHANK** PARKERSBURG, WV

PREP: 15 MIN. • **BAKE:** 30 MIN. + CHILLING
MAKES: 2 DOZEN

- 1 package yellow cake mix (regular size)
- 1 package (3.4 ounces) instant butterscotch pudding mix
- ⅓ cup canola oil
- 2 eggs
- 1 package (8 ounces) cream cheese, softened
- ⅓ cup sugar
- 1 cup brickle toffee bits, divided
- ½ cup butterscotch chips

1. Preheat oven to 350°. In a large bowl, combine cake mix, pudding mix, oil and 1 egg; mix until crumbly. Reserve 1 cup for topping. Press remaining mixture into an ungreased 13x9-in. baking pan. Bake 10 minutes. Cool completely on a wire rack.
2. In a small bowl, beat cream cheese and sugar until smooth. Add remaining egg; beat on low speed just until combined. Fold in ½ cup toffee bits. Spread over crust. Sprinkle with reserved crumb mixture. Bake 15-20 minutes or until filling is set.
3. Sprinkle with butterscotch chips and remaining toffee bits. Return to oven; bake 1 minute longer. Cool on a wire rack 1 hour. Refrigerate 2 hours or until cold. Cut into bars.

BLUEBERRY SHORTCAKE SUNDAES

BUTTERSCOTCH-TOFFEE CHEESECAKE BARS

Candy-Licious Fudge

A no-fuss fudge prepared in the microwave that tastes like a candy bar? It sounds too good to be true, but it's not!

—DEE LANCASTER OZARK, MO

PREP: 15 MIN. + CHILLING
MAKES: 2¼ POUNDS

- 1   teaspoon butter
- 1   can (14 ounces) sweetened condensed milk
- 1   package (11 ounces) peanut butter and milk chocolate chips
- 1   cup milk chocolate chips
- ⅔   cup milk chocolate English toffee bits
- 1   cup chopped pecans
- 2   teaspoons vanilla extract

1. Line a 9-in.-square baking pan with foil and grease the foil with butter; set aside.
2. In a large microwave-safe bowl combine milk, chips and toffee bits. Microwave, uncovered, on high for 1 minute; stir. Cook 1-2 minutes longer, stirring every minute, or until chips are melted. Stir in pecans and vanilla.
3. Transfer to prepared pan. Cover and chill at least 1 hour. Using foil, lift fudge out of pan. Gently peel off foil; cut into 1-in. squares. Store in an airtight container.
NOTE *This recipe was tested in a 1,100-watt microwave.*

---

(5)INGREDIENTS

Chocolate Banana Bundles

Banana and chocolate is such an irresistible combination that I make this quick dessert often.

—THOMAS FAGLON SOMERSET, NJ

START TO FINISH: 30 MIN.
MAKES: 4 SERVINGS

- 2   tablespoons butter
- ¼   cup packed brown sugar
- 2   medium ripe bananas, halved lengthwise

CANDY-LICIOUS FUDGE

- 1   sheet frozen puff pastry, thawed
- 4   ounces semisweet chocolate, melted
     Vanilla ice cream, optional

1. Preheat oven to 400°. In a large skillet, melt butter over medium heat. Stir in brown sugar until blended. Add bananas; stir to coat. Remove from heat; set aside.
2. Unfold puff pastry. Cut into four rectangles. Place a halved banana in center of each square. Overlap two opposite corners of pastry over banana; pinch tightly to seal. Place on parchment paper-lined baking sheets.
3. Bake 20-25 minutes or until golden brown. Drizzle with chocolate. Serve warm with ice cream if desired.

---

(5)INGREDIENTS

Easy Cherry Pockets

Here's a sweet treat your family is sure to delight in, and the best part is that it takes just minutes to make.

—TASTE OF HOME TEST KITCHEN

START TO FINISH: 20 MIN.
MAKES: 4 SERVINGS

- 1   tube (8 ounces) refrigerated crescent rolls
- 1   cup cherry pie filling
- ½   cup confectioners' sugar
- 1   to 2 tablespoons 2% milk

1. Preheat oven to 375°. Unroll crescent roll dough and separate into four squares; place on an ungreased baking sheet. Press seams and perforations together. Spoon ¼ pie filling in one corner of each square. Fold to make triangles; pinch to seal.
2. Bake 10-12 minutes or until golden. Combine the sugar and milk to achieve drizzling consistency. Drizzle over the turnovers; serve warm.

Chocolate Angel Cupcakes with Coconut Cream Frosting

Sweeten any meal with these fun, frosted chocolate cupcakes that take just minutes to make. The finger-licking flavor packs far fewer calories and fat than traditional desserts!

—**MANDY RIVERS** LEXINGTON, SC

PREP: 15 MIN. • **BAKE:** 15 MIN. + COOLING
MAKES: 2 DOZEN

- 1 package (16 ounces) angel food cake mix
- ¾ cup baking cocoa
- 1 cup (8 ounces) reduced-fat sour cream
- 1 cup confectioners' sugar
- ⅛ teaspoon coconut extract
- 2½ cups reduced-fat whipped topping
- ¾ cup flaked coconut, toasted

1. Preheat oven to 375°. Prepare cake mix according to package directions for cupcakes, adding cocoa when mixing.

2. Fill foil- or paper-lined muffin cups two-thirds full. Bake 11-15 minutes or until cake springs back when lightly touched and cracks feel dry. Cool 10 minutes before removing from pans to wire racks to cool completely.

3. For frosting, in a bowl, combine sour cream, confectioners' sugar and extract until smooth. Fold in whipped topping. Frost cupcakes. Sprinkle with coconut. Refrigerate leftovers.

TOP TIP

If you have any frosting left over from the cupcakes, spread some over a graham cracker or the flat side of a cookie such as a vanilla wafer or gingersnap. Top with another cookie.

CHOCOLATE BANANA BUNDLES

CHOCOLATE ANGEL CUPCAKES WITH COCONUT CREAM FROSTING

(5) INGREDIENTS
Banana Split Cookie Trifles

Layered with chocolate chip cookies, ice cream, sliced bananas and sundae toppings, this sweet and speedy trifle has it all.

—MARCI CARL
NORTHERN, CAMBRIA, PA

START TO FINISH: 15 MIN.
MAKES: 4 SERVINGS

- 4 soft chocolate chip cookies, crumbled
- 2 cups chocolate chip ice cream, softened
- 2 small bananas, halved lengthwise and cut into 1-inch pieces
- ½ cup whipped cream
- ⅔ cup hot fudge ice cream topping

Place 1 tablespoon cookie crumbs in each of four dessert dishes. Layer with half of the ice cream, bananas, whipped cream, fudge topping and remaining cookies. Repeat layers. Serve immediately.

Pretzel Cereal Crunch

A festive container of this salty-sweet treat was left in my mailbox several Christmases ago. My neighbor shared the quick and easy recipe. I've since added peanut butter because I love the flavor!

—CINDY LUND VALLEY CENTER, CA

PREP: 20 MIN. + COOLING
MAKES: ABOUT 9 CUPS

- 1¼ cups Golden Grahams
- 1¼ cups Apple Cinnamon Cheerios
- 1¼ cups miniature pretzels
- 1 cup chopped pecans, toasted
- 1 package (10 to 12 ounces) white baking chips
- 2 tablespoons creamy peanut butter

In a large bowl, combine the cereals, pretzels and pecans. In a microwave-safe bowl, melt chips; stir until smooth. Stir in peanut butter. Drizzle over cereal mixture; toss to coat. Spread evenly on a waxed paper-lined baking sheet. Cool completely; break into pieces. Store in an airtight container.

Melty Microwave Brownies

My rich fudgy brownies can't be beat for a quick dessert. The secret is baking them in the microwave oven.

—SUE GRONHOLZ BEAVER DAM, WI

PREP: 10 MIN. • **COOK:** 5 MIN. + COOLING
MAKES: 1 DOZEN

- ½ cup butter, cubed
- 2 ounces unsweetened chocolate, chopped
- 2 eggs
- ¾ cup sugar
- ½ cup all-purpose flour
- 1 teaspoon baking powder
- 1 teaspoon vanilla extract
- ½ cup semisweet chocolate chips
  Confectioners' sugar

1. In a microwave, melt butter and chocolate; stir until smooth. Cool slightly. In a large bowl, beat eggs 2 minutes. Gradually add sugar, beating until thick and pale yellow. Combine flour and baking powder; add to egg mixture. Stir in the melted chocolate mixture, vanilla and chips.
2. Pour into a greased 8-in.-square microwave-safe dish. Cook on high for 3½ to 4 minutes or until a toothpick inserted near the center comes out clean. Place on a wire rack; cool 10 minutes. Dust with confectioners' sugar.
NOTE *This recipe was tested in a 1,100-watt microwave.*

(5) INGREDIENTS
All-Star Ice Cream Sandwiches

Two popular treats are married together in a fun, cool, super-size ice cream sandwich.

—TASTE OF HOME TEST KITCHEN

PREP: 15 MIN. + FREEZING
MAKES: 4 SERVINGS

- ½ cup chocolate chip cookie dough ice cream, softened
- 8 Oreo cookies
- 6 ounces milk chocolate candy coating, melted
  Red, white and blue sprinkles

Spoon 2 tablespoons of ice cream onto half of the cookies. Top with remaining cookies. Spoon melted coating over tops. Decorate with sprinkles. Place on a baking sheet; freeze for at least 1 hour.

(5) INGREDIENTS
Chocolaty S'mores Bars

One night, my husband had some friends over to play poker and he requested these s'mores bars. They polished them off and asked for more!

—REBECCA SHIPP BEEBE, AR

PREP: 15 MIN. + COOLING
MAKES: 1½ DOZEN

- ¼ cup butter, cubed
- 1 package (10 ounces) large marshmallows
- 1 package (12 ounces) Golden Grahams
- ⅓ cup milk chocolate chips, melted

1. In a saucepan, melt butter over low heat. Add marshmallows; cook and stir until blended. Remove from heat. Stir in cereal until coated.
2. Using a buttered spatula, press evenly into a greased 13x9-in. pan. Drizzle with the melted chocolate chips. Cool completely. Cut into bars. Store in an airtight container.

ALL-STAR ICE CREAM SANDWICHES

CHOCOLATLY S'MORE BARS

**CONTEST-WINNING
EASY TIRAMISU**

(5) INGREDIENTS

Contest-Winning Easy Tiramisu

Here is a fun use for pudding snack cups. They make this treat truly effortless. It's great quick dessert for a special supper or anytime.

—**BETTY CLAYCOMB** ADVERTON, PA

START TO FINISH: 15 MIN.
MAKES: 4 SERVINGS

24 **vanilla wafers, divided**
2 **teaspoons instant coffee granules**
¼ **cup hot water**
4 **snack-size cups (3½ ounces each) vanilla pudding**
½ **cup whipped topping**
2 **teaspoons baking cocoa**

1. Set aside eight vanilla wafers; coarsely crush remaining wafers. Divide wafer crumbs between four dessert dishes.
2. In a small bowl, dissolve coffee granules in hot water. Drizzle over wafer crumbs. Spoon pudding into dessert dishes. Top with whipped topping; sprinkle with the cocoa. Garnish with the reserved vanilla wafers.

DID YOU KNOW?

Tiramisu translates to "pick me up." The shortcut version above is loosely based on the classic recipes, which use ladyfingers that are soaked in coffee, mascarpone cheese, zabaglione (a light Italian custard) and cocoa powder.

Apricot Crisp

These tropical cobbler cups with flaky coconut and a buttery crumb topping are a delicious way to use canned fruit.

—TASTE OF HOME TEST KITCHEN

START TO FINISH: 25 MIN.
MAKES: 4 SERVINGS

- 3 **cans (15 ounces each) reduced-sugar apricot halves, drained**
- 2 **tablespoons brown sugar**
- ½ **teaspoon ground ginger**
  TOPPING
- ¼ **cup all-purpose flour**
- 3 **tablespoons brown sugar**
- 3 **tablespoons quick-cooking oats**
- 2 **tablespoons flaked coconut**
- ¼ **cup cold butter, cubed**

1. Preheat oven to 400°. In a large bowl, combine apricots, brown sugar and ginger. Divide among four greased 8-oz. baking dishes.

2. In a bowl, combine the flour, brown sugar, oats and coconut. Cut in the butter until the mixture resembles coarse crumbs. Sprinkle over the apricots.

3. Bake 15 minutes or until filling is bubbly and top is golden brown.
NOTE *Crisp may be baked in a greased 8-in.-square baking dish 23-25 minutes.*

Strawberry Cheesecake Sundaes

This tastes like a frozen strawberry cheesecake, without the fuss of making a crust.

—TASTE OF HOME TEST KITCHEN

START TO FINISH: 15 MIN.
MAKES: 2 SERVINGS

- 1 **cup sliced fresh strawberries**
- 1 **tablespoon sugar**
- 1 **package (3 ounces) cream cheese, softened**
- ¼ **cup confectioners' sugar**
- 1 **tablespoon 2% milk**
- 1⅓ **cups vanilla ice cream**
- 2 **tablespoons graham cracker crumbs**
  Dash ground cinnamon

1. In a small bowl, combine the strawberries and sugar; set aside. In another bowl, beat the cream cheese, confectioners' sugar and milk until smooth.

2. Spoon ice cream into two dessert dishes; layer each with ¼ cup strawberries. Top with cream cheese mixture and remaining strawberries. Combine cracker crumbs and cinnamon; sprinkle over the sundaes.

5 INGREDIENTS
Chocolate Hazelnut Parfaits

Hazelnut coffee creamer adds great flavor to the chocolate pudding in my parfaits. Shortbread cookie crumbs and fresh strawberry slices always complete the layered desserts nicely.

—CHRISTY HINRICHS PARKVILLE, MO

PREP: 10 MIN. + CHILLING
MAKES: 8 SERVINGS

- 3 **cups cold milk**
- 1 **cup refrigerated hazelnut nondairy creamer**
- 2 **packages (3.9 ounces each) instant chocolate pudding mix**
- 1 **cup crushed shortbread cookies**
- 2 **cups sliced fresh strawberries**
  Whipped cream, optional

1. In a large bowl, whisk the milk, creamer and pudding mixes for 2 minutes. Let stand for 2 minutes or until soft-set.

2. Spoon ¼ cup pudding into each of eight parfait glasses; sprinkle each with 1 tablespoon cookie crumbs. Top with strawberries and remaining pudding and crumbs.

3. Refrigerate for 1 hour before serving. Garnish with whipped cream if desired.

APRICOT CRISP

Trail Mix Clusters

They may look naughty, but these chocolaty clusters are as nice as can be. The dried fruits, seeds and nuts are healthy foods and make a wholesome snack.

—ALINA NIEMI HONOLULU, HI

PREP: 25 MIN. + CHILLING
MAKES: 4 DOZEN

- 2 cups (12 ounces) semisweet chocolate chips
- ½ cup unsalted sunflower kernels
- ½ cup salted pumpkin seeds or pepitas
- ½ cup coarsely chopped cashews
- ½ cup coarsely chopped pecans
- ¼ cup flaked coconut
- ¼ cup finely chopped dried apricots
- ¼ cup dried cranberries
- ¼ cup dried cherries or blueberries

1. In a microwave-safe bowl, melt chocolate chips; stir until smooth. Stir in the remaining ingredients.
2. Drop mixture by tablespoonfuls onto waxed paper-lined baking sheets. Refrigerate until firm. Store in an airtight container in the refrigerator.

Makeover Dirt Dessert

This lightened-up dessert makes an amazing after-dinner treat. Break out the spoons and make sure you get a bite, because this is one dessert that won't be around for long!

—KRISTI LINTON BAY CITY, MI

PREP: 30 MIN. + CHILLING
MAKES: 20 SERVINGS

- 1 package (8 ounces) fat-free cream cheese
- 1 package (3 ounces) cream cheese, softened
- ¾ cup confectioners' sugar
- 3½ cups cold fat-free milk
- 2 packages (1 ounce each) sugar-free instant vanilla pudding mix
- 1 carton (12 ounces) frozen reduced-fat whipped topping, thawed
- 1 package (15½ ounces) reduced-fat Oreo cookies, crushed

1. In a large bowl, beat the cream cheeses and confectioners' sugar until smooth. In a large bowl, whisk milk and pudding mixes for 2 minutes; let stand for 2 minutes or until soft-set. Gradually stir into cream cheese mixture. Fold in the whipped topping.
2. Spread 1⅓ cups crushed cookies into an ungreased 13x9-in. dish. Layer with half of the pudding mixture and half of the remaining cookies. Repeat layers. Refrigerate at least 1 hour before serving.

(5)INGREDIENTS

Frozen Chocolate Monkey Treats

Everyone needs a fun, friendly way for kids to play with food. These "bites" are nutty and yummy. I just coat bananas in melted chocolate and dip them into peanuts, sprinkles or coconut.

—SUSAN HEIN BURLINGTON, WI

PREP: 15 MIN. + FREEZING • **COOK:** 5 MIN.
MAKES: 1½ DOZEN

- 3 medium bananas
- 1 cup (6 ounces) dark chocolate chips
- 2 teaspoons shortening
    Toppings: chopped peanuts, toasted flaked coconut and/ or colored jimmies

1. Cut each banana into six pieces (about 1 in.). Insert a toothpick into each piece; transfer to a waxed paper-lined baking sheet. Freeze until completely firm, about 1 hour.
2. In a microwave, melt chocolate and shortening; stir until smooth. Dip banana pieces in chocolate mixture; allow excess to drip off. Dip in toppings as desired; return to baking sheet. Freeze at least 30 minutes before serving.
NOTE *To toast coconut, spread in a 15x10x1-in. baking pan. Bake at 350° for 5-10 minutes or until golden brown, stirring frequently.*

TRAIL MIX CLUSTERS

MAKEOVER
DIRT DESSERT

FROZEN CHOCOLATE
MONKEY TREATS

Black Forest Cheesecake

My cheesecake is so popular that everyone just expects me to bring it to every gathering . And so I have for about the last 15 years.

—CHRISTINE OOYEN WINNEBAGO, IL

PREP: 20 MIN. + CHILLING
MAKES: 8 SERVINGS

- 1 **package (8 ounces) cream cheese, softened**
- ⅓ **cup sugar**
- 1 **cup (8 ounces) sour cream**
- 2 **teaspoons vanilla extract**
- 1 **carton (8 ounces) frozen whipped topping, thawed**
- 1 **chocolate crumb crust (8 inches)**
- ¼ **cup baking cocoa**
- 1 **tablespoon confectioners' sugar**
- 1 **can (21 ounces) cherry pie filling**

1. In a large bowl, beat cream cheese and sugar until smooth. Beat in sour cream and vanilla.

Fold in whipped topping. Spread half of the mixture evenly into the crust. Fold the cocoa and confectioners' sugar into the remaining whipped topping mixture; carefully spread over cream cheese layer. Refrigerate at least 4 hours.
2. Cut into slices; top each slice with cherry pie filling.

Honey-Oat Granola Bars

My husband and I enjoy these bars every day. It's a basic recipe to which you can add any of your favorite flavors...coconut or different kinds of chips, nuts and dried fruits.

—JEAN BOYCE NEW ULM, MN

PREP: 15 MIN. • **BAKE:** 15 MIN. + COOLING
MAKES: 3 DOZEN

- 4 **cups quick-cooking oats**
- 1 **cup packed brown sugar**
- 1 **cup chopped salted peanuts**
- 1 **cup (6 ounces) semisweet chocolate chips**
- ½ **cup sunflower kernels**

BLACK FOREST CHEESECAKE

- ¾ **cup butter, melted**
- ⅔ **cup honey**
- 1 **teaspoon vanilla extract**

1. Preheat oven to 350°. In a large bowl, combine oats, brown sugar, peanuts, chocolate chips and sunflower kernels. Stir in butter, honey and vanilla until combined (mixture will be crumbly). Press into a greased parchment paper-lined 15x10x1-in. baking pan.
2. Bake 15-20 minutes or until browned and bubbly. Cool for 15 minutes on a wire rack; cut into squares. Cool completely before removing from pan.

⑤ INGREDIENTS

Pistachio Cranberry Bark

This bark makes a lovely holiday gift from the kitchen. Fill a plate or cup with candy, then gather up clear cellophane around it and tie with red and green ribbons.

—SUSAN WACEK PLEASANTON, CA

PREP: 20 MIN. + CHILLING
MAKES: ABOUT 1 POUND

- 2 **cups (12 ounces) semisweet chocolate chips**
- 5 **ounces white candy coating, chopped**
- 1 **cup chopped pistachios, toasted, divided**
- ¾ **cup dried cranberries, divided**

1. In a microwave-safe bowl, melt semisweet chips; stir until smooth. Repeat with white candy coating.
2. Stir ¾ cup pistachios and half of the cranberries into semisweet chocolate. Thinly spread onto a waxed paper-lined baking sheet. Drizzle with candy coating.
3. Cut through with a knife to swirl. Sprinkle with remaining pistachios and cranberries. Chill until firm. Break into pieces. Store in an airtight container in the refrigerator.

Blueberry Crumble Tarts

Pop one in a lunch box, share a batch at work or wait until dessert—these are sweet anytime, anywhere. Sometimes, I refrigerate prepared tarts overnight and bake them while making dinner the following day.
—**CAROLE FRASER** NORTH YORK, ON

START TO FINISH: 30 MIN.
MAKES: 6 SERVINGS

- 2 **cups fresh blueberries**
- ¼ **cup sugar**
- 1 **tablespoon cornstarch**
- 1 **package (6 count) individual graham cracker tart shells**
- ¼ **cup all-purpose flour**
- ¼ **cup quick-cooking oats**
- ¼ **cup packed brown sugar**
- 2 **tablespoons cold butter**
  Ice cream or whipped cream, optional

1. Preheat oven to 375°. In a bowl, toss blueberries with sugar and cornstarch; spoon into tart shells. In a small bowl, mix flour, oats and brown sugar; cut in butter until crumbly. Sprinkle over blueberries.
2. Place tarts on a baking sheet. Bake 20-25 minutes or until topping is golden brown and filling is bubbly. Serve warm or at room temperature. If desired, top with ice cream.

PAIR IT!
Oven-Fried Chicken Drumsticks, page 105, and these tarts make a comforting meal.

BLUEBERRY CRUMBLE TARTS

(5) INGREDIENTS
Raspberry Lemon Trifles

This fancy and delicious dessert is so easy and quick to prepare that you can make it for unexpected guests. Substitute strawberries for the raspberries if you prefer.

—TASTE OF HOME TEST KITCHEN

START TO FINISH: 15 MIN.
MAKES: 4 SERVINGS

- 1¼ cups prepared vanilla pudding
- ¼ cup lemon curd
- 3 cups fresh raspberries

In a bowl, combine pudding and lemon curd. Spoon 2 tablespoons pudding mixture into each of four wine glasses or dessert dishes; sprinkle each with 1/4 cup raspberries. Repeat layers twice. Chill until serving.

(5) INGREDIENTS
Double-Chocolate Toffee Icebox Cake

My mother-in-law taught me that anything will taste good if you put enough butter, chocolate or cream in it. Sometimes I use chocolate graham crackers and stack up the layers in a 9-in-square pan.

—BEE ENGELHART
BLOOMFIELD TOWNSHIP, MI

PREP: 30 MIN. + CHILLING
MAKES: 8 SERVINGS

- 3 cups 2% milk
- 1 package (5.9 ounces) instant chocolate pudding mix
- 1½ cups heavy whipping cream
- 2 packages (9 ounces each) chocolate wafers
- 2 Heath candy bars (1.4 ounces each), crushed

1. In a large bowl, whisk milk and pudding mix 2 minutes. Let stand 2 minutes or until soft-set. In a large bowl, beat cream until stiff peaks form.
2. Arrange 20 cookies on bottom of an 8-in.-square baking dish. Spread a fourth of the chocolate pudding and a fourth of the whipped cream over the cookies. Repeat layers three times. Sprinkle with the crushed candy bars. Refrigerate overnight.

(5) INGREDIENTS
Triple Chip Cookies

Sweet and salty, just the way we like them! A tube of refrigerated peanut butter cookie dough is the base for these delightful cookies made with potato chips.

—TASTE OF HOME TEST KITCHEN

START TO FINISH: 30 MIN.
MAKES: 2½ DOZEN

- 1 tube (16½ ounces) refrigerated peanut butter cookie dough
- 1 cup coarsely crushed potato chips
- ½ cup butterscotch chips
- ½ cup swirled milk chocolate and peanut butter chips

1. Preheat oven to 350°. Let cookie dough stand at room temperature 5-10 minutes to soften. In a large bowl, combine the cookie dough and chips.
2. Drop by tablespoonfuls 2 in. apart onto ungreased baking sheets. Bake 10-12 minutes or until lightly browned. Remove the cookies to wire racks. Store in an airtight container.

No-Bake Brownies

Here are rich, fudge-like squares that are packed with marshmallows and nuts. The easy recipe makes eight brownies, but you'll want the extras to enjoy another time.

—HERMINE MUELLERLEILE
HYDE PARK, NY

PREP: 15 MIN. + CHILLING
MAKES: 8 SERVINGS

- ½ cup semisweet chocolate chips
- ¼ cup plus ½ teaspoon evaporated milk, divided
- ¾ cup crushed vanilla wafers (about 20 wafers)
- ½ cup miniature marshmallows
- ¼ cup confectioners' sugar
- ¼ cup chopped pecans or walnuts

1. In a microwave-safe bowl, melt the chocolate chips with ¼ cup milk; stir until smooth. Transfer 2 tablespoons to another bowl; stir in remaining milk and set aside for topping.
2. In a small bowl, combine the crushed wafers, marshmallows, confectioners' sugar and pecans; beat in the remaining chocolate mixture. Press into a 5¾x3x2-in. loaf pan coated with cooking spray. Spread with reserved chocolate mixture. Cover and refrigerate 1-2 hours or until firm. Cut into bars.

TOP TIP

For uniform bars or squares, use a ruler and make cut marks with the point of a sharp knife. Lay the ruler on top of the bars between the guide marks and use the edge as a cutting guide. If you're cutting the bars in the pan, remove a corner piece first, then the rest will be easier to lift out.

DOUBLE-CHOCOLATE TOFFEE ICEBOX CAKE

TRIPLE-CHIP COOKIES

NO-BAKE BROWNIES

**APPLE-CINNAMON
MINI PIES**

**MAPLE
MOCHA POPS**

**COFFEE WHIP
DESSERT**

Apple-Cinnamon Mini Pies

I came up with the idea for these little pies while snacking on applesauce one night and thought it would make a quick and delicious pie filling. They were a total hit. What's better than an apple pie that you can actually hold in your hand to eat?

—**KANDY BINGHAM** GREEN RIVER, WY

PREP: 20 MIN. • **BAKE:** 15 MIN.
MAKES: 1 DOZEN

- 1 **package (14.1 ounces) refrigerated pie pastry**
- ½ **cup chunky applesauce**
- 3 **teaspoons cinnamon-sugar, divided**
- 2 **tablespoons butter, cut into 12 pieces**
- 1 **tablespoon 2% milk, divided**

1. Preheat oven to 350°. On a lightly floured surface, unroll the pastry sheets. Using a floured 3½-in. round cookie cutter, cut six circles from each sheet.
2. In a small bowl, mix applesauce with 1½ teaspoons cinnamon-sugar. Place 2 teaspoons applesauce mixture on one half of each circle; dot with butter. Moisten pastry edges with some of the milk. Fold pastry over filling; press edges with a fork to seal.
3. Transfer to ungreased baking sheets. Brush tops with remaining milk; sprinkle with the remaining cinnamon-sugar. Bake for 12-15 minutes or until pastry is golden brown. Remove from the pans to wire racks. Serve warm or at room temperature.

Maple Mocha Pops

My husband says one is just not enough of these creamy pops. They're a breeze to make, and kids love them, too. For a more grownup presentation, freeze them in pretty serving cups and add a dollop of whipped cream.

—**CAROLINE SPERRY** ALLENTOWN, MI

PREP: 15 MIN. + FREEZING
MAKES: 1 DOZEN

- 2 **cups heavy whipping cream**
- ½ **cup half-and-half cream**
- ¼ **cup maple syrup**
- ¼ **cup chocolate syrup**
- 1 **tablespoon instant coffee granules**
- 12 **freezer pop molds or paper cups (3 ounces each) and wooden pop sticks**

1. In a large bowl, whisk whipping cream, half-and-half, maple syrup, chocolate syrup and coffee granules until the coffee dissolves.
2. Fill molds or cups with ¼ cup cream mixture; top with holders or insert sticks into cups. Freeze.

Coffee Whip Dessert

My luscious, silky coffee dessert is a smooth and creamy finale to an everyday meal or even a special occasion. It takes just a few minutes to prepare!

—**MARIAN PLATT** SEQUIM, WA

START TO FINISH: 30 MIN.
MAKES: 8 SERVINGS

- 1 **cup water**
- 2 **tablespoons instant coffee granules**
- 6½ **cups miniature marshmallows**
- 1 **cup heavy whipping cream**
  Whipped cream and additional instant coffee granules, optional

1. In a large saucepan, bring water to a boil. Remove from heat; stir in coffee. Add marshmallows; cook 5-6 minutes over low heat until marshmallows are melted, stirring occasionally. Pour into a large bowl; cover and refrigerate until slightly thickened.
2. In a small bowl, beat cream until soft peaks form; fold into marshmallow mixture. Spoon into dessert dishes. Garnish with whipped cream and additional coffee granules if desired.

Angel Toffee Dessert

Although this dessert has a light and airy texture, the flavor is undeniably rich. Purchase a prepared angel food cake or, if time allows, bake one from scratch or a boxed mix.

—*TASTE OF HOME* TEST KITCHEN

PREP: 15 MIN. + CHILLING
MAKES: 6-8 SERVINGS

- 2 **packages (3 ounces each) cream cheese, softened**
- ½ **cup confectioners' sugar**
- 2 **tablespoons milk**
- 1 **carton (8 ounces) frozen whipped topping, thawed**
- 5 **cups cubed angel food cake**
- ½ **cup chocolate syrup**
- ½ **cup English toffee bits or almond brickle chips, divided**

1. In a large bowl, beat cream cheese, sugar and milk until smooth. Fold in whipped topping. Arrange cake cubes in an ungreased 11x7-in. dish. Drizzle with chocolate syrup.
2. Set aside 1 tablespoon of toffee bits; sprinkle remaining toffee bits over chocolate. Spread cream cheese mixture over top. Sprinkle with remaining toffee bits. Cover and chill until serving. Store any leftovers in the refrigerator.

Chocolate-Raspberry Angel Food Torte

Here's a classic angel food cake dressed up in its holiday best. This no-fuss torte tastes as great as it looks.

—**LISA DORSEY** PUEBLO, CO

START TO FINISH: 20 MIN.
MAKES: 12 SERVINGS

- 1 **prepared angel food cake (8 to 10 ounces)**
- 1½ **cups heavy whipping cream**
- ¼ **cup confectioners' sugar**
- ¼ **cup baking cocoa**
- 1 **jar (12 ounces) seedless raspberry jam**
  Fresh raspberries and mint leaves

1. Divide cake horizontally into four layers. In a large bowl, beat the cream, confectioners' sugar and cocoa until stiff peaks form.

2. To assemble, place one cake layer on a serving plate; spread with a third of the raspberry jam. Repeat layers twice. Top with remaining cake layer. Spread frosting over top and sides of cake. Chill until serving. Just before serving, garnish with raspberries and mint leaves.

Cashew Clusters

I make this recipe for many bake sales at the local community college where I work. They are always the first to sell out.

—**BETSY GRANTIER** CHARLOTTESVILLE, VA

PREP: 20 MIN. + STANDING
MAKES: 6 DOZEN

- 1 **pound white candy coating, coarsely chopped**
- 1 **cup (6 ounces) semisweet chocolate chips**

- 4 **ounces German sweet chocolate, chopped**
- ⅓ **cup milk chocolate chips**
- 1 **can (9¾ ounces) salted whole cashews**
- 1 **can (9¼ ounces) salted cashew halves and pieces**

1. In a large microwave-safe bowl, combine the first four ingredients. Cover and microwave at 50% power until melted, stirring every 30 seconds.

2. Stir in cashews. Drop mixture by tablespoonfuls onto waxed paper-lined pans. Let stand until set. Store in an airtight container. **NOTE** *This recipe was tested in a 1,100-watt microwave.*

⑤ INGREDIENTS
Cheery Cherry Parfaits

For a change of pace, layer the creamy white chocolate pudding with peach, strawberry or blueberry pie filling.

—*TASTE OF HOME* TEST KITCHEN

PREP: 10 MIN. + CHILLING
MAKES: 4 SERVINGS

- 2 **cups whole milk**
- 1 **package (3.3 ounces) instant white chocolate pudding mix**
- 8 **date oatmeal cookies, coarsely crumbled**
- 1 **cup cherry pie filling**

1. In a small bowl, whisk milk and pudding mix 2 minutes. Let stand 2 minutes or until soft-set. Spoon ¼ cup pudding into each of four parfait glasses.

2. Layer each with ⅓ cup cookie crumbs and ¼ cup pie filling. Top with the remaining pudding and cookie crumbs. Refrigerate for 1 hour before serving.

CHOCOLATE-RASPBERRY ANGEL FOOD TORTE

PAIR IT!

Tater Tot-chos, page 60, and these bites will make a fun kid's meal.

PEANUT BUTTER BROWNIE BITES, 234

233

231

244

Treats for a Crowd

When you **need a dish** for a potluck, bake sale or classroom party, turn to the **yummy desserts** here...they're a **cinch to make.**

BUTTERSCOTCH TOFFEE COOKIES, 238

PEANUT BUTTER
SNOWBALLS

Easy Lemon Curd Bars

A cup of tea looks lonely without
something sweet beside it. These
bars are a nice accompaniment.
I love the combination of the nutty
crust and zippy lemon curd.

—**DONNA HARDIN** NEW VIRGINIA, IA

PREP: 30 MIN. • **BAKE:** 20 MIN. + COOLING
MAKES: 2 DOZEN

- 1 cup butter, softened
- 1 cup sugar
- 2 cups all-purpose flour
- ½ teaspoon baking soda
- 1 jar (10 ounces) lemon curd
- ⅔ cup flaked coconut
- ½ cup chopped almonds, toasted

1. Preheat oven to 350°. In a large
bowl, cream butter and sugar until
light and fluffy. Combine flour
and baking soda; gradually add to
creamed mixture and mix well.
2. Set aside 1 cup mixture for
topping; press remaining mixture
onto the bottom of a greased
13x9-in. baking dish. Bake 12-15
minutes or until edges are lightly
browned. Cool 10 minutes.
3. Spread lemon curd over crust.
In a small bowl, combine coconut,
almonds and reserved topping
mixture; sprinkle over lemon curd.
4. Bake 18-22 minutes or until
golden brown. Cool completely on
a wire rack. Cut into bars.

> **SWAP IT**
> Try these bars with
> lime curd and pecans
> for the lemon curd
> and almonds.

(5) INGREDIENTS

Peanut Butter Snowballs

These creamy treats are such a
nice change from the typical milk
chocolate and peanut butter
combination. The recipe is also an
easy one for children to help with.
I prepare the snowballs for bake sales
at my granddaughter's school and
put them in gift boxes when I share
with neighbors at Christmas.

—**WANDA REGULA** BIRMINGHAM, MI

PREP: 15 MIN. + CHILLING
MAKES: 2 DOZEN

- 1 cup confectioners' sugar
- ½ cup creamy peanut butter
- 3 tablespoons butter, softened
- 1 pound white candy coating,
  coarsely chopped

1. In a bowl, combine the sugar,
peanut butter and butter. Shape
into 1-in. balls and place on a waxed
paper-lined baking sheet. Chill for
30 minutes or until firm.
2. Meanwhile, melt the candy
coating in a microwave-safe bowl.

Dip balls in melted coating and
place on waxed paper to set.

(5) INGREDIENTS

Homemade Coconut Macaroons

Chewy, simple and oh, so good, these
bite-sized cookies are perfect for
bake sales—that is, if your family
doesn't eat them first!

—**SABRINA SHAFER** MINOOKA, IL

START TO FINISH: 25 MIN.
MAKES: 1½ DOZEN

- 2½ cups flaked coconut
- ⅓ cup all-purpose flour
- ⅛ teaspoon salt
- ⅔ cup sweetened condensed milk
- 1 teaspoon vanilla extract

1. Preheat oven to 350°. In a small
bowl, combine the coconut, flour
and salt. Add milk and vanilla; mix
well (batter will be stiff).
2. Drop by tablespoonfuls 1 in.
apart onto a greased baking sheet.
Bake 15-20 minutes or until golden
brown. Remove to wire racks.

**HOMEMADE
COCONUT MACAROONS**

**EASY LEMON
CURD BARS**

Marvelous Maple Fudge

Use this delicious, easy recipe for potlucks, large family gatherings or bake sales. Line your pan with foil to make removing the fudge a breeze.

—JEANNIE GALLANT
CHARLOTTETOWN, PEI

PREP: 10 MIN. • **COOK:** 20 MIN. + COOLING
MAKES: 1¾ POUNDS (64 PIECES)

- 1 teaspoon plus 1 cup butter, divided
- 2 cups packed brown sugar
- 1 can (5 ounces) evaporated milk
- 1 teaspoon maple flavoring
- ½ teaspoon vanilla extract
- ⅛ teaspoon salt
- 2 cups confectioners' sugar

1. Line an 8-in.-square pan with foil; grease the foil with 1 teaspoon butter.
2. Cube remaining butter. In a large saucepan, combine cubed butter, brown sugar and milk. Bring to a full boil over medium heat, stirring constantly. Cook 10 minutes, stirring frequently. Remove from heat.
3. Stir in maple flavoring, vanilla and salt. Add confectioners' sugar; beat on medium speed 2 minutes or until smooth. Immediately spread fudge into the prepared pan. Cool completely.
4. Using foil, lift fudge out of pan. Remove foil; cut into 1-in. squares. Store in an airtight container.

Easy Chocolate Chip Pumpkin Bars

This dessert is super simple to pull together, and the flavorful results will win you nothing but rave reviews.

—AIMEE RANSOM HOSCHTON, GA

PREP: 5 MIN. • **BAKE:** 30 MIN.
MAKES: 3 DOZEN

- 1 package spice cake mix (regular size)
- 1 can (15 ounces) solid-pack pumpkin
- 2 cups (12 ounces) semisweet chocolate chips, divided

1. Preheat oven to 350°. In a large bowl, combine cake mix and pumpkin; beat on low speed 30 seconds. Beat on medium 2 minutes. Fold in 1½ cups chocolate chips. Transfer to a greased 13x9-in. baking pan.
2. Bake 30-35 minutes or until a toothpick inserted in center comes out clean. Cool completely in pan on a wire rack.
3. In a microwave, melt the remaining chocolate chips; stir until smooth. Drizzle over bars. Let stand until set.

Almond Snack Cake

My oldest son was allergic to chocolate, so I had to find goodies to make without it. These treats filled the bill. In fact, my son is grown now, so I've been making this recipe for a long time! With its distinctive almond flavor, this snack cake is popular at bake sales.

—MARY LOU CRABILL PEYTON, CO

PREP: 10 MIN. • **BAKE:** 25 MIN. + COOLING
MAKES: 24 SERVINGS

- 4 eggs
- 2¼ cups sugar, divided
- 1 cup butter, melted
- 2 cups all-purpose flour
- ¼ teaspoon salt
- 1½ teaspoons almond extract
- ½ cup sliced almonds

1. Preheat oven to 350°. In a large bowl, beat eggs until light and lemon-colored. Gradually add 2 cups sugar, beating until combined. Stir in butter, flour, salt and extract.
2. Spread into a greased 13x9-in. baking pan. Sprinkle with almonds and remaining sugar. Bake 25-30 minutes or until a toothpick inserted near the center comes out clean. Cool on a wire rack.

MARVELOUS
MAPLE FUDGE

LEMON CRISP COOKIES

Lemon Crisp Cookies

Here's a quick-to-fix treat that's perfect to make when you've forgotten about a bake sale or a potluck. The cookies take only 10 minutes to whip up. The sunny yellow color, big lemon flavor and delightful crunch are sure to bring smiles.
—**JULIA LIVINGSTON** FROSTPROOF, FL

START TO FINISH: 30 MIN.
MAKES: ABOUT 4 DOZEN

- 1 **package lemon cake mix (regular size)**
- 1 **cup crisp rice cereal**
- ½ **cup butter, melted**
- 1 **egg, lightly beaten**
- 1 **teaspoon grated lemon peel**

1. Preheat oven to 350°. In a large bowl, combine all the ingredients (dough will be crumbly). Shape into 1-in. balls. Place 2 in. apart on ungreased baking sheets.
2. Bake 10-12 minutes or until set. Cool 1 minute; remove from pan to a wire rack to cool completely.

TOP TIP

Lemon zest is the outer peel or rind of the lemon (not including the bitter white membrane attached to the fruit). Zest is used often in bread and cake recipes. To remove the zest, peel thin strips with a small sharp knife, being careful not to include the white membrane, and mince finely. You can also take the whole fruit and rub it over a hand grater to remove the zest.

Lemon Angel Cake Bars

A neighbor gave me this recipe years ago and it's been in my baking rotation ever since. It can be made ahead and serves a bunch, so it's perfect for parties and potlucks.
—**MARINA CASTLE**
CANYON COUNTRY, CA

PREP: 15 MIN. • **BAKE:** 20 MIN. + CHILLING
MAKES: 4 DOZEN

- 1 **package (16 ounces) angel food cake mix**
- 1 **can (15¾ ounces) lemon pie filling**
- 1 **cup finely shredded unsweetened coconut**

FROSTING

- 1 **package (8 ounces) cream cheese, softened**
- ½ **cup butter, softened**
- 1 **teaspoon vanilla extract**
- 2½ **cups confectioners' sugar**
- 3 **teaspoons grated lemon peel**

1. Preheat oven to 350°. In a large bowl, mix cake mix, pie filling and coconut until blended; spread into a greased 15x10x1-in. baking pan.
2. Bake 20-25 minutes or until a toothpick inserted in center comes out clean. Cool completely in pan on a wire rack.
3. Meanwhile, in a large bowl, beat cream cheese, butter and vanilla until smooth. Gradually beat in confectioners' sugar. Spread over cooled bars; sprinkle with lemon peel. Refrigerate at least 4 hours. Cut into bars or triangles.
NOTE *Look for unsweetened coconut in the baking or health food section.*

LEMON ANGEL CAKE BARS

Chocolate-Coated Pretzels

My pretty pretzels are easy to prepare, and they're a smart way to get your sweet-and-salty fix.
—**VIRGINIA CHRONIC** ROBINSON, IL

PREP: 15 MIN. + STANDING
MAKES: 5-6 DOZEN

- 1 **to 1¼ pounds white and/or milk chocolate candy coating, coarsely chopped**
- 1 **package (8 ounces) miniature pretzels**
  Nonpariels, colored jimmies and colored sugar, optional

In a microwave, melt half of candy coating at a time; stir until smooth. Dip pretzels in coating; allow excess to drip off. Place on waxed paper; let stand until almost set. Garnish as desired; let stand until set.

Chocolate Peppermint Bark

These treats are a snap to make, but nobody seems to mind that I don't put in much effort—they just keep coming back for more.
—**KESLIE HOUSER** PASCO, WA

PREP: 15 MIN. + CHILLING
MAKES: ABOUT 1 POUND

- 6 **ounces white baking chocolate, chopped**
- 1 **cup crushed peppermint or spearmint candies, divided**
- 1 **cup (6 ounces) semisweet chocolate chips**

1. In a microwave, melt white chocolate at 70% power; stir until smooth. Stir in ⅓ cup crushed candies. Repeat with chocolate chips and an additional ⅓ cup candies. Alternately drop spoonfuls of chocolate and white chocolate mixtures onto a waxed paper-lined baking sheet.

2. Using a metal spatula, cut through candy to swirl and spread to ¼-in. thickness. Sprinkle with remaining crushed candies.

3. Refrigerate the bark until firm. Break into pieces. Store the bark between layers of waxed paper in an airtight container.

NOTE *This recipe was tested in a 1,100-watt microwave.*

Snickerdoodle Blondie Bars

When asked to bring a dessert for my boys' football team to share, I whipped up these unique blondies and was instantly named "the greatest mom."

—VALONDA SEWARD
COARSEGOLD, CA

PREP: 15 MIN. • **BAKE:** 35 MIN. + COOLING
MAKES: 20 SERVINGS

- 1 **cup butter, softened**
- 2 **cups packed brown sugar**
- 2 **eggs**
- 3 **teaspoons vanilla extract**
- 2⅔ **cups all-purpose flour**
- 2 **teaspoons baking powder**
- 1 **teaspoon ground cinnamon**
- ¼ **teaspoon ground nutmeg**
- ½ **teaspoon salt**

TOPPING
- 1½ **teaspoons sugar**
- ½ **teaspoon ground cinnamon**

1. Preheat oven to 350°. In a large bowl, cream butter and brown sugar until fluffy. Beat in eggs and vanilla. In another bowl, whisk flour, baking powder, spices and salt; gradually beat into creamed mixture. Spread into a greased 9-in.-square baking pan.

2. Mix topping ingredients; sprinkle over top. Bake 35-40 minutes or until set and golden brown. Cool in the pan on a wire rack. Cut into bars. Store in an airtight container.

CHOCOLATE PEPPERMINT BARK

SNICKERDOODLE BLONDIE BARS

Chocolate Caramel Cracker Bars

Made on Saturday and gone by Monday, these chocolate caramel bars with a cracker crust are just that good. Treat your family to the yummy treats as soon as you can!

—**ALLY BILLHORN** WILTON, IA

PREP: 15 MIN. • **COOK:** 10 MIN. + CHILLING
MAKES: 27 BARS

- 1 teaspoon plus ¾ cup butter, cubed
- 45 Club crackers (2½ x 1 inch)
- 1 can (14 ounces) sweetened condensed milk
- ½ cup packed brown sugar
- 3 tablespoons light corn syrup
- 1 cup (6 ounces) semisweet chocolate chips

1. Line a 9-in.-square baking pan with foil and grease the foil with 1 teaspoon butter. Arrange a single layer of crackers in pan.
2. In a large saucepan, combine the milk, brown sugar, corn syrup and remaining butter. Bring to a boil over medium heat, stirring occasionally. Reduce heat to maintain a low boil; cook and stir 7 minutes. Remove from heat. Evenly spread a third of the mixture over the crackers. Repeat cracker and caramel layers twice.
3. Immediately sprinkle chocolate chips over caramel; let stand 3-5 minutes or until glossy. Spread over top. Cover and refrigerate 2 hours or until chocolate is set. Using foil, lift layers out of pan; cut into 3x1-in. bars.

Peanut Butter Brownie Bites

I used to make these brownie bites with a cherry in the center. Then I discovered that my granddaughter Lily is big on peanut butter, so I switched it up. Now she loves to help me make them.

—**DONNA MCGINNIS** TAYLOR RIDGE, IL

PREP: 20 MIN. • **BAKE:** 20 MIN. + COOLING
MAKES: 3½ DOZEN

- 1 package fudge brownie mix (13x9-inch pan size)

FROSTING
- ½ cup creamy peanut butter
- 3 ounces cream cheese, softened
- 2 cups confectioners' sugar
- 4 teaspoons 2% milk
- 1 teaspoon vanilla extract
  Chopped salted peanuts, optional

1. Preheat oven to 350°. Line 42 mini-muffin cups with paper or foil liners.
2. Prepare brownie mix batter according to package directions. Fill prepared cups two-thirds full. Bake 18-22 minutes or until a toothpick inserted in center comes out clean (do not overbake).
3. Place pans on wire racks. Using the end of a wooden spoon handle, make a ½-in.-deep indentation in the center of each brownie. Cool 10 minutes before removing from pans.
4. For frosting, in a large bowl, beat peanut butter and cream cheese until blended. Gradually beat in confectioners' sugar, milk and vanilla until smooth. Fill or pipe frosting into indentations. If desired, sprinkle with chopped peanuts. Refrigerate leftovers.

Chocolate Caramel Cracker Bars $1.-

CHOCOLATE CARAMEL CRACKER BARS

**PEANUT BUTTER
BROWNIE BITES**

**SUGAR-CONE
CHOCOLATE CHIP COOKIES**

**SWEET &
SALTY CANDY**

**ROOT BEER FLOAT
FUDGE**

Sugar-Cone Chocolate Chip Cookies

If I could make a batch of cookies a day, I'd be in baking heaven. I made these for my boys when they were growing up, and now I treat my grandkids, too.

—**PAULA MARCHESI**
LENHARTSVILLE, PA

PREP: 25 MIN. • **BAKE:** 10 MIN./BATCH
MAKES: 6 DOZEN

- 1 cup butter, softened
- ¾ cup sugar
- ¾ cup packed brown sugar
- 2 eggs
- 3 teaspoons vanilla extract
- 2¼ cups all-purpose flour
- 1 teaspoon baking soda
- ½ teaspoon salt
- 2 cups milk chocolate chips
- 2 cups coarsely crushed ice cream sugar cones (about 16)
- 1 cup sprinkles

1. Preheat oven to 375°. In a large bowl, cream butter and sugars until light and fluffy. Beat in eggs and vanilla. In another bowl, whisk the flour, baking soda and salt; gradually beat into creamed mixture. Stir in chocolate chips, crushed sugar cones and sprinkles.
2. Drop by tablespoonfuls 2 in. apart onto ungreased baking sheets. Bake 8-10 minutes or until golden brown. Remove from pans to wire racks to cool.

Sweet & Salty Candy

I've been making this candy for the past few years and serving it at Teacher Appreciation lunches and bake sales. It's special because it never fails to win praise from everyone who tries it. For bake sales, I break the candy up and package it in little cellophane bags from the craft store.

—**ANNA GINSBERG** AUSTIN, TX

PREP: 15 MIN. • **BAKE:** 10 MIN. + COOLING
MAKES: ABOUT 1½ POUNDS

- 2 cups miniature pretzels, coarsely crushed
- ½ cup corn chips, coarsely crushed
- ½ cup salted peanuts
- ½ cup butter, cubed
- ½ cup packed brown sugar
- 1½ cups semisweet chocolate chips

1. Preheat oven to 350°. Line a 13x9-in. baking pan with foil and grease the foil; set aside. In a large bowl, combine the pretzels, corn chips and peanuts.
2. In a saucepan, melt butter. Stir in brown sugar until melted. Bring to a boil, stirring frequently. Boil 1 minute, stirring twice. Pour over the pretzel mixture; toss to coat. Transfer to prepared pan.
3. Bake 7 minutes. Sprinkle with chocolate chips. Bake 1-2 minutes longer or until chips are softened.

Spread over top. Cool on a wire rack 1 hour. Break into pieces. Store in an airtight container.

Root Beer Float Fudge

My children have always loved root beer floats, so I came up with this fudgy treat just for them. Sweet and creamy with that familiar root beer flavor, it's always a best-seller at school bake sales.

—**JENNIFER FISHER** AUSTIN, TX

PREP: 15 MIN. • **COOK:** 15 MIN. + CHILLING
MAKES: ABOUT 3 POUNDS

- 1 teaspoon plus ¾ cup butter, divided
- 3 cups sugar
- 1 can (5 ounces) evaporated milk
- 1 package (10 to 12 ounces) white baking chips
- 1 jar (7 ounces) marshmallow creme
- ½ teaspoon vanilla extract
- 2 teaspoons root beer concentrate

1. Line a 9-in.-square baking pan with foil; grease foil with 1 teaspoon butter. In a saucepan, combine sugar, milk and remaining butter. Bring to a rapid boil over medium heat, stirring constantly. Cook and stir 4 minutes.
2. Remove from heat. Stir in baking chips and marshmallow creme until melted. Pour one-third of the mixture into a bowl; stir in vanilla.
3. To remaining mixture, stir in root beer concentrate; immediately spread into prepared pan. Spread the vanilla mixture over the top. Refrigerate 1 hour or until firm.
4. Using foil, lift fudge out of pan. Remove foil; cut fudge into 1-in. squares. Store the fudge between layers of waxed paper in an airtight container in the refrigerator.
NOTE *This recipe was tested with McCormick root beer concentrate.*

HOW TO

FOIL A PAN FOR FUDGE

Fudge recipes often instruct you to line the pan with foil and to butter the foil before pouring in the fudge mixture. That way, when the fudge cools, you can easily lift foil and fudge out of the pan and cut the fudge into squares. Cutting the fudge outside the pan prevents the pan from being scratched by the knife and allows for more evenly cut pieces.

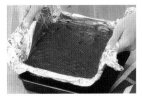

Raspberry Walnut Shortbread

A sweet raspberry filling is sandwiched between a crispy crust and a crunchy, nutty brown sugar topping in these satisfying bars.

—**PAT HABIGER** SPEARVILLE, KS

PREP: 15 MIN. • **BAKE:** 40 MIN. + COOLING
MAKES: 16 SERVINGS

- 1¼ **cups plus 2 tablespoons all-purpose flour, divided**
- ½ **cup sugar**
- ½ **cup cold butter**
- ½ **cup raspberry jam**
- 2 **eggs**
- ½ **cup packed brown sugar**
- 1 **teaspoon vanilla extract**
- ⅛ **teaspoon baking soda**
- 1 **cup finely chopped walnuts**

1. Preheat oven to 350°. In a bowl, combine 1¼ cups flour and sugar; cut in butter until crumbly. Press into a greased 9-in.-square baking pan. Bake 20-25 minutes or until edges are lightly browned. Place pan on a wire rack. Spread the jam over hot crust.

2. In a bowl, beat the eggs, brown sugar and vanilla. Combine baking soda and remaining flour; stir into egg mixture just until combined. Fold in walnuts. Spoon over the jam; spread evenly.

3. Bake 17-20 minutes longer or until top is golden brown and set. Cool completely on a wire rack before cutting.

Malted Milk Ball Brownies

You don't have to be a kid to love these delicious brownies! Malted milk balls in the batter and sprinkled on top make them special.

—**MITZI SENTIFF** ANNAPOLIS, MD

PREP: 15 MIN. • **BAKE:** 30 MIN. + COOLING
MAKES: 2 DOZEN

- 1 **package fudge brownie mix (13x9-inch pan size)**
- 1⅓ **cups chopped malted milk balls, divided**
- 1 **cup (6 ounces) semisweet chocolate chips**
- 2 **tablespoons butter**
- 2 **tablespoons milk**
- ¼ **teaspoon vanilla extract**

1. Preheat oven to 350°. Prepare brownie batter according to package directions; stir in 1 cup malted milk balls. Spread into a greased 13x9-in. baking pan.

2. Bake 28-30 minutes or until a toothpick inserted 2 in. from an edge comes out with moist crumbs. Cool completely on a wire rack.

3. In a microwave, melt chocolate chips and butter; stir until smooth. Cool slightly. Stir in the milk and vanilla. Spread over the brownies. Sprinkle with remaining malted milk balls. Refrigerate 10-15 minutes or until set. Cut into bars.

Sacher Bars

Is your mouth watering yet? This rich take on a Viennese classic using apricot preserves and chocolate left our tasters speechless. Unless you count "mmm."

—**LORRAINE CALAND** SHUNIAH, ON

PREP: 30 MIN. • **BAKE:** 15 MIN. + COOLING
MAKES: 6¼ DOZEN

- ¾ **cup butter, cubed**
- 3 **ounces unsweetened chocolate, chopped**
- 3 **eggs**
- 1½ **cups sugar**
- 1½ **teaspoons vanilla extract**
- 1¼ **cups all-purpose flour**
- ¾ **cup apricot preserves**
- 2 **ounces semisweet chocolate, chopped**

1. Preheat oven to 325°. Line a greased 15x10x1-in. baking pan with waxed paper. Grease and flour the paper; set aside. In a microwave, melt butter and the unsweetened chocolate; stir until smooth. In a bowl, beat eggs and sugar. Stir in vanilla and chocolate mixture. Gradually add flour.

2. Transfer to prepared pan. Bake 15-20 minutes or until a toothpick inserted near the center comes out clean (do not overbake). Cool 10 minutes before removing from pan to a wire rack to cool completely.

3. In a microwave, heat preserves until melted. Cut cake into four 7½x5-in. rectangles. Spread half of the preserves over two of the rectangles. Top each with the remaining cake and spread with remaining preserves. Cut into bars.

4. In a microwave, melt semisweet chocolate; stir until smooth. Drizzle over bars. Let stand until set. Store in an airtight container in the refrigerator.

(5) INGREDIENTS

Butterscotch Toffee Cookies

My cookie recipe, with its bold butterscotch flavor, stands out at events among all the chocolate. I like to enjoy one or two with a glass of milk or a cup of coffee.

—**ALLIE BLINDER** NORCROSS, GA

PREP: 10 MIN. • **BAKE:** 10 MIN./BATCH
MAKES: 5 DOZEN

- 2 **eggs**
- ½ **cup canola oil**
- 1 **package butter pecan cake mix (regular size)**
- 1 **package (10 to 11 ounces) butterscotch chips**
- 1 **package (8 ounces) milk chocolate English toffee bits**

1. Preheat oven to 350°. In a bowl, beat eggs and oil until blended; gradually add cake mix and mix well. Fold in chips and toffee bits.

2. Drop by tablespoonfuls 2 in. apart onto greased baking sheets. Bake 10-12 minutes or until golden brown. Cool cookies 1 minute before removing to wire racks.

SACHER BARS

BUTTERSCOTCH TOFFEE COOKIES

CARAMEL PRALINE TART

CAN'T LEAVE ALONE BARS

(5) INGREDIENTS
Can't Leave Alone Bars

I take these quick-and-easy treats to church meetings, potlucks and housewarming parties. I often make a double batch so we can enjoy some at home, too.
—**KIMBERLY BIEL** JAVA, SD

PREP: 20 MIN. • **BAKE:** 20 MIN. + COOLING
MAKES: 3 DOZEN

- 1 package white cake mix (regular size)
- 2 eggs
- ⅓ cup canola oil
- 1 can (14 ounces) sweetened condensed milk
- 1 cup (6 ounces) semisweet chocolate chips
- ¼ cup butter, cubed

1. Preheat oven to 350°. In a large bowl, combine the cake mix, eggs and oil. Press two-thirds of the mixture into a greased 13x9-in. baking pan. Set remaining cake mixture aside.

2. In a microwave-safe bowl, combine the milk, chocolate chips and butter. Microwave, uncovered, until chips and butter are melted; stir until smooth. Pour over crust.

3. Drop teaspoonfuls of remaining cake mixture over top. Bake 20-25 minutes or until lightly browned. Cool before cutting.

(5) INGREDIENTS
Caramel Praline Tart

This rich dessert is my own creation, and I'm very proud of it. It's easy enough to make for everyday, but special enough for company.
—**KATHLEEN SPECHT** CLINTON, MT

PREP: 35 MIN. + CHILLING
MAKES: 16 SERVINGS

- 1 sheet refrigerated pie pastry
- 36 caramels
- 1 cup heavy whipping cream, divided
- 3½ cups pecan halves
- ½ cup semisweet chocolate chips, melted

1. Preheat oven to 450°. Unroll pastry on a lightly floured surface. Transfer to an 11-in. fluted tart pan with removable bottom; trim edges.

2. Line unpricked pastry shell with a double thickness of heavy-duty foil. Bake 8 minutes. Remove foil; bake 5-6 minutes longer or until light golden brown. Cool on a wire rack.

3. In a large saucepan, combine the caramels and ½ cup cream. Cook and stir over medium-low heat until the caramels are melted. Stir in the pecans. Spread filling evenly into crust. Drizzle with the melted chocolate.

4. Refrigerate 30 minutes or until set. Whip remaining cream; serve with the tart.

SWAP IT
Use ½ cup melted white baking chips for the chocolate chips.

Gingerbread Fruitcake Cookies

Two of my favorite things, fruitcake and gingerbread, meet in a truly great cookie. You'd never know that this recipe starts with a mix. It bursts with fruit, nuts and gingerbread flavor, topped with a delightful orange glaze.
—JAMIE JONES MADISON, GA

PREP: 20 MIN.
BAKE: 10 MIN./BATCH + COOLING
MAKES: 3 DOZEN

- 1 package (14½ ounces) gingerbread cake/cookie mix
- ¼ cup butter, melted
- ¼ cup water
- 1 container (8 ounces) chopped mixed candied fruit
- ½ cup chopped pecans
- ½ cup raisins
- 1¼ cups confectioners' sugar
- 1 to 2 tablespoons orange juice

1. Preheat oven to 350°. In a large bowl, combine the cookie mix, melted butter and water to form a soft dough. Stir in the candied fruit, pecans and raisins. Drop dough by tablespoonfuls 2 in. apart onto ungreased baking sheets.
2. Bake 8-10 minutes or until set. Cool on pans 1 minute. Remove the cookies from the pans to wire racks to cool completely.
3. In a small bowl, combine the confectioners' sugar and enough orange juice to reach desired consistency. Spread or drizzle over cookies. Let stand until set.

TO MAKE AHEAD *Dough can be made 2 days in advance. Iced cookies can be stored in covered containers at room temperature 1 week or in the freezer up to 1 month.*

(5)INGREDIENTS
Caramel Marshmallow Delights

Our children like to take these sweet and chewy treats to school to share on their birthdays.
—SUSAN KERR CROWN POINT, IN

PREP: 25 MIN. + CHILLING
MAKES: 5-6 DOZEN

- 1 package (10 ounces) Rice Krispies
- 1 can (14 ounces) sweetened condensed milk
- ½ cup butter, cubed
- 1 package (14 ounces) caramels
- 1 package (16 ounces) large marshmallows

1. Place cereal in a shallow bowl; set aside. In a double boiler or metal bowl over simmering water, combine the milk, butter and caramels, stirring until smooth. Remove from heat.
2. With a fork, quickly dip marshmallows into hot mixture; allow excess to drip off. Roll in cereal. Place on a foil-lined pan; chill 30 minutes. Remove from the pan and refrigerate in an airtight container.

GINGERBREAD FRUITCAKE COOKIES

SWEET & SALTY
MARSHMALLOW
POPCORN TREATS

DATE-WALNUT
PINWHEELS

(5) INGREDIENTS
Sweet & Salty Marshmallow Popcorn Treats

Popcorn balls get sweet, salty and crunchy when you add a little chocolate and then go nuts.
—**NINA VILHAUER** MINA, SD

PREP: 20 MIN. + COOLING
MAKES: ABOUT 5 DOZEN

- 4 **quarts popped popcorn**
- 3 **cups salted peanuts**
- 1 **package (12.6 ounces) milk chocolate M&M's**
- 1 **package (16 ounces) large marshmallows**
- 1 **cup butter, cubed**

1. In a bowl, combine popcorn, peanuts and M&M's. In a large saucepan, combine marshmallows and butter. Cook and stir over medium-low heat until melted. Add to popcorn mixture; mix well.
2. When cool enough to handle, shape into 2-in. popcorn balls. Let stand until firm before wrapping in plastic.

Date-Walnut Pinwheels

Every time someone drops in for coffee, I bake up a batch of these fruit and nut cookies—I always have the ingredients in my pantry.
—**LORI MCLAIN** DENTON, TX

START TO FINISH: 25 MIN.
MAKES: 1 DOZEN

- 3 **tablespoons sugar**
- ½ **teaspoon ground cinnamon**
- 1 **refrigerated pie pastry**
- 1 **tablespoon apricot preserves**
- ⅔ **cup finely chopped pitted dates**
- ½ **cup finely chopped walnuts**

1. Preheat oven to 350°. Mix the sugar and cinnamon. On a lightly floured surface, unroll pastry sheet; roll pastry into a 12-in. square. Spread preserves over top; sprinkle with dates, walnuts and cinnamon-sugar.
2. Roll up jelly-roll style; pinch seam to seal. Cut crosswise into 12 slices, about 1 in. thick. Place 1 in. apart on an ungreased baking sheet. Bake 12-14 minutes or until

golden brown. Remove from pan to a wire rack to cool.

Sweet Cereal Clusters

I think my crunchy combination of peanuts, pretzels and cereal, covered with white candy coating, makes a fun snack.
—**SUE YOUNT** MCBAIN, MI

START TO FINISH: 30 MIN.
MAKES: ABOUT 4½ POUNDS

- 6 **cups Corn Chex**
- 3 **cups miniature pretzels**
- 1 **jar (16 ounces) dry roasted peanuts**
- 2¼ **cups milk chocolate M&M's**
- 1 **cup raisins**
- 1½ **pounds white candy coating, melted**

In a bowl, mix first five ingredients. Pour candy coating over the cereal mixture; stir until coated. Spread onto waxed paper-lined baking sheets. Refrigerate 15 minutes or until set. Break into pieces. Store in an airtight container.

**CHOCOLATE-DIPPED
CANDY CANES**

(5)INGREDIENTS

Chocolate-Dipped Candy Canes

I couldn't resist combining my two loves in this recipe—peppermint and chocolate! These are so easy, but if one breaks in the process, just pop it in your mouth.

—SANDRA BAUMGARTEN

VANCOUVER, WA

PREP: 20 MIN. + STANDING • **COOK:** 5 MIN.
MAKES: 1 DOZEN

  1 **cup semisweet chocolate chips**
12 **candy canes (6 inches each)**
  3 **ounces white baking chocolate,
    chopped**
    **Optional toppings: assorted
      colored sugars or sprinkles
      and crushed candies**

1. In a microwave, melt chocolate chips; stir until smooth. Dip curved ends of candy canes in chocolate; allow excess to drip off. Place on waxed paper.
2. In a microwave, melt white baking chocolate; stir until smooth. Drizzle over chocolate. If desired, decorate with toppings. Let stand until set.
3. Use to stir servings of hot cocoa.

DID YOU KNOW?

Candy canes are said to have been the ingenious idea of a choirmaster at a cathedral in Germany in the 1670s. He took sugar stick candy and bent each to resemble a shepherd's staff. They were handed out to the children to help keep them quiet during the very long Christmas services. Stripes did not appear in candy canes until after 1900.

(5) INGREDIENTS

Microwave Marshmallow Fudge

With only five ingredients from your pantry and fridge, this decadent delight is perfect for any occasion!

—**SUE ROSS** CASA GRANDE, AZ

PREP: 15 MIN. + CHILLING
MAKES: ABOUT 2 POUNDS

- 1 **teaspoon butter**
- 1 **can (16 ounces) chocolate frosting**
- 2 **cups (12 ounces) semisweet chocolate chips**
- ½ **cup chopped walnuts**
- ½ **cup miniature marshmallows**

1. Line a 9-in.-square pan with foil and grease the foil with butter; set aside. In a microwave, melt the frosting and chocolate chips; stir until smooth. Stir in the walnuts; cool for 10 minutes. Stir in the marshmallows. Transfer the fudge to the prepared pan. Cover and refrigerate until firm.

2. Using foil, lift the fudge out of the pan. Discard the foil; cut the fudge into 1-in. squares. Store the fudge in an airtight container in the refrigerator.

Angela's XOXO Shortbread Brownies

It seems that everyone loves brownies. This version has a buttery crust, with a sweet finish thanks to the touch of candy on top.

—**ANGELA KAMAKANA BAPTISTA** HILO, HI

PREP: 15 MIN. • **BAKE:** 45 MIN. + COOLING
MAKES: 16 SERVINGS

- 2 **cups all-purpose flour**
- ½ **cup sugar**
- 1 **cup cold butter, cubed**
- 1 **package fudge brownie mix (13x9-inch pan size)**
- 8 **striped chocolate kisses, unwrapped**
- 8 **milk chocolate kisses, unwrapped**
- ½ **cup M&M's Minis**

MICROWAVE MARSHMALLOW FUDGE

1. Preheat oven to 350°. In a large bowl, mix flour and sugar; cut in butter until crumbly. Press onto the bottom of a greased 13x9-in. baking pan. Bake 17-20 minutes or until lightly browned. Cool on a wire rack.

2. Prepare brownie mix batter according to package directions; spread over crust. Bake 23-28 minutes longer or until a toothpick inserted in center comes out clean (do not overbake). Immediately top with kisses and M&M's, spacing evenly and pressing down lightly to adhere. Cool in pan on a wire rack.

Caramel Candy Bars

Everyone adores these layered caramel bars. They're so rich that a small portion is enough to satisfy a sweet tooth—but watch out! They still disappear in a flash!

—**JEANNIE KLUGH** LANCASTER, PA

PREP: 20 MIN. • **BAKE:** 15 MIN. + CHILLING
MAKES: 2 DOZEN

- ½ **cup butter, softened**
- ½ **cup packed brown sugar**
- 1⅓ **cups all-purpose flour**

CARAMEL LAYER
- 1 **package (14 ounces) caramels**
- ⅓ **cup butter, cubed**
- ⅓ **cup evaporated milk**
- 1⅔ **cups confectioners' sugar**
- 1 **cup chopped pecans**

CHOCOLATE DRIZZLE
- ¼ **cup semisweet chocolate chips**
- 1 **teaspoon shortening**

1. Preheat oven to 350°. In a large bowl, cream the butter and brown sugar until light and fluffy. Beat in the flour until blended. Press into a greased 13x9-in. baking dish. Bake 12-15 minutes or until the bars are golden brown.

2. In a small saucepan over medium-low heat, melt caramels and butter with milk until smooth, stirring occasionally. Remove from heat; stir in confectioners' sugar and pecans. Spread over crust.

3. In a microwave, melt chocolate chips and shortening; stir until smooth. Drizzle over caramel layer. Cover and refrigerate 2 hours or until firm. Cut into bars.

Mocha Pecan Balls

Dusted in either confectioners' sugar or cocoa, this six-ingredient dough rolls up into truffle-like treats—no baking is required.

—LORRAINE DAROCHA
MOUNTAIN CITY, TN

START TO FINISH: 25 MIN.
MAKES: 4 DOZEN

- 2½ **cups crushed vanilla wafers (about 65 wafers)**
- 2 **cups plus ¼ cup confectioners' sugar, divided**
- ⅔ **cup finely chopped pecans, toasted**
- 2 **tablespoons baking cocoa**
- ¼ **cup reduced-fat evaporated milk**
- ¼ **cup cold strong brewed coffee**
  Additional baking cocoa, optional

1. In a bowl, combine the wafer crumbs, 2 cups confectioners' sugar, pecans and cocoa. Stir in milk and coffee (mixture will be sticky).

2. With hands dusted with some confectioners' sugar, shape dough into ¾-in. balls; roll in remaining confectioners' sugar or additional baking cocoa if desired. Store in an airtight container.

CARAMEL CANDY BARS

MOCHA PECAN BALLS